I0103030

# Ruth Hubbard and Gilles Paquet

## Driving the Fake Out of Public Administration

Detoxing HR in the Canadian Federal Public Sector

# Collaborative Decentred Metagovernance Series

T his series of books is designed to define cumulatively the contours of collaborative decentred metagovernance. At this time, there is still no canonical version of this paradigm: it is *en émergence*. This series intends to be one of many 'construction sites' to experiment with various dimensions of an effective and practical version of this new approach.

Metagovernance is the art of combining different forms or styles of governance, experimented with in the private, public and social sectors, to ensure effective coordination when power, resources and information are widely distributed, and the governing is of necessity decentred and collaborative.

The series invites conceptual and practical contributions focused on different issue domains, policy fields, *causes célèbres*, functional processes, etc. to the extent that they contribute to sharpening the new apparatus associated with collaborative decentred metagovernance.

In the last few decades, there has been a need felt for a more sophisticated understanding of the governing of the private, public and social sectors: for less compartmentalization among sectors that have much in common; and for new conceptual tools to suggest new relevant questions and new ways to carry out the business of governing, by creatively recombining the tools of governance that have proven successful in all these sectors. These efforts have generated experiments that have been sufficiently rich and wide-ranging in the various laboratories to warrant efforts to pull together what we know at this stage.

This twelfth volume deals with the fake at the origin of much unwarranted waste and inefficiency in the Canadian federal public administration. The authors propose that it has its sources in the progressivist cosmology that has displaced the primary concern of government from coordination to distribution. They probe the world of human resources (HR) as an illustration of the malefits entailed by this displacement of focus which occurred dramatically in 1967 when the Government of Canada decided to care less about performance and more about being a 'model employer'. An MRI of the HR systems helps to guide a process of modernisation of the HR regimes. But the reader is sharply reminded in the conclusion that one cannot detox the HR regimes without tackling the progressivist cosmology.

Interested parties are invited to join the Chautauqua.

– Editorial Board

Other titles published by INVENIRE are listed at the end of this book.

# Ruth Hubbard and Gilles Paquet

## Driving the Fake Out of Public Administration

Detoxing HR in the Canadian Federal Public Sector

INVENIRE

Ottawa, Canada

2016

University of Ottawa **Press**
Les **Presses** de l'Université d'Ottawa

The University of Ottawa Press (UOP) is proud to be the oldest of the francophone university presses in Canada and the oldest bilingual university publisher in North America. Since 1936, UOP has been enriching intellectual and cultural discourse by producing peer-reviewed and award-winning books in the humanities and social sciences, in French and in English.

**www.Press.uOttawa.ca**

**Library and Archives Canada Cataloguing in Publication**

Title: Driving the fake out of public administration : detoxing HR in the Canadian federal public sector / Ruth Hubbard and Gilles Paquet.
Names: Hubbard, Ruth, 1942- author. | Paquet, Gilles, author.
Description: Reprint. Originally published: Ottawa, Canada : Invenire, 2016. | Includes bibliographical references.
Identifiers: Canadiana (print) 20220399050 | Canadiana (ebook) 20220399085 | ISBN 9780776638348 (softcover) | ISBN 9780776638355 (PDF) | ISBN 9780776638362 (EPUB)
Subjects: LCSH: Civil service—Canada—Personnel management. | LCSH: Public administration — Canada.
Classification: LCC JL108 .H85 2022 | DDC 352.6/30971—dc23

Legal Deposit: Library and Archives Canada, Third Quarter 2022
© University of Ottawa Press 2022, all rights reserved.

This book was initially published by Invenire Books in 2016 in the Collaborative Decentered Metagovernance Series. The cover design, layout and design were produced by Sandy Lynch. The University of Ottawa Press reissued this book thanks to the support of Ontario Creates.

## Invenire

Invenire Books, an Ottawa-based idea factory that operated from 2010 to 2019, specialized in collaborative governance and stewardship. Invenire and its authors provide creative practical and stimulating responses to the challenges and opportunities faced by today's organizations. The list is now carried by the University of Ottawa Press.

Profession: Public Servant
The Entrepreneurial Effect: Practical Ideas from Your Own Virtual Board of Advisors
La flotte blanche : histoire de la compagnie de navigation du Richelieu et d'Ontario
Tableau d'avancement II : essais exploratoires sur la gouvernance d'un certain Canada français
The Entrepreneurial Effect: Waterloo
The Unimagined Canadian Capital: Challenges for the Federal Capital Region
The State in Transition: Challenges for Canadian Federalism
Cities as Crucibles: Reflections on Canada's Urban Future
Gouvernance communautaire : innovations dans le Canada français hors Québec
Through the Detox Prism: Exploring Organizational Failures and Design Responses
Cities and Languages: Governance and Policy – An International Symposium
Villes et langues : gouvernance et politiques – symposium international
Moderato Cantabile: Toward Principled Governance for Canada's Immigration Policy
Stewardship: Collaborative Decentred Metagovernance and Inquiring Systems
Challenges in Public Health Governance: The Canadian Experience
Innovation in Canada: Why We Need More and What We Must Do to Get It
Challenges of Minority Governments in Canada
Gouvernance corporative : une entrée en matières

Tackling Wicked Policy Problems: Equality, Diversity and Sustainability
50 ans de bilinguisme officiel : défis, analyses et témoignages
Unusual Suspects: Essays on Social Learning
Probing the Bureaucratic Mind: About Canadian Federal Executives
Tableau d'avancement III : pour une diaspora canadienne-française antifragile
Autour de Chantal Mouffe : le politique en conflit
Town and Crown: An Illustrated History of Canada's Capital
The Tainted-Blood Tragedy in Canada: A Cascade of Governance Failures
Intelligent Governance: A Prototype for Social Coordination
Driving the Fake Out of Public Administration: Detoxing HR in the Canadian Federal Public Sector
Tableau d'avancement IV : un Canada français à ré-inventer
A Future for Economics: More Encompassing, More Institutional, More Practical
Pasquinade en F : essais à rebrousse-poil
Building Bridges: Case Studies in Collaborative Governance in Canada
Scheming Virtuously: The Road to Collaborative Governance
A Lantern on the Bow: A History of the Science Council of Canada and its Contributions to the Science and Innovation Policy Debate
Fifty Years of Official Bilingualism: Challenges, Analyses and Testimonies
Irregular Governance: A Plea for Bold Organizational Experimentation
Pasquinade en E: Slaughtering Some Sacred Cows

The University of Ottawa Press gratefully acknowledges the support extended to its publishing list by the Government of Canada, the Canada Council for the Arts, the Ontario Arts Council, the Social Sciences and Humanities Research Council and the Canadian Federation for the Humanities and Social Sciences through the Awards to Scholarly Publications Program, and by the University of Ottawa.

ONTARIO ARTS COUNCIL
CONSEIL DES ARTS DE L'ONTARIO
an Ontario government agency
un organisme du gouvernement de l'Ontario

Canada Council   Conseil des arts
for the Arts      du Canada

Canada

uOttawa

"To fake: to contrive so as to deceive."
*Webster's Encyclopedic Dictionary*

# | Table of Contents

# | The Storyline: It Is All a Matter of Coordination

## Gilles Paquet

*"L'association, la coopération, toutes les formes
de l'assurance offrent des ressources sans fin."*
*Alain*

This short book is about coordination. It argues that when coordination ceases to be the primary concern in organizations, and is displaced by another dominant guiding principle (egalitarianism, absolute hierarchy, etc.), a debacle follows: inefficiency and ineffectiveness ensue, fake creeps in, and toxic behaviour, structures and habits crystallize. As a result, performance deteriorates, and distributive coalitions impose noxious practices in the name of their own interest. Then, these practices have a tendency to persist and to cripple wider and wider zones of our socio-economy. Over time such practices become habituated, and come to be regarded as normal.

The fear of such a disastrous cascade may suffice to entice collaboration, but it may also not. The Great Depression, World War II, and the challenges of victory (and defeat) in different countries – with the need for reconstruction – have put a good deal of pressure on most national economies in the second quarter of the last century. But the following 30 years of seemingly effortless extensive growth led many Western, so-called advanced socio-economies to become somewhat "aged and arterio-sclerotic" – running out of steam and overtaken by the virus of egalitarianism and internecine redistribution. Redistribution concerns came to displace the more challenging coordination concerns. This cultural shift has had a phenomenal impact on all aspects of the modern socio-economies (Kindleberger 1978; Olson 1984).

Some socio-economies recognized early the need for a fountain of youth to dissolve the social arterio-sclerotic structures of the body politic – as Kindleberger would put it – but most experienced "galloping senility" after 1973. It translated into a worldwide decline in productivity.

The way in which the human resources have been handled in the federal public sector in Canada, in particular after 1967, is an echo effect of this cultural shift. The guiding principle in the human resources management (HRM) of the federal public sector became the principle of the model employer. Even after unionization had begun to permeate the public sector, the employer remained determined to regard its role *not* as having to extract as much value-adding and innovation as possible from its labour force, but to act with culpable benevolence and insouciance *vis-à-vis* the public sector workers – thereby giving a very bad example to all other sectors of the nation.

This resulted in some 50 years in which the elected officials betrayed the fiduciary role entrusted to them by the citizenry, enabling and allowing the unionized federal public service (and also the super-bureaucracy that routinely emerged from it) to extract increasingly more generous and unwarranted pay and fringe benefits for the provision of rather poor quality services.

Why has this been allowed to happen?

This book suggests that it is the result of the new 'progressivist' *ethos* – with politically-invented social rights of all sorts, and undue deference to compassion-ordained precedence of egalitarian goals over any productivity and innovation concerns. This materialized through the demise of critical thinking with regard to human resources arrangements and the crystallization of an endemic failure to confront inefficiency and waste as a Canadian cultural trait. This trait has been responsible for the success of waves of populist and ill-founded redistributive schemes rooted in ideology and propagated by the *pouvoir social* – in the sense the word has been used by Tocqueville. This sweeping *pouvoir social* – embodied in mechanisms of diffusion of opinion – produced dogmas that were dominant to such an extent that even political power was intimidated and discretely censored. Fundamentally incapable of frontally opposing such unwarranted 'progressive' views, the state and the opinion molders allowed the populist forces to softly 'impose' the dominium of egalitarianism over value-adding and effectiveness concerns (Boudon 2005).

In Part I of this volume, we document sketchily the sad state of affairs of the federal public service that has ensued, and we underscore the important role of the failure to confront in the deplorable drift of the Canadian order.

In Part II, we sketch an alternative approach to human resources (HR) and HR management at the federal level that might detox HR in the Canadian federal public service. These corrective measures would give back its fully warranted valence to the coordination game and give the employer enough leverage to ensure that it can extract value-adding and innovative contributions from its employees. This requires, however, that a new philosophy of efficiency and effectiveness be restored, and that the employer prove ready to shoulder his burden of office and act with gumption to ensure appropriate cognitive capabilities are recruited, appropriate organizational architectures are put in place, and the requisite armature of moral contracts are negotiated with the employees so that the various tasks the government is charged to despatch are provided with a high degree of efficiency, effectiveness and intelligence. This would flow from a significant cultural change.

It is not possible to explore the full range of instruments that might have to be put in place in the range of HR and HRM schemes best adapted to the burden of office of the different portions of the federal government apparatus, but we have set the stage for an inquiry system that would help design prototypes for the diverse schemes required in the many different sections of the federal public service.

Part III provides rich illustrations of the ways in which the array of instruments envisaged (capabilities, organizational structures and moral contracts) may be put in place.

This cannot be accomplished by sheer plumbing repairs. What is required is a new philosophy of HR anchored in the priority of making the highest and best use of the most capable resources, and real organizational changes – involving the transformation of the roles of major actors and the full use of the full range of instruments and levers needed, intelligently and differentially, in the diverse portions of the federal public service.

The conclusion emphasizes the need to construct a variety of HR arrangements for the pluralist governance of a plural federal public service. The design of such HR and HRM will present quite a challenge: it will require nothing less than a new paradigm of public administration – one that would escape the conceit of the model employer, and tame the deceits of the progressive cosmology. Our short book is an invitation to initiate social experimentations now.

# References

Boudon, Raymond. 2005. *Tocqueville aujourd'hui*. Paris, FR: Odile Jacob, pp. 167ff.

Kindleberger, Charles P. 1978. *The Aging Economy*. Kiel, DE: Institut fur Weltwirtschaft an der Universitat Kiel.

Olson, Mancur. 1984. *The Rise and Decline of Nations: Economic Growth, Stagflation, and Social Rigidities*. New Haven, CN: Yale University Press.

INTRODUCTION

# | The Priority Should Be Performance, Not Being a Model Employer

## Ruth Hubbard

*"L'administrateur administre la maladie; il ne la guérit point."*
*Alain*

The label 'public administration' should have generated some suspicion when it was invented. Implicitly, it suggests that there is something fundamentally different about the way in which public affairs are conducted as opposed to other forms of affairs or organizations. While no substantial rationale has ever been persuasively evoked as to why public administration should claim exceptionalism *vis-à-vis* any aspect of ordinary sound management, the new label invited such claims to be made. The rest is history: a long list of 'excuses' have been invented to rationalize public administration being exempted from the rigour of sound management, always in the name of some higher-order 'progressive' concern that is purported to swamp out mere interests in efficiency, effectiveness, economy, etc.

The history of public administration in most countries has been marred by a plague of such *ad hoc* relaxations of sound management rules in the name of ideologically selected norms. This sort of under-mining of sound management and governance has eroded the very foundation of 'stateness', i.e., the capacities enabling the state to perform functions sufficiently well that it may be possible for it to hope to survive in the long run.

Over time, the cumulative effect of these relaxations has been toxic. In the recent past, Francis Fukuyama (2004) has referred to the "black hole of public administration" to connote the sad state of public administration, both in theory and in practice. We concur as outlined in a book we published in 2010 (Hubbard and Paquet 2010).

## Culture governance shift

Culture governance connotes the underpinning of beliefs and propensities to act in certain directions that is only slowly and cumulatively swayed by the accumulation of experiences. This undergrowth influences the ways in which individuals and groups, conditioned by these evolving sentiments, react to new circumstances. The *ethos* of the time is usually absorbed and articulated by opinion molders and the media, and they tend to maintain and reinforce *l'air du temps* (Bang 2003).

A recent book by Paquet and Wilson (2016), building on a decade of forensic work analyzing governance failures of all sorts by private, public and social concerns, has proposed an approach to intelligent governance likely to counter the sort of erosion that has plagued public administration. It has drawn attention to the important culture governance shifts in modern socio-economies like Canada over the last 70 years. In particular, in their chapter 7, they argue that there has been a shift in culture governance "from a focus and priority on coordination and performance to a focus and priority on redistribution and egalitarianism," and that this has had toxic effects in the case of Canada.

After the Second World War, concern for coordination was still central (even if redistribution tools were used for stabilization purposes – as in the case of family allowances), but the results of state action on the coordination front were sufficiently unimpressive, especially from the 1970s on, to provoke a dramatic switch away from a coordination focus. Given a perceived incapacity to deal with the coordination problem *ex ante*, the ensuing social and personal costs of such a poorly coordinated and arterio-sclerotic socio-economy, and the exponential growth of the entitlement mentality with the welfare state, governments embraced a culture governance, focusing on redistribution schemes to correct both real and imaginary 'malefits' inflicted by an imperfectly coordinated socio-economy.

This increased the propensity of groups on all sides in countries like Canada to shift their attention away from the daunting and frustrating efforts to repair and transform the 'coordination game' to ensure the highest and best uses of all resources, toward investing their energy in making the highest and best use of the state in the 'redistribution game' – to ensure both protection from anything that could be declared a 'malefit' (and claim requisite compensation when this could not be done), and maximize the capture of all possible entitlements, rents, privileges and compensatory state transfers (whether morally defensible or not). This redirected the bulk of the artillery of citizen criticisms away from pressing the government to reform the coordination terrain towards pressing the government to become ever more involved in fuelling the redistribution of tangible and symbolic benefits to compensate for real or imaginary disadvantages.

As a consequence, redistribution came to be more and more important in the national discourse, and, by the 1990s, redistribution had become somewhat sacralised:

- being regarded as the only really effective tool available to government in an era of increasing complexity to correct (after the fact) the impacts of governance pathologies that could not be prevented beforehand; and
- the general acceptance of all the redistributive and entitlement mechanisms becoming deeply-rooted in a 'no-fault' culture that authorizes the forgiveness of governments for the lack of *ex ante* wisdom in their

interventions as long as 'appropriate' compensation is provided for those claiming to have been hurt.

Throughout this transubstantiation process, most governments remained blithely unconscious of and oblivious to the social rigidities and mental prisons that such a perspective was generating. In particular, governments failed to grasp that redistributing property rights is addictive, and that, even more importantly, the redistributive *ethos* easily becomes sufficiently powerful to mollify all efforts to ever get the coordination house in order.

Canada's drift in that direction was particularly notable.

## HR as a crucial arena

The coordination game pertains to all informational, human, organizational and material resources, but this volume focuses mainly on human and organizational resources. Human resources (HR) and the organizational arrangements to ensure maximum value-adding are not the only meaningful resources, but their relative importance in the overall socio-economy is immense. This is also the case in the public sector. This is why we have decided to tackle the issue of coordination failures in public administration through a closer look at the current state of affairs of the Canadian federal bureaucracy and the HR regime. There are other dimensions where coordination failures are flagrant (finances, information, etc.) in all sectors, but the problem would appear to be most toxic in the case of human resources. This is why we have decided, in this first stab at driving the fake out of public administration, to focus on human resources management (HRM). Other dimensions of the problem may be tackled later.

The Canadian public sector workforce is a central engine of the Canadian state. It constitutes the major tool of the Canadian government to help it appraise and monitor the Canadian situation at any given time, and to design and deliver effective responses to detected problems in the workings and structure of the governance of the Canadian socio-economy. As the Canadian state grew in size and responsibilities in the second half of the 20th century, the Canadian federal public sector workforce grew commensurably. The HR regime had to adjust to these new circumstances, and, whether it adjusted well or badly was bound to have a fundamental impact on the performance of the apparatus of governance of the Canadian socio-economy. To put it differently, governance failures in handling human resources could only have disastrous effects on the Canadian economy as a whole.

There would appear to be an agreement (at least outside the tribe of public administration *aficionados* where a grave case of cognitive dissonance and denial prevails about their own deficiencies)[1] on the sad state of the Canadian federal public sector workforce. In a recently published interview in the *Ottawa Citizen* (May 2016a) on the occasion of the presentation of the *Twenty-Third Annual Report to the Prime Minister on the Public Service of Canada* (Wernick 2016), the new Clerk of the Privy Council suggested that the federal public service is in very sad shape and much in need of repair.

Wernick describes a public service that is unproductive ("loads of rules, bureaucracy and process that isn't productive"); that is lacking in agility (structures and processes that make it so difficult to "move dollars, people and information around, within and across departments"); that is somewhat learning impaired (hobbled by structures that make it too slow, rigid and risk-averse); that it is worn out (where "we are too slow and not very nimble," and exists within a public service workplace that is old, outdated and tired).

---

[1] Whenever public administration academics allow themselves to pay any attention to the state of Canadian federal public administration, they indulge in what Vaclav Havel calls "evasive thinking," i.e., waxing generalities about the bureaucracy having to be refurbished, while providing no indication about how it might have to change. This sort of airy-fairy toothless commentary (that does not qualify as critical thinking at all) is often immersed in a flow of persiflage and verbiage dutifully transcribed from the foam of whitecaps generated by the daily press. This has become the genre in good currency in the public administration literature. In any other domain, this genre would be regarded as 'analysis lite', but, in public administration circles, it earns praise and prize as scholarship.

It is hardly surprising that the citizens and the politicians feel not very well served by such a technocracy, and that the compact of crucial public sector actors (citizens-politicians-bureaucrats) is beginning to face effective competition from non-state actors offering not only to provide more cheaply better quality services than what the state can offer, but also to provide alternative infrastructural arrangements as substitutes for those the state has in place (Paquet and Wilson 2016).

The federal government is the largest employer in Canada, with more than 260,000 core employees, nearly 90 percent of which are permanent employees. Recent analysis by the Canadian Federation of Independent Business (CFIB) reports that Canadians are paying more than a 15 percent premium in wages for federal workers over their private sector counterparts in similar occupations – using a basic analysis not disputed by government experts (CFIB 2008).[2]

This premium amounts to $4.5 billion of an annual wage bill for the core employees alone that was estimated at nearly $26 billion at that time.[3] This is more than the entire annual minimum savings objective of $4 billion by 2014-15, outlined in the 2012 federal budget for its departmental spending review. In

[2] The study (CFIB 2008) uses 2006 Census data and a comparison of narrowly defined occupational groups in the federal public sector using a core methodology that is said not to be disputed by Treasury Board Secretariat (TBS) experts. Its estimate for comparable occupations (i.e., not the total core) was 17.6%. The study estimates a premium of over 40% of paid and unpaid benefits (e.g. pensions and vacation/time off) are included as well. About an earlier CFIB report, TBS noted in 2006 that "[w]hatever the actual absolute difference in salary levels between the federal public sector and other sectors, our own analysis in this report confirms a relatively rapid and unprecedented rate of increase in real average salaries in the federal public sector. If federal public sector average salaries continue to grow faster than salaries in the private sector or elsewhere in the economy, a substantial wage premium will certainly open up in favour of the federal public sector" (Lahey 2006: chapter 6, p. 11-17).

[3] The annual wage bill for the core was estimated at $25.8 billion in the CFIB study using 2006 Census data. The estimate of $4.5 billion used here was obtained by applying 15% to the CFIB annual wage bill figure. The wage bill was reported at $43 billion in May 2013 (May 2013). The premium being paid based on those data has not been revealed.

addition, a confidential government report completed in mid-2011 estimated absenteeism in the federal public service at 2.5 times the average rate in the Canadian private sector, costing a further $1 billion in unwarranted outlays (Weston 2012).

As for the quality of work provided by the Canadian federal work force, it is difficult to make a authoritative statement on the basis of the information available for the whole enterprise, but recent studies about the quality of the work of executives in the Canadian federal public sector has been questionable (Hubbard and Paquet 2014).

A fundamental source of this costliness and ineffectiveness must be ascribed to a human resource regime that is less effective than it ought to be. This is an indictment that has been uttered in the *Seventh Report of the Prime Minister's Advisory Committee on the Public Service*, issued in March 2013, that diagnosed the situation this way: "[t]he Public Service employment model is outmoded in almost every respect – from performance management to classification to labour relations and total compensation" (Tellier and Emmerson 2013: 3). It is therefore reasonable to accept this global statement as a working hypothesis.

The HR regime of a government like Canada's federal government exists to ensure that there is an adequate set of capable and motivated people – now and in the future – to ensure that it is able to do, in as efficient and effective a way as possible, the things that it was elected to do. In other words, the government personnel must enable and support the link between the performance of those hired to work in one of the nearly 90 core departments and agencies (the "public service") and the mission of the department/agency where they work. Why has it not?

## Fifty years ago the HR regime went off track: the model employer conceit

We have chastised in very strong terms in earlier writings (Hubbard and Paquet 2015: Introduction) the strong tradition of 'conservatorship' that has plagued Canadian public administration – a tradition that has led, over time, the bureaucracy's 'need to preserve' to overshadow the 'need to serve'. This conservatorship attitude has become a toxic mental prison and has considerably crippled the work of the public sector.

This tendency was exacerbated in the post-World War II decades, when a generation of politicians, emerging from the public service, contributed significantly to sacralising the role of the bureaucracy as guardian of the fundamental principles of democracy. This distractive focus on the central importance of the bureaucracy led the elected governors to neglect their primary role as fiduciaries working first and foremost on behalf of the citizens.

As a result, in the 'progressivist' era of post-World War II that seemed to make any profligacy or imprudence less ominous than it was, Canada, under the influence of the Universal Declaration of Human Rights and the philosophy underpinning it, allowed a most toxic virus to contaminate the HRM world of the Canadian federal government: the focus on performance of the technocracy was lost.

Some 50 years ago, on the occasion of an illegal strike by the Canadian Union of Postal Workers (CUPW), the Pearson government (against the advice of many experts) decided not to respond to such an illegal strike with force and vigour but by granting, in the most servile manner, not only the right to strike to the CUPW members, but, in the same swoop, to the whole of the federal public service – all this in the name of its doctrine of 'model employer' ('Pearsonian conceit'). This irresponsible concession – granting the upper hand in negotiations to the unions so that they could take citizens as hostages – was to corrupt the labour-management interaction on the federal public sector scene in Canada for generations.

In the euphoria of the welfare state, "showing the way for other employers" (i.e., being a 'model employer') (Bach and Kessler 2008: 133) had become an idea in good currency. The Canadian federal government's radical version of this credo led to its losing focus on what the government was actually hiring people to do. Instead of keeping its eye firmly on the performance ball, it became primarily concerned with the happiness of its employees. This started them down a road leading to trouble – trouble that persists to today.

(1) In 1967, the government of the day convinced Parliament to grant collective bargaining – including the right to strike – for many terms and conditions of employment for the vast majority of its employees (currently about 85 percent). Although the right to strike has proven effective in the private sector to settle disputes (i.e., 'trial by combat'), in this case it was being applied in an arena in which there is, by definition, no marketplace to discipline either party's behaviour (Lahey 2006: chapter 15, p. 4).

(2) At the same time, the link between individual performance of public sector employees and departmental/agency missions was eroded both directly (e.g. by failing to link remuneration to performance)[4] and indirectly (e.g. by making it much tougher to adapt the occupational group structure – and corresponding

---

[4] The idea of linking some part of remuneration to mission-related performance is both attractive and logical in the private sector, but "[t]he dominant historical practice in the Canadian federal public service compensation ... has been to avoid any explicit link to performance in establishing pay ... many employees and most unions oppose the adoption of any form of pay for performance" (Lahey 2006: v1-14, p. 6-7). The long road to establish the link began in 2006-7 but no public information is available as of May 2013 about any current efforts to move in this direction for the 85% of workers covered by collective agreements. In early 2011, the Treasury Board Secretariat noted that "[t]he Clerk of the Privy Council has made strengthening performance management a key part of his agenda to renew the Public Service. A phased approach is being used with an initial focus on certain senior positions ... . The goal is to expand to a broader population of senior excluded or unrepresented individuals in 2009-10 [now in place] and, potentially, to represented managers in subsequent years." (http://www.tbs-sct.gc.ca/faq/pmcse-eng.asp) [Accessed May 22, 2013]. There is currently a degree of "pay at risk" in place for the Executive Category. In 2011, 25% was to be tied to the government's "one year 'strategic review' of operating expenses" (http://www.bloomberg.com/news/2011-10-07/canada-to-tie-public-servant-performance-pay-to-spending-cuts.html) [Accessed May 22, 2013].

bargaining unit structure – to something that might fit well with the nature of evolving department/agency missions).[5]

(3) This amounted to the federal government betraying its role as fiduciary on behalf of the citizens for the good governance of the public household. The Charter of Rights made things even worse when it erected a document marred by evasive thinking as the reference point in the final determination of what rights had priority over others in a variety of circumstances where conflicting rights issues emerged. The weight of this philosophy of 'model employer' over the next decades has been immense.

The Harper government was the first one to seriously attempt to regain the capacity to manage the public household in a manner that would ensure better performance with Bill C-4 that re-established fundamental management rights. The philosophy of the Harper government was best expressed in a document tabled by Minister Tony Clements (quoted in May 2014) as a preamble to the forthcoming HRM negotiations.

The employer indicated that it would like to initiate its efforts to make the public service more effective by insisting on four basic competencies ("showing integrity and respect; thinking things through; working effectively with others; taking initiative and being action-oriented") (May 2014) – all matters focused on performance. To capture the *zeitgeist* of the times, it may suffice to say that the knee-jerk reaction of 17 Canadian federal public service unions was to bring the employer to court for trying to impose "disguised discipline".

[5] It is very important to "bring together employees who can see the common interests they share, and to establish meaningful comparisons with the external labour market" (Lahey 2006: v1-14, p. 2). Nevertheless, it will be tougher to adapt the occupational group structure as required (notwithstanding it is collectively bargained) because of potential conflicts between unions that might lose members. For example, if two occupational groups ought to be combined to "make sense" for the employees as well as to enable meaningful comparisons with the external labour market, but they are currently represented by different bargaining agents, one of those agents would lose membership by that action and one would gain.

This juvenile reaction of the public sector unions to the most commonsensical efforts to deal with widely acknowledged problems of inefficiency and ineffectiveness in the federal public service was accompanied by a self-righteous defence of the least defensible practices of their members and of their most outrageous privileges, and a denial that any dysfunctionality of the federal public service could be ascribable to the employees. Yet such an insane reaction by the public sector unions did not yield a scintilla of criticism of the union attitude in the media or in the commentaries of the intelligentsia. Fifty years of indoctrination in the 'progressivist gospel' that unions are always right, and management is always wrong had permeated the culture thoroughly.

As if to symbolically consecrate the Kafkaesque situation that had ensued in Canada, in 2015, a majority judgment of the Supreme Court took the extraordinary step of adjudicating (with significant opposition from a number of Supreme Court judges) that in the case of Saskatchewan's essential services legislation, the right to strike of the Saskatoon employees took precedence over the right to essential services for the citizens. Again, the media and the intelligentsia were mute.

The Harper government went to defeat in the fall of 2015. Only the most naïve observers were surprised when, in the spring of 2016, Treasury Board President, Scott Brison, announced his intention to rescind C-4: he charmingly called this major step backward a restoration of fair and balanced labour laws and "protecting workers' rights and strengthening the middle class" (May 2016b). In clear language, the new Trudeau government abolished the first significant effort in 50 years to put the government back in the driver's seat in the management of its workforce. Instead, it chose to restore the grossly unbalanced 1967 arrangements that, through the Pearson conceit, had put the unions in the driver's seat.

The sophistry of the Trudeau government in associating the power of the aristocracy of labour in the public sector with the fate of the middle class in Canadian society is totally disingenuous. It amounts to a purely ideological rant. Failing to put an end to the Pearsonian conceit is going to be immensely costly financially. But more importantly maybe, it is also condemning the federal public sector to wallow in its own ineffectiveness, and Canadians to continue to be served poorly by the federal workforce: the Trudeau government would appear, in full cognizance of the toxic effects of the Pearsonian conceit, to be continuing to sacrifice the public interest to pandering to the unions.

Consequently, there would no longer appear to be even limited possibility of significant reforms 'from within' that might refurbish the federal public sector HR system in the near future. Could it be that the only alternative is some certainty that revolutionary technological forces might dispense with a portion of the federal public service 'from without' (Paquet and Wilson 2016)?

## Envoi

This book owes much to the collaboration of Fellows of the Centre on Governance over the years. For this collegiality, we would like to express our appreciation. It also owes much to the Centre of Governance and Invenire for its financial, material and moral support.

## References

Bach, S. and I. Kessler. 2008. "HRM and the New Public Management" in *The Oxford Handbook of Human Resource Management*. P. Boxall *et al.* (eds). Oxford, NY: Oxford University Press, chapter 23, p. 133.

Bang, Henrik P. 2003 (ed.). *Governance as Social and Political Communication*. Manchester UK: Manchester University Press.

Cartwright, S. 2011. *Report of the Review of the Public Service Modernization Act, 2003*. Ottawa, ON: Government of Canada, 19 pp, http://www.tbs-sct.gc.ca/reports-rapports/psma-lmfp/psma-lmfp00-eng.asp [Accessed April 26, 2013].

Canadian Federation of Independent Business (CFIB). 2008. *Wage Watch: A Comparison of Public-sector and Private-sector wages.* Ottawa, ON: Canadian Federation of Independent Business (www.cfib.ca) [Accessed March 14, 2012].

Canada Revenue Agency. 2011. *Canada Revenue Agency: Creating a Performance-oriented Culture.* Ottawa, ON: Canada Revenue Agency, June. Private copy.

Fukuyama, Francis. 2004. *State-building – Governance and World Order in the 21ˢᵗ Century.* Ithaca, NY: Cornell University Press.

Havel, Vaclav. 1991. *OPEN LETTERS.* London, UK: Faber & Faber.

Hubbard, R. 2003. "Public Service Modernization: Fixing the Cart May Not Suffice," *www.optimumonline.ca*, 33(2): 8-15.

Hubbard, Ruth and Gilles Paquet. 2010. *The Black Hole of Public Administration.* Ottawa, ON: University of Ottawa Press.

Hubbard, Ruth and Gilles Paquet. 2014. *Probing the Bureaucratic Mind – About Canadian Federal Executives.* Ottawa, ON: Invenire.

Hubbard, Ruth and Gilles Paquet. 2015. *Irregular Governance: A Plea for Bold Organizational Experimentation.* Ottawa, ON: Invenire.

Lahey, J. 2006. *Expenditure Review of Federal Public Sector – Volume 1 - The Analytical Report and Recommendation.* Ottawa: Treasury Board Secretariat, v1-9, (17 pp), http://www.tbs-sct.gc.ca/report/orp/2007/er-ed/vol1/vol107-eng.asp, v1-4 (24 pp), http://www.tbs-sct.gc.ca/report/orp/2007/er-ed/vol1/vol114-eng.asp & v1-16 (23 pp), http://www.tbs-sct.gc.ca/report/orp/2007/er-ed/vol1/vol116-eng.asp [Accessed Dec 12, 2012].

Lynch, K. 2009. *Sixteenth Annual Report to the Prime Minister on the Public Service of Canada.* Ottawa, ON: Privy Council Office. http://www.clerk.gc.ca/eng/feature.asp?mode=preview&pageid=221 [Accessed March 23, 2013].

May, Kathryn. 2013. "A 'new beginning' for public service," *Ottawa Citizen*, Wednesday, May 29, A1.

May, Kathryn. 2014. "Unions grieve new PS performance rules," *Ottawa Citizen*, April 7.

May, Kathryn. 2016a. "PS needs to pick up pace of reforms: Privy Council Clerk," *Ottawa Citizen*, March 25.

May, Kathryn. 2016b. "Public service news: Liberals to repeal hated Tory legislation on PS Bargaining," *Ottawa Citizen*, May 26.

Paquet, Gilles and Christopher Wilson 2016. *Intelligent Governance – A Prototype for Social Coordination*. Ottawa, ON: Invenire.

Tellier, P. and D. Emmerson. 2013. "Modernizing the employment model is the key challenge facing the Public Service today," *Seventh Report of the Prime Minister's Advisory Committee on the Public Service*. Ottawa, ON: Government of Canada, March, 7 pp., http://www.clerk.gc.ca/eng/feature. asp?pageId=314 [Accessed August 16, 2016].

Wernick, Michael. 2016. *Twenty-Third Annual Report to the Prime Minister on the Public Service of Canada*. Ottawa, ON: Privy Council Office, March 31, http://www.clerk.gc.ca/eng/feature. asp?pageId=431 [Accessed August 16, 2016].

Weston, Greg. 2012. "Public Sick days cost $1B a year," CBC News, June 20.

# PART I

# Cleansing the Augean Stables

The vocation of Part I is not to exhaustively report on the multitude of initiatives that have been launched over the last 50 years to repair the damages inflicted by the 1967 silent surrender by the Pearson government. This sort of autopsy is only of historical interest at this time. What is undeniable is that, as of this early portion of the 21st century, nothing has been repaired, and most of the so-called specialists in public administration remain in denial in the face of the flagrant evidence of poor performance by the Canadian federal public sector workforce.

In chapter 1, our focus will be on the inanity of the recent diagnoses provided by the public administration tribe, and the very limited utility of the feeble efforts at repairs that they have inspired. This skeptical outlook may appear to be somewhat negative. This is not the case. What we have in mind is pointing to the superficiality of those initiatives in order to establish what should be regarded as avenues that lack promise. It should prepare the reader's mind to focus on more promising approaches.

However, this sanitization of the field of operations cannot suffice. Much of the failure of the enterprise to come up with meaningful strategies of repair is not ascribable to the sole complexity of the field of operations. It is rather ascribable to the broad cultural environment that has dramatically crippled critical thinking in public administration and also in much of the Canadian intellectual scene. Consequently, it will not suffice to reflect on the design of new governance principles and mechanisms to bring forth improved governance architecture and plumbing. One must also tackle the 'crippling cultural *ethos'* that prevents even informed observers from approaching the field of operations of the Canadian federal public service in a critical way.

In chapter 2, our focus will be on the toxic nature of the present crippling public administration perspective. We will track it down to the degradation of the common public culture. This does not apply only to human resources management issues. Indeed we will illustrate, in passing, its impact on entirely different fields of operations where the same crippling failure to confront wicked problems has had very toxic impacts indeed.

This dual approach – mechanical/organizational and cultural – to the governance failures in Canadian society is crucial, for the blockages on the road to effective repairs are as much in the distorted eye of the observers as in the complexity of the tasks with which one has to cope.

So, at the end of this book, we must be ready not only to tackle the awesome task of transforming the whole capabilities and organizational architecture of the federal public sector, and also the modification of the public service culture, but ultimately the whole idea of public administration, if one is to hope that this enterprise will be less impotent when the whole Canadian federal public sector (and other levels of governance) goes through the next phase of its continual evolving experience.

CHAPTER 1

# | Tinkering Can No Longer Suffice

## Ruth Hubbard and Gilles Paquet

"Let's go ... " (scenic note: nobody moves).
(the last line of the play *Waiting for Godot*)
*Samuel Beckett*

## Introduction

For decades, the authors of this chapter, in different capacities and from different perspectives, have been observing the Canadian federal public service and its executives with a view to gauging their performance, to diagnosing the sources of their ineffectiveness, and to proposing some repairs. Already by the early 1990s, it was obvious that the Canadian federal public service was too costly by any standard, and very cost-ineffective. Moreover, it was also known that a substantial portion of the federal bureaucracy was not even "showing up" – having "mentally opted out," failing to bring the requisite *affectio societatis* to the despatch of their work, and failing to meet the requirements of their burden of office, etc. (Paquet 1991-92).

By March 2015, even officials of the association representing Canada's federal public service executives (APEX) confirmed that almost one third of the Canada's federal executives had "mentally checked out" and that the engagement of the other two-thirds had fallen over the years (May 2015b).

Blueprint 2020 (the 2013 document about what the Canadian public service should be now and in the future) was a *cri d'alarme*, and, over the last year or so, one would think that this would have been a wake-up call. Indeed, a number of organizations have appeared to show some concern for these issues in terms that are more or less disingenuous. They have volunteered their own diagnoses about the source of the triple problem of disengagement, inefficiency and ineffectiveness of the Canadian federal public bureaucracy, and have suggested ways to tackle it. These documents (or rants in some cases) have been unequally perceptive or helpful.

Some documents emanated from the core agency purportedly charged with the governance and management of the Canadian federal public service – the Treasury Board Secretariat. Others have emerged from a mushy collection of central places in the federal administrative apparatus that are supposed to have concerns for the performance of the Canadian federal public service (the Office of the Clerk of the Privy Council/Secretary to Cabinet as titular Head of the Public Service, etc.). In addition there have been studies from the Association of Professional Executives of the Public Service of Canada (APEX) and statements from the public service unions. Views from the employees have been forthcoming through survey results – most recently in 2014 (Public Service Employee Survey (PSES)).

To this array of points of view set out by closely concerned interest groups, one might add a number of studies emerging from academic or think tank circles – more or less closely associated with some branch or other of the federal public sector, and as a result more or less allowed to exert critical thinking and, therefore, more or less capable or willing to assign blame where blame is due.

We have not attempted to review all these documents with the same care.

Of the various initiatives, some were conducted at too much of a cloud-nine level, and cast in fundamentalist molds to such an extent that they could not be considered as leading to anything practical. Even though some of these philosophical disquisitions denounced promiscuity between politicians and bureaucrats in thunderous terms, even damning individuals by name in some cases, they appear to be faulting flawed structures and unacceptable behaviours for most ailments but remaining too metaphysical in their search for a panacea (the negotiation of a charter of the public service). This may have been inspiring but led to nothing more than a sort of other-worldly Ponce de Leon's quest for a fountain of youth strategy to dissolve all the arterio-sclerosis of the Canadian public service. For example, we have put aside the Heintzman (2014) paper as *hors champs*: it would deserve special treatment.

Of these various groups, the public service unions (to a different degree one must admit depending on the particular union) have brought forth the most corporatist diagnosis and the most sophomoric cure. If one were to believe the utterances and the advertising campaigns of some, the unionized public service clergy at the federal level cannot be held responsible for any of the difficulties noted. All the problems are ascribable to the Harper government and its political epigones, and the cure is simply to get rid of them. Public service unions have developed a juvenile antagonistic perspective *vis-à-vis* the federal employer that has led them to blindly and self-righteously stand up for the least defensible practices of their members and their most outrageous privileges, to deny any dysfunctionality of the federal public service ascribable to the employees, and to react to the most commonsensical efforts to deal with widely acknowledged problems by the most obtuse resistance and sophistry. We have ignored these rants in preparing this paper.

The other groups have not completely escaped *l'esprit du temps* – a spirit that we analyzed in some of our writings as marked by conservatorship (Hubbard and Paquet 2015), social learning disabilities and pneumopathology (Paquet 2014) – but the ratio of noise to signal in their messages has been less prohibitive.

In the next section, we sketch in a very succinct but critical way the diagnoses and the cures emanating from documents produced by the Treasury Board Secretariat and by the Office of the Clerk of Privy Council, in the various publications of APEX, in the latest survey of employees (PSES), and the proposals set out in the study of Lahey and Goldenberg (2014). We also mention the diagnosis and the cure suggested by our own inquiries (Hubbard and Paquet 2014a, 2015).

Let us begin with a report on the work of two think tanks: the Public Policy Forum and Canada 2020.

In the following section, we try to show how to tackle the problem head on by developing a 'synoptic perspective' and by pulling together practical suggestions that go beyond superficial tweaking. We do so, building on our own earlier work (Hubbard and Paquet 2014a: conclusion) and also keeping in mind a wise remark from Ian Clark (2001), suggesting that fundamental reforms of the public service require an alignment of many agendas.

It is our view that for any incoming government of whatever political stripe, this composite cure is a *sine qua non* if it truly wishes to be able to deliver what is on its own agenda – whatever that might be.

In the final section, we suggest that at the core of this compendium of actions would be the decision by the Canadian government to put in place a powerful infrastructure to combat the fundamental and endemic inertia of the system – a Ministry of Governance and Public Service – capable of quarterbacking such important reforms of the governance apparatus and of human resource management in concert with a few core partners in the current governing institutions. The Australian experience is presented as a potential model for a process likely to bring forth such reforms.

# Vignettes of diagnoses and cures
# from different perspectives

Loud and clear dissatisfaction with the performance of the Canadian federal public service has been recorded since the 1970s. This has led to various waves of putative reforms (Nielsen's task forces, Tellier's PS 2000, Program Review, etc.), but none has generated a substantial refurbishment of the governing apparatus triggering the installation of the requisite capacity to transform the Canadian federal public service.

The main reason for these failures has been the lack of gumption that has presided over all these enterprises: they all ended up being nothing more than wishy-washy patching up exercises, entirely dominated by temporary fiscal restraint objectives, and completely ignoring the governance and management imperatives that should have been given priority.

They all ignored the new technological and moral imperatives that are redefining the way public administration is conducted. Such cost-cutting 'rear-view-mirror' perspectives are inadequate when one is trying to shape the public service of the future, and to anchor its capacity to perform efficiently, effectively and innovatively in the mastering of a capacity to transform that will keep it not only up-to-date and abreast with the new technologies, and in keeping with the new mores, but also and most importantly make it *antifragile* (Taleb 2012) – i.e., capable of growing stronger and more capable of dealing with ever more daunting challenges.

This is the only way to ensure that the public service will thrive in the future: not being satisfied with mere resilience (that allows it to spring back unscathed after a shock), but aiming at continually becoming better equipped to handle ever more challenging difficulties.

This increasingly dynamic capability to cope with ever more technologically and morally demanding circumstances means that, in systems terms, the public sector labour force needs to acquire a capacity to transform and to improve in the face of an environment plagued with more and more nasty and unpredictable wicked problems and avalanches. At the same time, of course, there needs to be the same sort of improvement in its human capital, knowledge capital, knowhow, and wisdom – something analogous to what is expected from licenced professionals if they wish to maintain their designation and continue to practice their profession in medicine, law, engineering, etc.

This is what one can legitimately expect from public sector employees who are charged by the state to deliver life-and-death services and deal with ever more wicked problems (Brown *et al.* 2010).

What follows is a comment on a series of documents (A) defining the kind of public service that is needed, according to the Blueprint 2020 document of the Clerk in 2013. The next four comments (B through E) provide different perspectives on the problem and suggest responses of varying sorts. The last piece (F) paints a picture of what is needed most starkly, and sets the stage for what needs to follow.

A. **Blueprint 2020** (Clerk of the Privy Council 2013) was an ambitious invitation to transform along these lines. Full of lofty ideals, it would appear to recognize that the ground was in motion, and that the environment required innovation, agility, more productivity, and antifragility from the federal public service. This has produced efforts to drive the fake out of public administration through specific action on these fronts by the Treasury Board Secretariat.

Perhaps for tactical reasons, the lofty objectives of Blueprint 2020 were translated into somewhat toned-down and tweak-sounding operational objectives. Even these scaled-down 'objectives' have generated a good deal of dogged resistance. The public sector unions attacked those commonsensical, performance-seeking aspects of its action as "disguised discipline." But unions were not the only *saboteurs*. Other groups have contributed in many subtle ways to rein in or to derail the Blueprint 2020 debate toward certain very particular sub-aspects of poor performance, in order to defang its ambitious demands.

B. One such subtle enterprise of defanging has been the work of the then **Clerk of Privy Council** (Janice Charette). By softening the objectives of Blueprint 2020 considerably, and focusing on more tame or operational issues like reinvigorating recruitment, building a healthful environment, and reinforcing the policy community, the new Clerk has unfortunately contributed to deflecting attention altogether from the oblique but stinging indictment of the present system contained in Blueprint 2020.

The "we will try to do better" tone adopted by Janice Charette in her annual report to the Prime Minister on the state of the public service erased the scintilla of odium of the ever so polite indictment of the existing apparatus contained in Blueprint 2020. It has allowed all the stark resistance to any fundamental change to attach its wagon to that Charette locomotive, and to transform the demand for a cure that would effect a transformation of the Canadian federal public service system into a mere need for tweaking.

For some observers, this sort of language game may not appear to be dramatically important. This is so only because they remain blind to the coxswain role of the Clerk (as Head of the Public Service) as the final arbiter to whom all senior officials turn before deciding if the general directions chosen by the former Clerk are to be taken seriously.

C. **APEX** has resisted the gospel of Blueprint 2020 much less obliquely and much more pointedly, but equally subtly, by a series of documents. They deflected the probing of the causes and sources of the whole malaise of the public service as fundamentally and dynamically deficient into narrower avenues anchored in work pressure generating mental health issues and in a lack of respect and civility that prevented executives from serving well. This shifted the attention away from the core indictment of Blueprint 2020 that the federal public service in its present form is ill-equipped to cope with the new challenges and the new demands it faces and needs a massive transformation. In a nutshell, the incapacity and failure to deliver adequate services by the Canadian federal public service may well be a cause rather than a consequence of mental stress even though APEX insists on the alternative explanation.

The documents written for and by APEX have marshalled various arguments that ascribe all the difficulties of the Canadian federal public service (if they exist) to the disengagement and disempowerment of executives due to:

- a centralization of power in the hands of unpredictable and unreliable politicians;
- continual reduction of resources and authorities;
- a lack of respect of executives by politicians that provokes disengagement;
- the ensuing mental pressure, and development of mental health issues; and
- all of this leading executives to "check out" as a strategy of survival.

APEX claims that executives have all the skills and knowledge they need, and that what prevents them from performing is beyond their control: they are "victims" – caused in particular by the lack of civility, and the lack of respect of the employer, thereby generating mental stress and mental health problems for them and those they supervise. The cure – more civility, respect and tender care – would appear rather unpersuasive if the failing capabilities of the bureaucracy to serve governments well when facing more wicked policy problems are the real difficulty that needs curing.

APEX wants to tackle the disempowerment, disrespect, incivility, mental pressure, etc., as if they were exogenously generated. But what if the federal public executives "check out" because they cannot shoulder the burden of their office, and are really victimized because of these incapacities and inabilities?

D. **The Public Service Employee Survey** does not quite tell the same story. The employee survey conducted in late 2014 is obviously not meant to provide an articulate response to Blueprint 2020, but it does reveal directly the perception of a broad cross-section of public servants with respect to certain themes that are related to the general malaise of the Canadian federal public service at present.

One of the major findings, for our purposes, is the extent to which dissatisfaction is recorded by public servants at large, with finger pointing at certain sources of difficulties having to do with the executives of the federal bureaucracy. Three statistics appear to indicate that public servants in general have some concern about the performance of executives: only 53 percent have confidence in senior managers, only 46 percent feel that executives try to resolve problems that concern them, and only 38 percent say that unsatisfactory performance is managed effectively by their superiors.

This focuses the attention on the ineffectiveness of executives – a matter more or less denied in the perspective set out by their representatives.

E. The recent **Lahey and Goldenberg study** (2014) is a perplexing document. On the one hand, it focuses only on ADMs, but on the other hand, it casts an eye rather broadly on the changes and dynamic of the broader environment for the Canadian federal public service. Ascertaining not only how demands on the ADMs are changing, the study also pays attention to the demands on the whole public service, as well as on how the skills of the executives (as they are) may not match the sort of capabilities required by the new challenges faced by the executives – especially, but not only, by the ADMs.

The Lahey and Goldenberg text is crafted in politically correct language, sanitized to a great extent, but also robustly sprinkled with statements made by interviewees that reveal more discord than the tone of the text tries to convey. The ADMs are not fully exonerated for their declining status and fate, but they are not either explicitly indicted in a fundamental way. Readers will find in this study anything they need to develop contradictory arguments on this front.

A whole array of factors is invoked (centralization of the decision-making process that has squeezed the ADMs out of their traditional niches, etc.), but there is some palpable hesitation to declare what would appear to be flagrant: the ADMs are ill-equipped to deal with the more complex issues with which they are now confronted. They do not have the skills and depth required. Consequently, the demand for their services has naturally declined because they are not capable of providing them effectively.

Lahey and Goldenberg dare to raise real questions about the skills (but not about the competencies) of the ADMs, allowing the impression that such lack of "competencies" might be easily repaired with some tweaking. By contrast, when Lahey and Goldenberg identify some structural flaws that in no way can be ascribed as the responsibility of the executives (too many layers of hierarchies, churn, etc.), they immediately seize upon these features in making recommendations. But again, this is formulated in a very tame manner: delayering is a form of tweaking.

In the final analysis, a reader would have to be forgiven if he/she were to remember "delayering and clarifying" as the focal point of the message – rather than the lack of needed competencies by the incumbents that emerges from the interviews and testimonies.

The Lahey and Goldenberg document is neither as simplistic as the obfuscating counter-attack of APEX (so the document could not easily be used to support the sort of dogged resistance to anything dramatic that is being undertaken in response to Blueprint 2020), nor is it stark enough in pointing to the existing deficiencies of the executives to allow those in authority (who have developed a great capacity for selective reading) to use it to quash the sort of resistance that has already materialized and prevents any serious reforming action from being taken as a result of Blueprint 2020.[1]

As a result of its determination never to conclude that the system is flawed and the personnel incompetent, but to defend a relatively 'easy to accept' cure – all this without completely occluding some toxic findings – the document is both comforting and frustrating.

F. Between 2008 and 2014, **Hubbard and Paquet** have showered their colleagues with a variety of papers and books that have pointed the finger directly at the lack of competencies of the Canadian federal public service, and to the need to design a less ineffective alternative to the mythical Westminster system structure, if one is to hope to have in place a performance-oriented bureaucracy that is capable of responding to the daunting challenges of the 21st century.

In effect, between 2006 and 2009, Hubbard and Paquet held some 44 sessions on 24 taboo topics with approximately 100 senior executives of the Canadian federal government under the auspices of APEX. With those executives, they probed a certain number of issues that were designed to elicit a display of the capacities and effectiveness of the group to gauge and solve problems of increasing complexity and requiring *seriatim*:

- the capacity to cope with difficult issues;
- the capacity to engage intelligently with more complex issues;
- the capacity to collibrate, or tinker with, yet more thorny problems; and

[1] This artful elusiveness of the Lahey and Goldenberg document deserves blame when their study carefully avoids even mentioning recent other studies that have squarely indicted the competencies of the executives of the Canadian federal public service (Hubbard and Paquet 2010, 2014a, b) or ignores suggestions that have been floating around for years about the need for some redesign to drive the fake out of the management vacuum that plagues the federal bureaucracy (Heintzman and Juillet 2012) while carefully recording the banalities of a literature dedicated to the conservatorship of antiquated structures and a gospel of tweaking.

- the capacity to reframe the problem definitions when wicked problems could not be tackled effectively otherwise.

Progressively, as the sequence of sessions unfolded, it became clear that the best of the federal public executives (for we feel that we were facing some of the best of the lot who were keenly interested in the challenges they were facing) may be able to handle the first two levels of difficulties, but they were not well prepared to handle effectively the latter two groups of daunting problems.

We first reported on the strengths and weaknesses in the capabilities of these executives in *The Black Hole of Public Administration* (Hubbard and Paquet 2010: chapter 3) and "Competencies: part of the governance vacuum" (Hubbard and Paquet 2014b). For a summary of the weaknesses revealed in our discussions with EXs as we progressed through more and more complex problems, see "Competencies" (Hubbard and Paquet 2014b: 118) where a list is starkly presented. We reproduce it below:

- decline in open critical thinking,
- lack of gumption,
- willful blindness in the face of mental prisons and neuroses,
- incapacity/unwillingness to take the initiative,
- impatience with systemic issues and propensity to focus on operational details,
- cognitive dissonance,
- presence of latent fear,
- moral vacancy, crippling epistemologies,
- risk aversion and fear of experimentation, and
- disinterest in the face of new perspectives difficult to understand.

This led Hubbard and Paquet to point to the sort of way forward likely to shepherd the Canadian federal bureaucracy out of this predicament: first in a most general way in the conclusion of *Probing the Bureaucratic Mind: About Canadian*

*Federal Executives* (Hubbard and Paquet 2014a), and then to focus on the major planks of this platform in *Irregular Governance: A Plea for Bold Organizational Experimentation* (Hubbard and Paquet 2015: Part III).

* * *

One may attach different weights to these action studies that question the qualifications and competencies of the public sector executives to varying degrees, and indict the governance and management structures in place in the Canadian federal public sector more or less vehemently. Depending on the nature of the diagnosis arrived at, a range of responses – from doing nothing, to tinkering, to a dramatic refurbishment of the Canadian federal public service and an equally fundamental transformation of the structures of management to deal with the present management vacuum – may be suggested.

The cognate victimhood attitude carefully crafted by APEX may be less crude than the "anybody but Harper" of the public sector unions, but it may not deserve more credibility and attention. It is a refusal to look at the factum developed over time about the ineffectiveness and poor performance of the federal public sector employees, and a failure to recognize that a significant portion of such poor performance can and should be credibly ascribed to the flaws of the executives and the organizational forms with which they have accepted to work. This sentiment was confirmed by the federal employees in the survey.

With a slightly different focus – ADMs for Lahey and Goldenberg, and EXs for Hubbard and Paquet – the so-called academic studies have the merit of recognizing *a priori* the responsibility of the executive class with respect to the poor performance of the federal public sector. The two groups use softer and harsher language respectively; they search for an easy out in the first case by being satisfied to demand upfront much more than delayering, while the second group suggests nothing less than a refoundation of both the human resource (HR) regime (at the executive level at the very least), and a transformation of the governance structure to take the fake out of public administration.

Lahey and Goldenberg are not very specific except when it comes to delayering. Hubbard and Paquet have been bolder and have developed in the conclusions of *Probing the Bureaucratic Mind* (Hubbard and Paquet 2014a) some guidelines for action on the capacities refurbishment front; and in the chapter 6 of *Irregular Governance* (Hubbard and Paquet 2015), a sketch of what is required both on the capacities front and on the governance structure front – suggesting the idea of boards of management to complement the traditional structure of departments and agencies.

Some of these ideas have been talked about for decades, and they have received the support of many a public administration expert. But they have been fiercely fought by the clergy of federal public administrators and their close academic allies – both groups mesmerized by the fantasies of Westminster and dedicated to its conservatorship – a bias that leads bureaucracies to give precedence to the need to preserve over the need to serve (Terry 2003: 29). For these modern Quixotes, the idea and the model of Westminster is more real than the reality they are facing everyday – for them *"le réel n'a pas eu lieu"* (Onfray 2014). Consequently, the canonical literature they distill is completely immunized against both the new reality and the new ideas others might develop about it.

## Evasive thinking

Two recent documents that obliquely purport to deal with flaws in the preparation of senior federal executives might illustrate our contention.[2] The first escapes the problem of

---

[2] We use the word obliquely because of the fact that neither of the two reports clearly admits that senior executives are ill-prepared to do their jobs well. They only hint that the present situation may be less than perfect or may become so. This subtlety is quite important for it reveals the aura of perfection and holiness that is meticulously maintained about the quality of the federal senior public service.

present inadequacies of the senior executives by shifting the debate to problems of individual leadership in the future. The second shifts the focus to an even higher level of abstraction by insisting that the core problem is at the level of the political-bureaucratic interface.

## A. Canada's Public Policy Forum (2014)

A first intriguing example of this sort of *fuite en avant* is a recent publication of Canada's Public Policy Forum (CPPF 2014) based on the "insights from over 130 *emerging and established leaders* within and outside the public sector" (our emphasis). The document escapes from the difficult world of the problems of capabilities and competencies of the Canadian federal executives through an elevation of the debates to the fanciful world of 'leadership', and by focusing on so-called future problems rather than on the ones we face now. It would appear to suggest that the problem is not one of capabilities and competencies but one of leadership. Consequently, it occludes completely the inadequacies of the senior federal executives now, and focuses on the ruminations of these "insightful" persons about the ten top skills that the leader of the future must have.

It is obviously much easier to focus on leaders but this can only be valid if one assumes that if the leadership problems are resolved, then the problems of the organization will automatically be resolved too. This presumes that the organization is adequate and fit to begin with. The only thing missing would be heroic leaders guiding competent followers into doing the right thing. The competency problem is therefore made to disappear by assumption. The table presenting the 10 leadership skills elicited from consultation with insightful leaders is reproduced in Table 1. The future leaders equipped with these skills would repair any putative flaws in the public service – if such flaws might ever be detected.

TABLE 1.

## Canada's Public Policy Forum:
## Speculations About the Skills of the Future Leader

| Astute Strategist | Empathetic Facilitator | Pragmatic Technophile | Catalyzing Agent | Prudent Manager |
|---|---|---|---|---|
| • Understands complexity<br>• Possesses broad knowledge<br>• Is a quick thinker<br>• Has good judgement | • Builds relationships<br>• Communicates effectively<br>• Finds common ground<br>• Manages expectations | • Embraces innovation<br>• Continues learning about new technology<br>• Seeks opportunities to leverage technologies<br>• Understands risks | • Adapts to change<br>• Drives outcomes<br>• Seizes opportunities<br>• Motivates others to act | • Manages budgets<br>• Is business savvy<br>• Takes a balanced approach<br>• Is resourceful |

| Persuasive Entrepreneur | Shrewd Diplomat | Fearless Advisor | Passionate Talent Scout | Inspirational Team Captain |
|---|---|---|---|---|
| • Has a curious mind<br>• Thinks creatively<br>• Believes that change is possible<br>• Knows how to sell an idea | • Possesses political acuity<br>• Is thick-skinned<br>• Manages multiple priorities<br>• Is a good negotiator | • Filtres relevant information<br>• Provides honest advice<br>• Has integrity<br>• Understands when to push and when to step back | • Is enthusiastic about work<br>• Plays an active role in talent management<br>• Values leadership at all levels<br>• Embraces and leverages diversity | • Leads by example<br>• Demonstrates authenticity<br>• Has a positive attitude<br>• Is a team player |

Source: Canada's Public Policy Forum, 2014, p. iv.

It is difficult to disagree with the fact that the attributes mentioned in Table 1 might be useful and desirable. The difficulty has to do with the fact that the attributes listed are strictly 'leadership competencies', and that they seem to suggest that these top-down skills are the only components that matter.

This sleight of hand (through which the competency problems have been transformed into leadership problems) is all the more surprising because it is proposed at the very moment when it has become widely recognized that heroic leadership is dying as a necessary and sufficient condition in all organizations. The priority is more and more on tackling governing issues not in a "Big G" top-down world, but in a "small g" governance world where nobody is in charge, and the competencies of all partners are becoming most important.[3]

In the complex world of ours, few (if any) have all the information, power and resources to provide individual heroic leadership. Information, power and resources are widely distributed over many persons and groups, and 'stewardship' (an ensemble of mechanisms ensuring effective coordination in the manner of an automatic pilot) – and not 'personal leadership' – is required to ensure that those in possession of portions of the information, power and resources work collaboratively to steer the organization in directions promising resilience, antifragility and progress.

The reductive twist perpetrated by the CPPF to transform complex concerns about competencies, capabilities and performance into simple concerns about personal leadership is deceitful. What is required for an organization to perform

---

[3] In this, the CPPF follows here the lead of the professional Canadian public service which has had a fixation on key leadership skills and not on competencies over the last decades: the CPPF "emerging and established leaders" have simply relayed the perspective in good currency in the Canadian bureaucracy. The underlying model of governing is still "Big G" government: a view built on the perception that all the required power, resources and information are in the hands of leaders who (if effective leaders) are able to control the process of communication through which their orders will be carried out, and thereby guide the organization to success.

well is a mix of *savoir-faire*, qualifications, expertise, skills, competencies all around, certain behavioural characteristics, but also particular organizational and institutional re-arrangements to ensure a good match between the complexity of the task and the capacities of office holders and effective stewardship (Hubbard *et al.* 2012).

In this "small g" governance world, the cosmology of leadership is quite toxic. Despite the CPPF claim upfront that the future will require flat, flexible and forward thinking, the skill set that emerges from this psychoanalysis of emerging and established leaders is, not surprisingly, skills demanded in a hierarchical world, and purported to generate top-down decisions to be taken – for it is assumed that someone is in charge, that this someone has all the information, resources and power to effect a satisfactory strategy, and that the only problem is that this someone should be able to issue the right orders. There would appear to be no need for the leader to learn to begin with and to redesign anything. The cognitive abilities of the office holder are assumed to match the complexity of the tasks to be tackled. All that matters is to select the polymath charismatic leader – the rest (performance included) will follow automatically. The CPPF has squeezed out of a *coterie* of emergent and established leaders a list of the 29 generic skills and attributes to look for in these leaders (CPPF 2014: 8).[4] Happy hunting!

---

[4] SKILLS: business acumen, change management, collaborative intelligence, cultural competency, entrepreneurial thinking, global awareness, organizational skills, political acuity, problem solving, relationship building, strategic analysis, technological fluency; ATTRIBUTES: adaptability, broad knowledge, confidence, creativity, curiosity, decisiveness, dedication, emotional intelligence, foresight, good judgment, initiative, integrity, passion, perseverance, persuasiveness, pragmatism, receptivity, tact.

## B. Canada 2020

An even more recent document, penned by Ralph Heintzman for Canada 2020, shifts the debate to an even more ethereal level: according to that document, the core issue that cripples the present state of affairs in the Canadian senior public service is the relationship between elected and non-elected officials. The problem is therefore not one of competencies (nor even one of individual leadership skills), but lies with the "promiscuity" between public service executives and elected officials as the source of evil.[5]

Heintzman chooses to illustrate the toxic dimension of such promiscuity by reference to two specific events: the first one is a clearly condemnable intervention of the Office of the Clerk of Privy Council to prevent an assistant deputy minister (ADM) from stopping wrongdoing by senior federal public servants at the time of the sponsorship affair – this was obviously reprehensible since it purported to stop action against criminal activities of a political nature;[6] the second one is the much more debatable case of the Clerk of the Privy Council taking a stand against the Parliamentary Budget Officer (PBO) (and in favour of the government) in a matter where the PBO had made what was regarded by many observers as a very contestable request for the tabling of documents on emerging policies that had not been finalized. In discussing this second case, Heintzman would appear to suggest that any collaboration between the senior bureaucracy and the politicians is potentially *a priori* reprehensible or at least suspect. By extension, one may infer that the senior bureaucracy has a responsibility to defend a notion of the public interest that is different from the one held by the elected officials, and that this

[5] The word promiscuity is borrowed somewhat uncritically by Heintzman but has been used in a most cavalier way by many public administration specialists from Britain (Wilson and Barker 2003) and Canada (Lindquist and Rasmussen 2012). It would appear to be a pillar of Heintzman's diagnosis.

[6] This is a matter on which we have commented in Hubbard and Paquet, 2007, p. 48.

technocratic view is seemingly more legitimate than the elected officials' view.

This doctrine may even appear to legitimize the disloyalty of the bureaucratic tribe of senior executives *vis-à-vis* the elected government, and to suggest that, for the technocrat, loyalty to the bureaucratic tribe would appear to take precedence over the loyalty to the elected government.

As a grand solution, Heintzman suggests that what is required is a Charter of Public Service that would establish the boundaries of separate facilities that politicians have to respect in dealing with the bureaucracy, and vice versa. Another way of interpreting such a document might be to regard it as a strengthening of the role of the technocracy, and a suggestion that it has greater moral authority than the elected officials. In effect, the Canada 2020 position is ascribing the difficulties of the public service to its being unduly influenced by the politicians, and its response to the malaise is therefore to ensure a stronger firewall between them, and a more firmly established role for the technocracy in our governance.

\* \* \*

Elegant though these explorations may be, they do not address the central issue of the underperformance of the federal senior executives in the face of a world of greater complexity and uncertainty. They provide sermons when what is needed is a more down-to-earth effort to make public sector bureaucracies more effective and efficient.

The literature on governance has shown over the last decades that, in our world plagued by complexity and uncertainty, public sector bureaucracies are confronted with new difficulties:

- the problem definition for many of the issues they face is not given to them necessarily *ab ovo*;
- the requisite power, resources and information necessary to understand these issues and to imagine effective ways to deal with them are not in the hands of one person most of the time;

- the result is that one has to launch an inquiring system to ascertain the nature of the problem and to uncover what sort of communication and collaborative arrangements are likely to be required to cope with the problems at hand;
- this, in turn, will lead to major design work to ensure that the necessary apparatus is in place to steward the system in a reasonably effective direction (Paquet 2013).

None of the required crucial cognitive, inquiring, social learning and designing abilities or capacities would appear to have been given much prominence in the kinds of ratiocinations that the CPPF and Canada 2020 propose. As a result, one has to wonder about the magical process through which such wonderful heroic individual bureaucratic leaders (free from any political pressure) will ever find their way in a world where an inquiring system has to be constructed to elicit a reasoned diagnosis, and to design collaborative governing – if one cannot count on a broad competent cadre of senior executives well-suited to the complexities of the tasks to play their part in all those operations.

The proposals, interesting as they may be, are therefore unlikely to do much to repair the competency deficiencies that have been observed. Like the early maps of the 15th century, they may be elegant but not helpful to navigation.

## Tackling the problem head on

This very succinct review of a selection of documents that were produced recently has presented alternative diagnoses and cures for the ailments of the Canadian federal public service. It does not point to a convergent strategy.

When Ian Clark (Clark 2001) looked back reflectively at the early waves of the reform effort in countries and provinces with Westminster roots from the 1980s on, he pointed out that for major public service reform to be successful, two things are necessary. First, an alignment is needed at the political level of the policy, fiscal and management agendas, and second, intense political interest must exist in the management agenda itself (*Ibid.*: 85).

The agendas may have seemed aligned in the first years of the present decade (e.g. amending labour laws and improving control over total compensation costs), when the then Clerk (Wayne Wouters) launched Blueprint 2020, and when he followed it up with a national validation and engagement process involving all public servants (seeking their ideas) that was called 'impressive and unprecedented' by the Prime Minister. Direction 2020 tasked its executive heads with 'making it happen' by implementing the necessary changes.

But this process also allowed the senior bureaucracy's vested interest in resisting change to materialize. This is when the wheels came off the cart. A confederacy of bureaucrats and consorts succeeded in defanging the process by trivializing it so to speak, i.e., deflecting action toward scaled-down objectives and operational issues. This more-timid pathway has taken the wind out of Blueprint 2020 sails.

For the kind of fundamental transformation expressed in Blueprint 2020 to be successful in repositioning the public service in such a way that it can effectively do its job of serving Canadians and the governments of the day, politicians have to become fully conscious (and it has to be clearly explained to the citizenry) that the policy, fiscal and management agendas of the government require (of necessity) a dramatic transformation of the antiquated Canadian federal public service – a trans-substantiation of the bureaucracy. Otherwise the elected governments, whatever their stripe, will not be able to deliver on the agendas that they professed prior to the election because the bureaucracy will prove incapable of delivering for them.

What is missing at the present time is a recognition by all parties that reforming the Canadian federal bureaucracy is a *sine qua non* for any government that wishes to ensure that it has the capacity to deliver on its agendas. This would appear not to be acknowledged by any of the key players at the present time.

A minister of the Machinery of Governance and the Public Service – some sort of aggrandized, enhanced, enriched, souped-up version of Treasury Board Secretariat – in charge of a super department with the resources necessary to ensure the required coordination – would send a clear signal that a transformation of the Canadian federal public service is now recognized at the top as essential. Such a key player would be a legitimate voice at the Cabinet table, able to speak to the broad perspective that is necessary to ensure that appropriate governance and management structures are in place and that competent human resources are found and developed to ensure that the job is done effectively.

Putting the right person in this sort of right job at the right time may be necessary at the political level, necessary but not sufficient to create the conditions for the revolution called for by Blueprint 2020 to materialize and succeed.

In this context, the Australian experience may be interesting. It may appear to be too straightforward and practical to be acceptable in the Canadian context, yet it holds some lessons as to the sort of process that needs to be put in place.

In Australia, it all began with the Australian Public Service Commission (2007) – with a mandate quite different from the mandate of the Canadian PSC – producing a briefing paper applying the Rittel and Webber (1973) wicked problem approach to national policy fields. This was an eye-opening experiment.

First, it brought the characteristics of wicked problems identified by Rittel and Webber into visibility in national debates in all issue domains:

- multiple interpretations with no one version being right or wrong;
- interdependencies, multiple causality and trade-offs between conflicting goals;
- addressing the problem leading to unforeseen consequences;
- problem definition not stable but a moving target;
- no definitive solution;
- great social complexity;
- rarely tractable within one discipline, or organization, so difficult to position responsibility; and

- resolution involving personal and social behavioural changes.

Second, it also revealed that such wicked problems cannot be generalized outside their contexts, that they rest on underlying paradoxes (self-contradictory statements in which both propositions are true), and that they contain multiple worldviews, multiple ways of constructing knowledge and multiple ethical positions. In a word, it requires a different sort of inquiring system, much different from the standard linear approaches in good currency in public administration (Brown *et al.* 2010: 62-64).

Third, in part as an echo effect of this initiative by the Australian Public Service Commission, a research team at the Australian National University got involved in developing guiding principles for an open, critical, transdisciplinary, collective and imagination-fuelled systemic approach in dealing with wicked policy problems. While their interest was largely focused on sustainability, it has put in place the foundations of a broader approach, capable of tackling wicked policy problems of all sorts.

This approach has been summarized synthetically by Jacqueline Y. Russell (2010: 56-58) as anchored in:
- the partiality, plurality and provisionality of knowing;
- the reliability of knowledge being gauged by critical and intersubjective assessment;
- the awareness of the purposes, agendas and values with respect to the inquiring process;
- including both facts and values in the inquiry process; and
- openness to the ontological, epistemological and ethical rationalities.

It has been suggested that the sort of inquiring system required is to proceed in four stages (Brown *et al.* 2010: 78):
- identify the range of worldviews that make up the context of the problem;
- establish the validity of the evidence that each of the knowledges can provide;

- create the conditions that sponsor creativity among the diverse participants; and
- develop a strategy that allows all the contributing knowledges to share possible actions for the future.

This may appear to be rather sketchy, but it proposes a genuinely unconventional and innovative approach that has been able to generate illuminating results in a large number of case studies (Brown *et al.* 2010: Part II), and that later has been stylized in the form of a textbook that shows the way, step by step, to design collective learning for transformational change (Brown and Lambert 2013).

Such an approach – open to different worldviews, transdisciplinary, critical, collective and allowing imagination to play its role in the design of future arrangements – would appear to pave the way for the development of a more comprehensive approach to the challenges they face, and to suggest the contours of a new covenant for senior executives in the public service if they are to meet the Friedmann-Abonyi test (1976): guided by the need to establish that their initiatives are technically feasible, socially acceptable, not too destabilizing, and implementable to begin with.

A social learning approach, built on cognate intentions, has been developed in parallel at the Centre on Governance at the University of Ottawa. It has also been applied to wicked policy problems of all sorts on the broad public administration scene over the years (Paquet 1999, 2013). But it has never met any interest in Canada on the part of the public administration community. We were told that it was difficult to understand. What is clear is that the stimulus for change must come from outside the public administration tribe, but from a position that has some 'skin in the game' – the game being necessarily broader than the field of interest of the federal senior executives alone.

Up to now, a venture such as the one that was kick-started by the Australian Public Service Commission would have been considered unworkable in Canada. A more oblique form of attack on the governance and management vacuum and on the incapabilities of senior executives may need to be envisaged – one that at first blush would not appear to require the development of such a new *outillage mental*.

In Canada, critical thinking is not our cup of tea in this issue domain: obliquity is *de rigueur* (Kay 2010) ... but is it really impossible to proceed as the Australians did? We would say that, with a few design adjustments, this is a process that might be worth the experimentation.

## References

ADP Research Institute. 2012. *Employee Satisfaction vs. Employee Engagement: Are They the Same Thing?* http://www.adp.com/~/media/RI/whitepapers/Employee%20Engagement%20vs%20Employee%20Satisfaction%20White%20Paper.ashx [Accessed July 21, 2015].

Advisory Committee on The Public Service. 2014. *Eighth Report to the Prime Minister.* http://www.clerk.gc.ca/eng/feature.asp?pageId-369 [Accessed April 28, 2014].

Advisory Committee on The Public Service. 2015. *Ninth Report to The Prime Minister.* http://www.clerk.gc.ca/eng/feature.asp?pageId=405 [Accessed September 1, 2015].

Advisory Committee on The Public Service. 2015. *Twenty-second Annual Report To The Prime Minister On The Public Service Of Canada.* http://www.clerk.gc.ca/eng/feature.asp?/pageid=408 [Accessed July 27, 2015].

Allan, L. 2015. *Top Leadership Perspectives on Performance Management.* http://www.businessperform.com/articles/performance-management/leadership-performance-management.html [Accessed July 21, 2015].

APEX. 2013. *2012 APEX Work and Health Survey: Synopsis.* http://www.apex.gc.ca/uploads/key%20priorities/health/2012%20health%20survey%20results%20-%20eng.pdf [Accessed July 21, 2015].

APEX. 2014. *Blueprint 2020 Report to Clerk of Privy Council.* http://www.apex.gc.ca/en/publications/consultations#workexs [Accessed July 21, 2015].

APEX. 2015. *2014 Public Service Employee Survey Results for Executives.* http://www.apex.gc.ca/en/publications/consultations#workexs [Accessed July 21, 2015].

APEX. 2015. *Perspectives of Public Service Executives on Their Evolving Work.* http://www.apex.gc.ca/en/publications/consultations#workexs [Accessed July 21, 2015].

Appiah, K. Anthony. 2010. *The Honor Code – How Moral Revolutions Happen.* New York, NY: Norton.

Australian Public Service Commission. 2007. *Tackling Wicked Problems: A Public Policy Perspective.* Canberra, AU: Australian Government.

Beck, Randall and Jim Harter. 2014. "Why Great Managers are so Rare – Companies fail to choose the candidate with the right talent for the job 82% of the time, GALLUP finds," *Business Journal,* March 25, http://www.gallup.com/businessjournal/167975/why-great-managers-rare.aspx?version=print [Accessed July 27, 2015].

Boland, Richard J. and Fred Collopy. 2004. *Managing by Design.* Stanford, CA: Stanford University Press.

Brown, Valerie A. *et al.* (eds.). 2010. *Tackling Wicked Problems – Through Transdisciplinary Imagination.* London, UK: Earthscan.

Brown, Valerie A. and Judith A. Lambert. 2013. *Collective Learning for Transformational Change – A Guide to Collaborative Action.* London, UK: Routledge.

Canada's Public Policy Forum. 2014. "Flat, flexible, and forward-thinking: Public Service Next," March, https://www.ppforum.ca/sites/default/files/Flat%20Forward%20Flexible%20Final%20Report_EN.pdf [Accessed August 22, 2016].

Charette, Janice. 2015. *Twenty-second Annual Report To The Prime Minister On The Public Service Of Canada*. http://www.clerk. gc.ca/eng/feature.asp?/pageid=408 [Accessed July 27, 2015].

Charette, Janice. 2015. "Preparing Canada's Public Service To Meet The Challenge," *Policy Options*, July-August, p. 100-101.

Chartered Institute of Personnel Development. 2015. *Employee Outlook Spring 2015*. http://www.cipd.co.uk/binaries/ employee-outlook_2015-spring.pdf [Accessed July 21, 2015].

Clark, Ian D. 2001. "Distant Reflections on Federal Public Service reform in the 1990s," *Public Service Management Reform: Progress, Setbacks and Challenges*. February. http:// portal.publicpolicy.utoronto.ca/en/ianclark/Documents/ DistantReflectionsInOAGReport.pdf [Accessed July 27, 2015].

Clerk of the Privy Council (Wouters, Wayne). 2013. *Blueprint 2020 – Introduction*. http://www.clerk.gc.ca/eng/feature. asp?pageId=350 [Accessed July 25, 2015]. 2p.

Clerk of the Privy Council (Wouters, Wayne). 2013. *Blueprint 2020 – Getting Started – Getting Your Views*. http://www.clerk. gc.ca/eng/feature.asp?pageId=349 [Accessed July 23, 2015].

Cuisinier, Vincent. 2008. *L'affectio societatis*. Paris, FR: Lexis-Nexis Litec.

Dowden, Craig. 2015. *Civility Matters!* http://www.apex.gc.ca/ en/publications/whitepapers [Accessed July 21, 2015].

Dowden, Craig. 2015. *Maximizing Employee Engagement Within the Federal Public Service*. http://www.apex.gc.ca/en/publications/ whitepapers [Accessed July 26, 2015].

Duhigg, Charles. 2012. *The Power of Habit – Why we do what we do in life and business*. Toronto, ON: Doubleday.

Flade, P., J. Harter and J. Asplund. 2014. "Seven Things Great Employers Do (That Others Don't)," *Business Journal*, April 15, http://www.gallup.com/businessjournal/168407/seven-things-great-employers-others-don.aspx?version=print [Accessed July 27, 2015].

Friedmann, John. 1978. "The Epistemology of Social Practice," *Theory and Society*, 6(1): 75-92.

Friedmann, John and George Abonyi. 1976. "Social Learning: A Model for Policy Research," *Environment & Planning*, A8, p. 927-940.

Heintzman, Ralph. 2014. *Renewal of the Federal Public Service: Toward a Charter of Public Service*. Ottawa, ON: Canada 2020.

Heintzman, Ralph and Luc Juillet. 2012. "Searching for New Instruments of Accountability: New Political Governance and the Dialectics of Democratic Accountability" in H. Bakvis and M.D. Jarvis (eds.). *From New Public Management to New Political Governance*. Montreal, QC: McGill-Queen's University Press, p. 342-379.

Herrman, Chris. "Poor Performance Reward and Recognition," *Business Performance*, http://www.businessperform.com/ articles/performance-management/poor_performance_ reward.html [Accessed July 21, 2015].

Hubbard, Ruth and Gilles Paquet. 2007. *Gomery's Blinders and Canadian Federalism*. Ottawa, ON: University of Ottawa Press.

Hubbard, Ruth and Gilles Paquet. 2010. *The Black Hole of Public Administration*. Ottawa, ON: University of Ottawa Press.

Hubbard, Ruth and Gilles Paquet. 2014a. *Probing the Bureaucratic Mind – About Canadian Federal Executives*. Ottawa, ON: Invenire.

Hubbard, Ruth and Paquet, Gilles. 2014b. "Competencies: part of the governance vacuum," *www.optimumonline.ca*, 44(3): 58-73.

Hubbard, Ruth and Paquet, Gilles. 2015. *Irregular Governance – A Plea for Bold Organizational Experimentation*. Ottawa, ON: Invenire.

Hubbard, Ruth *et al.* 2012. *Stewardship: Collective Decentered Metagovernance and Inquiring Systems*. Ottawa, ON: Invenire.

Kay, John. 2010. *Obliquity – Why our goals are best achieved indirectly*. London, UK: The Penguin Press.

Lahey, James and Mark Goldenberg. 2014. *Assistant Deputy Ministers in the Canadian Public Service.* Ottawa, ON: University of Ottawa, Centre on Public Management and Policy, http://socialsciences.uottawa.ca/cgpp-cpmp/eng/documents/Report_ADM_study_2014_e.pdf [Accessed August 8, 2015].

Lindquist, Evert and Ken Rasmussen. 2012. "Deputy Ministers and New Political Governance: From Neutral Competence to Promiscuous Partisans to a New Balance?" in Herman Bakvis and Mark D. Jarvis (eds.). *From New Public Management to New Political Governance: Essays in Honour of Peter C. Aucoin.* Montreal, QC and Kingston, ON: McGill-Queen's University Press, p. 179-203.

Lipman, V. 2013. "Surprising, Disturbing Facts From the Mother of All Employee Engagement Surveys," *Forbes,* September 23, http://www.forbes.com/sites/victorlipman/2013/09/23/surprising-disturbing-facts-from-the-mother-of-all-employee-engagement-surveys/ [Accessed July 21, 2015].

Mann, A. and R. Darby. 2014. "Should Managers Focus On Performance or Engagement? Gallup examined this question and found that the answer isn't as "either/or" as most companies might think," *Gallup Business Journal,* August 5, http://www.gallup.com/businessjournal/174197/managers-focus-performance-engagement.aspx?version=print [Accessed July 27, 2015].

May, Kathryn. 2014. "Unions grieve new PS performance rules," *Ottawa Citizen,* April 7, A1-2.

May, K. 2015a. "Senior Bureaucrats feel role as 'true execs' has declined," *Ottawa Citizen,* July 8, A9.

May, K. 2015b. "Study urges changes of top bureaucracy," *Ottawa Citizen,* July 14, A6.

May, K. 2015c. "PS executives 'disengaged'," *Ottawa Citizen,* July 15, A1.

Normann, Richard. 2001. *Reframing Business.* Chichester, UK: Wiley.

Onfray, Michel. 2014. *Le réel n'a pas eu lieu – le principe de Don Quichotte*. Paris, FR: Autrement.

Paquet, Gilles. 1991-92. "Betting on Moral Contracts," *Optimum*, 22(3): 45-53.

Paquet, Gilles. 1999. "Tackling Wicked Problems" in G. Paquet, *Governance Through Social Learning*. Ottawa, ON: University of Ottawa Press, chapter 2.

Paquet, Gilles. 2012. "La gouvernance, science de l'imprécis," *Organisations & Territoires*, 21(3): 5-17.

Paquet, Gilles. 2013. *Tackling Wicked Policy Problems – Equality, Diversity and Sustainability*. Ottawa, ON: Invenire.

Paquet, Gilles. 2014. *Unusual Suspects – Essays on Social Learning Disabilities*. Ottawa, ON: Invenire.

Paquet, Gilles and Christopher Wilson. 2011. "Collaborative Co-governance and Inquiring Systems," *www.optimumonline.ca*, 41(2): 1-12.

Pritchett, Lant. 2013. *The Rebirth of Education – Schooling ain't Learning*. Washington, DC: Brookings Institution.

Public Service Commission (New South Wales Government). 2014. *People Matter Employee Survey 2014: Main Findings Report*, http://www.psc.nsw.gov.au/about-the-public-sector/people-matter-employee-survey/people-matter-employee-survey-2014 [Accessed August 2, 2015].

Rein, L. 2014. "Federal employees unhappy with senior leaders, suffer low morale, survey shows," *Washington Post*, Oct. 24, http://www.washingtonpost.com/politics/federal-employees-unhappy-with-senior-leaders-suffer-low-moral-survey-shows/2014/10/24/0b4a414c-5ba9-11e4-b812-38518ae74c67_story.html [Accessed August 17, 2016].

Rittel, H. and M. Webber. 1973. "Dilemmas in a General Theory of Planning," *Policy Sciences*, 4, p. 155-169.

Russell, Jacqueline Y. 2010. "A Philosohical Framework for an Open and Critical Transdisciplinary Inquiry" in Brown,

Valerie A. *et al.* (eds.). *Tackling Wicked Problems – Through Transdisciplinary Imagination.* London, UK: Earthscan, p. 31-60.

Sabel, Charles F. 2001. "A Quiet Revolution of Democratic Governance: Towards Democratic Experimentalism" in *Governance in the 21st Century.* Paris, FR: OECD, p. 121-148.

Sunohara, D. 2014. "TBS & Performance Management: Hit & Miss?" February 5, http://deltapartners.ca/blog/tbs-performance-management-hit-miss [Accessed August 2, 2015].

Taleb, Nassim N. 2012. *Antifragile – Things that gain from disorder.* New York, NY: Random House.

Terry, Larry D. 2003. *Leadership of Public Bureaucracies – The Administrator as Conservator.* Armonk, NY: M.E. Sharpe.

Treasury Board Secretariat. 2005. *Executive (EX) group qualification standard,* https://www.tbs-sct.gc.ca/dev/qual-eng. asp [Accessed July 20, 2015].

Treasury Board Secretariat. 2008. *Directive on the Performance Management Program (PMP) for Executives.* http://www.tbs-sct. gc.ca/pol/doc-eng.aspx?id=14226 [Accessed August 9, 2015].

Treasury Board Secretariat. 2015. "Office of the Chief Human Resource Officer." Use index at http://www.tbs-sct.gc.ca/tbs-sct/organization-organisation/organization-organisation-eng. asp [Accessed July 26, 2014].

Treasury Board Secretariat. 2015. *2014 Public Service Employee Survey – Focus Series*, subsets dealing with employee engagement, performance management, senior management, and values and ethics. For focus index, see http://www.tbs-sct.gc.ca/psm-fpfm/modernizing-modernisation/pses-saff/focus-regard-eng.asp [Accessed August 8, 2015].

Treasury Board Secretariat. 2015. *The New Key Leadership Competencies*, http://www.tbs-sct.gc.ca/psm-fpfm/learning-apprentissage/pdps-ppfp/klc-ccl/klcp-pccl-eng.asp [Accessed August 8, 2015].

Treasury Board Secretariat. 2015. *Qualification standard for the Executive (EX) group – Frequently asked questions*, http://www.tbs-sct.gc.ca/psm-fpfm/learning-apprentissage/pdps-ppfp/klc-ccl/faq/qualexfaq-eng.asp.

Treasury Board Secretariat. 2015. *Performance Management Program (PMP) for Executives*, http://www.tbs-sct.gc.ca/psm-fpfm/learning-apprentissage/ptm-grt/mran-eng.asp [Accessed August 9, 2015].

United States Office of Personnel Management. 2014. *2014 Federal Employee Viewpoint Survey Results*, http://www.fedview.opm.gov/2014FILES/2014_Governmentwide_Management_Report.pdf [Accessed July 21, 2015].

Wilson, Graham and Anthony Barker. 2003. "Bureaucrats and Politicians in Britain," *Governance*, 16(3): 349-372.

# CHAPTER 2

# | Failure To Confront

## Gilles Paquet

"Politeness is a way of not talking. When we are
being polite, we say what we think we should say …
Politeness maintains the *status quo*."
*Adam Kahane*

Allow me to take the reader away from the minutiae of
human resources (HR) and the Canadian federal public
service *stricto sensu*, for a moment, to probe the mind
of those observers who have been looking at these issues in
Canada in recent times. Chapter 1 suggested that, for all sorts
of reasons, these observers have not been quite as observant
as they should have been. This was ascribed, without much
explanation, to a culture of excessive tolerance and excessive
politeness, to a demise of critical thinking in Canada these days.

Earlier, I have had occasion to draw attention to the toxic
impact of the lack of critical thinking (Paquet 2014a: chapters
1, 5) and to denounce the ways in which this has become an
epidemic in Canada. This scourge has imposed much damage
to this country, and goes a long way toward explaining why
a significant pathology, like the model employer conceit, has
gone unchallenged, very much like many other 'progressive'
contraptions and impostures.

It has much to do with the strength of *pouvoir social* – a concept used by Tocqueville to grapple with the ensemble of mechanisms through which, on some topics, an opinion comes to prevail (whether it is reasonable or not) that leaves political power somewhat mesmerized and paralyzed, and any sort of opposing view gets somewhat censured (Boudon 2005: 168ff). In a culture of excessive tolerance and unreasonable accommodation, this sort of crowd effect, like the contagion of public opinion, operates with the force of a hurricane and carries much devastation.

In this sort of world, failure to confront unwarranted assumptions, flawed arguments, and deceitful and disingenuous persons or groups is toxic, for silence transforms mute bystanders into passive carriers of the virus and full accomplices in exercises of intellectual imposture – be it in matters of HR and public services or in any other matters.

In this chapter, I suggest first that failure to confront is a major source of the Canadian malaise crippling the country these days. Second, I illustrate the toxic nature of such a phenomenon by probing the important damage it has perpetrated in two issue domains. Third, I argue for an injection of a significant amount of gumption in conversations about issues of concern in Canada as the only way to ensure that the necessary degree of confrontation materializes. The explicit intent is to make the case for such courageous action in the HR mess described in chapter 1.

## The degradation of the common public culture

Robin Higham and I have denounced the perfect, quiet, cultural capitulation of Canadians into failure to confront (Higham and Paquet 2013). The major source of such blindness and inertia is Canadians' congenital failure to effectively confront unwarranted assumptions, flawed arguments, and deceitful and disingenuous persons and groups. This is ascribable to a process of degradation of the common public culture, as a result of the nexus of three families of forces: the installation of a culture of entitlement, the demise of critical thinking, and a certain cult of atonement.

## Culture of entitlement[1]

In a world of surprises, accelerated change, and required adaptation to constantly changing circumstances, the quest for stability and certainty may be illusory, but it is nevertheless a constant human aspiration. Over time, the natural preference for not having one's life disturbed has come to be regarded as a widely-shared reasonable priority. But this quest for stability has been consequential: it has induced groups of citizens (with the complicity of governments, which are always seeking ways to please voters) to allow these preferences for certainty to be transubstantiated into some version of human rights, and those rights to be translated, in turn, into the citizens' entitlements to have protection provided by their governments against undesirable circumstances.

With the Universal Declaration of Human Rights, the post-World-War II egalitarian doctrine argued that any citizen, *qua* citizen, is as meritorious and deserving as the next citizen. This has made it possible for the view to emerge that any form of differential outcome is odious. Indeed, in radical circles, it has been argued that if one citizen cannot have access to a service, others should not have it either – in the name of equality of outcome. This doctrine has triggered an exponential growth of entitlements, related not just to basic needs, but also, and most vociferously, to "positional goods" (Hirsch 1976: 66) – goods or services that are associated with a higher status. Envy has become a barometer of legitimate expectations, and any form of inequality of outcomes denounced as illegitimate. Such a view has been labeled 'progressive'.

Once preferences are relabeled as rights and entitlements, they quickly morph into a set of demands for guarantees that the state will meet these 'needs' regarded as having been earned (*des acquis*), and these preferences are expected to be satisfied by the state in perpetuity.

[1] This section draws freely on an argument presented in Higham and Paquet, 2013.

Some 50 years of such cumulative entitlements – what Nicholas Eberstadt has referred to as an "entitlement epidemic" (Eberstadt 2012) – has been an exponential increase in state transfers to individuals, a growing dependency of citizens on such transfers, and the parallel growth of a "culture of entitlement" that would appear to make this growth likely to continue unabated. Toxic effects can be expected: on governments, for which this might become unaffordable; but also on the citizens themselves – for whom such arrangements may generate learned dependency and helplessness, or an erosion of their burden of office as citizens, or even an erosion of their moral character and sense of responsibility as members of a liberal democracy.

Indeed, according to some observers, moral agency has already been undermined, as governments have begun to take over tasks that individuals used to manage themselves. The very idea of vulnerability "has become such a cannibal that it now covers not only the victims of misfortune or delinquency but even the delinquents themselves" (Minogue 2010: 9).

## The demise of critical thinking

This entitlement epidemic has contributed, at least in part, to the demise of critical thinking. As individuals developed a bloated notion of what they were entitled to, many of the arrangements that underpinned such an edifice became sacred cows. Those sacred cows were "placed outside public discussion" (as Gottfried (2002) would put it), and immunized from any criticism as part of the 'progressive' apparatus: i.e., arrangements not necessarily rationally defensible on social, economic, or political grounds, but regarded as legitimized by the hegemonic reference to compassion, and therefore not to be questioned except perhaps by the odd 'counter-progressive' individual – a condemnation without appeal as intellectually and morally deficient.

The notion of 'progressive' has now permeated the conventional wisdom, and immunized a whole range of policies and arrangements from any meaningful scrutiny. This has resulted in the exclusion of critical thinking from vast territories of public affairs.

When whole portions of human activity are out of bounds for critical thinking, ideologies run amok, and moral relativism becomes the new creed. Every judgment is made on the basis of ideology, and everything is as good as anything else, depending on the ideology invoked. No order of precedence is regarded as defensible, and any ordering at all is defined as contingent and illegitimate.[2] This new frame of mind has been vigorously propounded under all sorts of labels (post-modernism being the most celebrated), and any standard or ordering has come to be regarded as no more legitimate or worthy than any other.

There are problems generated by the failures to apply critical thinking to human affairs.

What do critical thinkers do? They raise vital questions, formulate them clearly, gather relevant information and interpret it effectively, come to well-reasoned conclusions and decisions, test them on relevant criteria, think open-mindedly about alternative perspectives, assess their assumptions and consequences, and communicate effectively with others in coming to solutions.

More succinctly, critical thinking is "reasonable, reflective, responsible, and skillful thinking that is focused on deciding what to believe or do" (Schafersman 1991: 3). More analytically, critical thinking combines – thinking skills (analyzing, interpreting, explaining, evaluating, and recognizing logical fallacies), a skeptic's worldview (recognizing that things are not always entirely what they seem), and intellectual due process (more integrity, humility, tolerance of uncertainty, and raw courage than most of us find easy to summon) (Gabennesch 2006).

As a result of generalized entitlements, and the deliquescence of all critical perspectives and reference points

---

[2] This decline in critical thinking in the federal public service in Canada has been documented in Hubbard and Paquet, 2014.

as contingent, the whole notion of critically appraising anything as better or more valuable than something else has been put into question. Given that opposition to anything is deemed simply the result of adopting a different ideology or perspective, presumed to be superior to the one in good currency, such opposition is summarily regarded as ill-founded and pretentious. It is hardly surprising, under such circumstances, that critical thinkers feel that they can enter the fray only at their peril.

## Cult of atonement

The sense that any ordering is illegitimate, and therefore the result of operations that are indefensible, has injected a sense of apprehended guilt into those tempted to call a spade a spade. Indeed, this sentiment has been distorted and exploited by the righteous few who make "a show of good conscience by apologizing for collective sins – and by exhorting the state to enact compulsory penance" (Gottfried 2002: 95). A self-censorship has emerged that has tended to emasculate public discourse, action and interaction. Indeed, apprehended denunciation, and the consciousness of having to expiate sins of critical thinking, have begun to inhabit the public mind and to inhibit public discourse in a significant way.

These forces have translated into behavioural modification of the most untoward sort: a sanitization of public language, a refusal to confront even the worst sophistry and deception, and a sheepish acceptance of even the most unreasonable accommodation in the name of tolerance – which is often a code word for the expiation for imagined sin.

This generic habituation to a *modus operandi* marked by a congenital failure to confront has emerged in different incarnations:

### 1. Political correctness

This guilt at asserting any form of ordering or at suggesting any assessment of limitations and flaws in existing arrangements, or at pointing out the sources and causes of such flaws, has led to the language being purged of anything that might be regarded as sharp or stark statements about certain issues. Adverbs were mobilized to attenuate any statement to the point of making it trite and vacuous. Civility, which is the primary virtue enabling conversation and dialogue, was perverted to the point where it became a systematic avoidance of any critical view, and where all negative words were somewhat liquefied, so as to become meaningless. The first victim of this erosion of language was free speech, and the banishment of contrarian views. The magic of dialogue was killed, and social learning was disempowered.

## 2. Failure to confront *stricto sensu*
Not only was language enfeebled, but action was neutered as well. Even the outrageous abuses of the rules of *vivre-ensemble* remain unchallenged. Challenges to the authority of the criminal code by Sharia promoters were narrowly defeated by Premier McGuinty's intervention in Ontario; but, in other cases, there was the abject capitulation of Gatineau City Council that withdrew – on the sole basis of one immigrant's protest – a manual to help newcomers to better adjust to Canadian ways, prepared by the foreign-born and long-term Canadian resident city council member Mireille Apollon, in consultation with provincial officials.

How can we defend our ways of *vivre-ensemble* if no view can be regarded as more deserving than any other in our morally relativist world?

This, as might be expected, has led to ever more egregious abuses by groups who found that their very marginality should suffice to immunize them from sanction. Such hyper-tolerance has become incorporated into practices, and practices into rules. Over time, the fuss generated by any potential dissent has become sufficient to deter confrontation, however serious the matter in question.

## 3. Unreasonable accommodation
Perhaps even worse, because of the systematic failure to confront, there has been a silent refurbishment of the rules of *vivre-ensemble* in good currency to accommodate the most unreasonable requests. Traditions rooted in centuries of *vivre-*

*ensemble* were blithely offered up as contingent nuisances, to be casually sacrificed in order not to offend one minority or another. This has led to a tyranny of the minorities: servile accommodation to the unreasonable wishes and preferences of marginal groups for the sole purpose of avoiding the confrontation that would bring with it automatic odium.

Some particularly vivid examples might be useful: the tolerance of polygamy in Bountiful, BC; the schools for Blacks only in Toronto; the refusal to monitor, during their period of qualification for citizenship, the true presence in Canada of persons with permanent resident requirements; the criminal timidity with which any member of a majority group feels obliged to respond to any asinine request by a member of a minority group, etc.

## Failure to confront in action

The intent is not of preparing a list of instances where failure to confront (and its variants – political correctness and unreasonable accommodation) have killed the process of natural conversation and critical thinking among individual citizens. This is an overwhelming if not impossible task because this virus has come to cripple social intercourse in every aspect of our way of life, and to become a determining source of social dysfunction, often by materializing in different ways in different domains.

The intent here is to deal with cases where the virus has allowed significant impostures to take hold, and some flawed arguments and some toxic views to acquire canonical status and to be immunized from warranted debunking as a result of a protective belt provided by a lack of critical probing ascribable to some odium attached to anyone being perceived as daring to question these mythical stories.

In one case (S.O.S. Montfort), the imposture has only had a local echo, even though it has led to much myth-making on the part of its perpetrators, while in another case (mass immigration and multiculturalism), the imposture has had a national impact and may be regarded as an unheralded mystification that remains to this day a *coup d'état épistémologique* of immense consequence generally unrecognized and even denied by its perpetrators.

## *Imposture I:*

## *The failure to confront S.O.S. Montfort and the subtractive bilingualism assumption*

In the latter half of the 1990s, the Ontario government set up a commission to examine the possibility of restructuring the health care system in the province. In the Ottawa-Carleton sub-region, as a result of improved medical technology and of a turn toward ambulatory care and home care, some 20 percent of the hospital beds in the region were closed between 1989 and 1996. This had entailed an increase in fixed and operating costs per bed in the region, and seemed to call for a re-allocation of resources between research hospitals (where costs per procedure were 30 percent higher) and community hospitals.

The preliminary report of the Commission underlined the excess capacity of the regional health care system, the decrepit state of the plant at the Civic Hospital and very limited scope for expansion there, and the need to expand the capacity of community hospitals to take care of routine and simpler cases, and prevent overflowing to costlier tertiary hospitals.

Yet the Commission, on the basis of this sound diagnosis, brought forth some rather astonishing recommendations: making the Civic Hospital the privileged teaching and research hospital, closing three community hospitals (Montfort, Grace, Riverside), and making the General Hospital (the most modern tertiary institution, located close to the Faculty of Medicine of the University of Ottawa, and with much space for expansion) into a super-community hospital.

In the face of flagrant *non sequitur* between analysis and recommendations, the reactions were vivid.[3]

---

[3] The rest of this section is based on an extensive literature that can be readily consulted in Paquet 2001, 2002, 2014d: chapter 9.

On the one hand, there was a reasonable strategy, proposed by the General Hospital and the Riverside Hospital, suggesting that the preliminary report was incoherent, that occult political forces emanating from the Civic Hospital seemed to have influenced the recommendations unduly, and that the recommendations that did not flow naturally from the analysis should be revisited.

On the other hand, there was an alternative approach developed on the basis of the assumption that the preliminary report was the final report. On that basis, it was decided by the Montfort that only a crusade based on affect and emotions by Francophones could break the will of the Commission and of the Ontario government, and save the Montfort.

S.O.S. Montfort – the crusading arm of the Montfort – decided to fight for the survival of the Montfort in the name of linguistic rights of Francophones without paying any attention to the incoherence of the report or to what was happening in the rest of the region.

S.O.S. Montfort argued that Francophones had an absolute right to health care in institutions operating exclusively in French, and, by politically mobilizing a segment of the Franco-Ontarian community from Eastern Ontario, demanded preferential treatment for the Montfort by demonizing bilingual hospitals. This passionate strategy generated a vehement protest movement, generalized disinformation, and delirious arguments. This ethnic/linguistic focus sideswiped any effort to conduct a cohesive action to force the Commission to provide a less inadequate solution for the region than the one it had originally proposed. The fact that the broad health care community did not speak with one voice meant that the Commission did not feel the need to respond to all concerns, and ended up with a modified report, stuffed with evasive suggestions in many areas when very strongly formulated and clear recommendations were in order.

The revised report accomplished little. The Grace Hospital was closed. As for the rest of the system (except for the Montfort and Queensway-Carleton), it was amalgamated into the Ottawa

Hospital with very general suggestions as to its governance but with no clear timetable and much vagueness. The Montfort remained open with its own management and governance like Queensway-Carleton. Since the Montfort was dissatisfied with the reduced mandate devolved to it by the Commission, it was led to go to court to receive recognition of "the fundamental unwritten constitutional principle protecting the minorities."

The fragile argument of S.O.S Montfort is presented in an affidavit of Roger Bernard (2000) and can be summarized as follows:

Major premise: "The survival of a culture depends on the dynamism of language" (*Ibid.*: 37).

Minor premise (1): The dynamism of a language is eroded by any bilingual context (i.e., a context that is not exclusively Francophone) for such a context creates a low probability that the Franco-Ontarians would demand that they be addressed in French. Consequently, bilingual institutions tend to generate a "subtractive bilingualism and a secondarization of the status of French" (*Ibid.*, p. 47). This leads to acculturation, assimilation, and threatens the survival of the community (*Ibid.*: 48).

Minor premise (2): Montfort as a general hospital is "an institution that embodies the French presence in Ontario" and is "a symbol of the force and vitality of the Franco-Ontarian community" (*Ibid.*: 49).

Conclusion: Any minorization of the role of Montfort or any concession to bilingualism is bound to accelerate the assimilation process and "the loss will be irrevocable and heavily consequential for the survival of French Ontario" (*Ibid.*: 50).

As I explain in detail in Paquet (2002), this reasoning is flawed.

The major premise is built on a problematic link between culture and language. The two minor premises are simply false in the sense that they assign an undue role, importance and significance to the Montfort. From this follows a conclusion that is a *non sequitur* – a statement that would suggest that any erosion of the status of the Montfort (a clinic of 200 beds that can never even hope to respond to anything but an infinitely small portion of the needs of the Franco-Ontarian population of the sub-region of Eastern Ontario) would entail dramatic consequences for the survival of the Franco-Ontario community in its totality.

This S.O.S. Montfort radical message was simple: linguistic apartheid, everything in French at the Montfort or it will be assimilation for the whole of French Ontario. This did not correspond at all to the opinion of the community, but only to the view of a fundamentalist local gentility. Yet it was sufficient to trigger an immense amount of disinformation, 'group think', delirious statements and purges to get rid of those who could not be intimidated into falling into line with the new gospel.

In Eastern Ontario, those who remain unintimidated (and rather argued for more service in French in bilingual hospitals) were called *collaborateurs* on the front page of *Le Droit* – a French daily of Eastern Ontario which, with Radio-Canada Ottawa-Gatineau, was a main source of systematic disinformation on this file. This environment explains why many a skeptic did not dare to take a chance, and felt that they had to indulge in grand standing in favour of the 'cause' for fear of being ostracized.

As for the courts, the Superior Court of Ontario was itself intimidated into making ubuesque statements in the November 29, 1999 judgment supporting the S.O.S. Montfort position (Paquet 2014d: 215), but the Ontario Court of Appeal quashed this judgment on December 7, 2001. It declared the Charter argument invalid, and only recognized that, since the Commission had explicitly (and stupidly) stated that it had not taken into account the existence of Law 8 on the services in French in Ontario in its work, this administrative snafu was sufficient for the Court of Appeal to quash also the recommendation of the Commission about reducing the mandate of the Montfort.

Even though it may be said that this toxic storm did not have much impact outside of Eastern Ontario, it would be silly to think that it did not contaminate the public mind. Each year since those surreal events, a memorial service celebrates with pomp the myth of the great accomplishments of S.O.S. Montfort to save French Ontario.

Indeed every occasion for mobilization *pour la cause* would appear to have a scent of S.O.S. Montfort: the same players, the same recriminatory tone, the denunciation of traitors for their lack of engagement, the same excesses of language and unreason still burn – as was seen in the fall of 2014 with the mini-movement to make Ottawa officially bilingual (Paquet 2014b, 2014c) – even including the re-emergence of the vocabulary about *collaborateurs linguistiques* (Cornellier 2014).

Myth-making is not inconsequential.

What was at first a simple lie in the heat of action gets, as time goes by, to congeal into a fairy tale and to acquire a certain degree of concreteness in the collective memory. This is not unlike the fantasies that crystallized around two mythical figures in French Canada's history (Dollard des Ormeaux or Madeleine de Verchères) consecrated in the primary school history books of yesteryear in Quebec until their quiet debunking when their phony aura was burst. Through the ritual retelling of their tall tales as facts, the main actors of the S.O.S. Montfort have transformed their moments of disinformation and weakness of will – *la lâcheté de désinformer pour la cause* of 2000 – into acts of courage *à la* Corneille. Quite an ethical somersault!

### Imposture II:

### The failure to confront and expose the so-called Canadian consensus on multiculturalim and on indiscriminate massive immigration

If Imposture I was perpetrated locally in Eastern Ontario, and therefore may have created only local damage, Imposture II was perpetrated on the national scene, and is having dramatic impacts on the whole Canadian society.

Over the last 20 years, Canada has adopted an immigration policy based on a "faith in the long term benefits of high levels of immigration," although no evidence or meaningful argument has ever been put forward to justify this faith (Green and Green 2004), and there are reasons to believe that it serves neither the newcomers nor Canadian society well.[4]

The only political rationale to explain this new philosophy of immigration is that it appears to have been a seductive tactic to get the vote of the roughly 20 percent of the Canadian population that is foreign-born – a segment of the population that is purported to benefit from family reunification and the chain immigration this process underpins.

This new era followed decades when the Canadian immigration policy had been defined in keeping with what was called 'the absorptive capacity of the Canadian socio-economy'. Such a stance seems to have served both Canada and the newcomers well, since it can be demonstrated that the Canadian experience of integration of immigrants was quite successful: newcomers integrated into the Canadian socio-economy well and relatively quickly, and contributed significantly and positively to their new homeland.

Surprisingly, this act of faith in the long-term benefits of much higher levels of immigration has not been challenged as one might have expected, even though economists have argued for more than 20 years that economic benefits of this policy are likely to be very small (Economic Council of Canada 1991). This unfounded assertion continues to be presented as self-evident by many stakeholders and so-called 'progressives'. It has even come to be consecrated by some political scientists like Keith Banting as corresponding to "a Canadian consensus" (quoted in O'Neill 2010).

According to Jeffrey Reitz, this "Canadian consensus in support of massive indiscriminate immigration" is supposedly based on two pillars (*The Economist* 2011; Reitz 2011): first, "belief in immigration as [an] economic benefit" (because they have been told repeatedly that, through the operation of the point system selection process, the newcomers are highly skilled and therefore must be net contributors to Canadian wealth enhancement); and second, "pride in Canadian

---

[4] This material draws freely from Gilles Paquet, 2012, chapter 1.

multiculturalism" because, supposedly, Canadians have been persuaded by the 'multiculturalism commitment' to view 'diversity *per se* as a very important primary good', and have developed a pride in this becoming a Canadian brand. So even if the positive economic benefits might be put in doubt, such accelerated immigration inflows could still be presumed to have, by definition, an overall positive impact since they contribute to the diversity objective.

As a matter of consequence, any suggestion that such an immigration regime could have a negative impact on the security and health of Canadians, on solidarity and the Canadian social fabric, or on the commitment to the welfare state or other fundamental institutions in the host society, has been merrily discounted.

This Panglossian view, based on ill-founded assumptions but robust state propaganda, has been contested in some circles (Paquet 1989, 2008, 2012: chapter 2). But much of the criticism has been denounced as racist, nativist and even fascist in 'progressive' circles and the media, and, in official circles, as politically incorrect.

I would claim that Canadians have been (1) 'disinformed' systematically by officials and the media about the real impact on the economy of massive immigration, and about its use as an effective way to counter the effects of the aging of the Canadian population; and (2) 'hoodwinked' by state-sponsored multiculturalism propaganda into accepting diversity as an unbounded blessing when, in fact, the optimum amount of diversity is not necessarily maximum diversity – for maximum diversity could have negative impacts on many aspects of the host society, including the common public culture.

These unfounded assumptions have been presented as self-evident by a diffuse coalition of immigration activists and naïve academics (with the complicity of politicians) to fuel a vicious cycle: the high percentage of foreign-born in the population triggering more pressure for increased immigration (whatever the consequences) as politicians tried to capture the electoral support of these new Canadians.

The lack of critical debate about mass immigration is consequential not only because of enormously greater economic costs than benefits, but also because massive and indiscriminate immigration is being allowed to somewhat irresponsibly redefine the very Canadian common public culture – its references, norms and social codes. The deity of diversity and the state-promoted multiculturalism as ideological programming about cultural relativism, equality of cultures, and the commitment to the "preservation and enhancement of the multicultural heritage of Canadians" (from Section 27 of the Charter) have transformed Canada's self-image, its identity, and even the way in which public institutions would appear to react to critical events.

This second imposture promises to have a fundamental impact on the fabric of Canada. The multiculturalism conceit continues to serve as the rationale for massive indiscriminate immigration in Canada in the name of two lies: (1) that immigration generates immense benefits, and (2) that multiculturalism entails that optimum diversity is maximum diversity. Both these propositions are false, but they are both repeated *ad nauseam* by the Canadian federal government propaganda and its 'progressive bureaucracy', and by federal politicians who are worried that if they act responsibly in modulating immigration, they will be accused of racism, bigotry, and anti-immigration sentiment, and would suffer at the polls in a country where one citizen out of five has been born outside Canada – one of two in Toronto (Paquet 2008, 2012).

It might appear to be a distraction to have so many paragraphs about indiscriminate massive immigration and multiculturalism as Imposture II in a book that is purporting to focus on Imposture III – the 1967 Pearson conceit about the HR regime of the Canadian public sector. My reason for such insistence is that Imposture II may be regarded as the most important hoodwinking operation perpetrated on this country in the second half of the 20th century, and that it has become the cornerstone of the social philosophy of Trudeau *le jeune*.

It is also an imposture that is likely to carry the most toxic impact of the three impostures discussed here.[5]

My argument[6] suggests that:

(1) there can be no denial that the current Canadian immigration and refugee regime supports massive and indiscriminate immigration;

(2) there is something puzzling about the so-called 'pan-Canadian consensus' that materialized between the mid-1990s and the mid-2000s (from a position where two-thirds of Canadians polled consistently found immigration levels to be too high, to a position where two-thirds of Canadians polled disagreed with this statement). This reversal of position is most certainly not evidence-based, and it happened at a time of increasing immigration flows, and increasing difficulties of integration for newcomers. There are reasons to believe that it has been nurtured by naïve multiculturalists, immigration activists, and the state deepening multiculturalist propaganda. As Andrew Cohen suggests, "if enough people tell you this, you come to believe it" (Cohen 2007: 158).

(3) while the federal Liberal Party played a key role in early targeting the vote of the foreign-born by favouring mass immigration, by the end of the first decade of the 21st century all political parties had been forced to follow suit for these same electoral reasons; an examination of the electoral literature of all parties in the May 2011 federal election is illuminating;

---

[5] The case of the first one, about SOS Montfort, had only a local impact. In the case of the third one, the Pearson conceit, there is still a possibility of extinguishing it (indeed we almost did it with C-4). In the case of the second one, about indiscriminate massive immigration and multiculturalism, it seems that Canadians have fallen prey to its sophistry and any critical thinking about it is by now censored. It would appear that Canadians will awaken to its full toxic impact only when it is too late to do anything about it.

[6] I have fully developed my argument elsewhere (Paquet 2008, 2012, 2013).

(4) many serious cost-benefit analyses of the new policy reveal that the costs are greater than the benefits, and that therefore it is welfare-reducing for Canadian society; in addition, there are other deleterious effects in terms of health, security, solidarity, etc.;

(5) there has been much sophistry and deception in defending the new policy by sheer disinformation; yet it is surreptitiously redefining the Canadian identity, and, in the name of political correctness, there is a systematic suppression of any critical discussion about the new norms;

(6) much administrative pathology has developed as a result of this new policy being recklessly carried out – e.g. an ever more lax selection process, fraud, etc. ascribable to administrative overload, etc.

The following sample of puzzling (and potentially bothersome) features of the Canadian immigration and refugee regimes is common knowledge. These facts have been documented (and at times denounced) over the years in various studies (Collacott 2003; Grubel 2009):

- for the past 20 years, we have been accepting numbers close to one percent of our population as official immigrants each year: i.e., circa 280,000 recently (without counting temporary workers, foreign students and refugees);
- in the last 25 years, the number of immigrants has increased systematically without any regard to the employment and economic conditions in Canada;
- the United States admits half as many official immigrants on a per capita basis as Canada, and their best experts have recommended that their immigration flow should be cut in half (Borjas 1999), because it is not helping economic growth;
- 80 percent of our official immigrants are not in the "skilled worker" category;
- only 17 percent of the 'principal' applicants in the selected worker category are chosen for their potential to enter the workforce;

- only 20 perent of the selected immigrants are met face to face and interviewed by a visa officer before their being admitted to the country;
- the economic situation of the more recent cohorts of immigrants *vis-à-vis* the Canadian-born has dramatically deteriorated over the past 20 years, thereby revealing growing difficulties of integration;
- the rate of refugee acceptance in Canada is three times the average of other countries, including a large number who would not even be considered as genuine refugees by other countries (e.g. those coming from the United States, the United Kingdom, Germany, Sweden etc. – countries considered to have democratic regimes and sound rule of law).

Finally, the laxity of the admissibility criteria related to health, criminality, security, etc. (that have plagued the immigration and refugee regimes since the 1990s) has been denounced vehemently by the Office of the Auditor General (Collacott 2003: 26-33). This laxity has made it more and more painful for the newcomers to integrate effectively into the labour market, and it has led to growing frustrations. Consequently, even some immigrant groups have come to favour a reduction in the immigration levels, and, by a proportion of over 70 percent in some Canadian polls, are supporting the recommendation that the selection process be tightened by, for instance, requiring newcomers to be competent in English or French when they arrive (Collacott 2010).

Information that has become available over the last 20 years has been explicitly ignored and occluded because it fits badly with the new paradigm that underpins the state indoctrination program in Canada. This has been the case for research that showed that what Canadians would gain from immigration in terms of economic benefits is very small, and for the work of demographers who have argued that immigration cannot be expected to compensate for an aging population in Canada either in the short term or the long term. Yet statements to the contrary continue to be repeated by politicians, officials, 'progressive academics', and the media. This is systematic disinformation.

Another important quantity of carefully unacknowledged information has to do with the current immigration regime resulting in an excess supply of unskilled labour, thus making integration in the Canadian labour market much more difficult, and at much lower levels of compensation. Indeed, Statistics Canada has shown that the recent cohorts have found their integration more painful, and their earnings in relation to native Canadians significantly lower and continuing to deteriorate even further (Picot *et al.* 2007). And this is true not only at the lower end of the scale. Green and Green have also shown that there has been downward pressure on wages paid even to well-educated workers, with the immigrants themselves "struggling – with declining success – to find jobs commensurate with their knowledge and experience, [need for] good incomes and decent affordable housing" (Green and Green 2004: 134). As Michael Valpy put it, this poses a question about the 'morality' of admitting that many immigrants (quoted in Bissett 2009: 11).

Finally, there are also pernicious costs associated with the current immigration regime: discouraging efforts to train and put to work Canadians who are unemployed or underemployed (e.g. Aboriginals), and the negative impact of the immigration regime on the development of more effective methods of production in Canada because cheap labour is available (Stoffman 2008).

## *Imposture III:*
## *The failure to confront the 1967 Pearson conceit*

Much has been presented earlier about the forces at work that prevented a reversal of the insane decision to adopt a 'model employer' stance in the face of increasingly combative public sector unions. Much of this failure to confront is ascribable to the Post World War II *ethos* and the impact of the *pouvoir social* that has come to contaminate public opinion with the virus of progressivity.

This may have been the result of a euphoric wealth effect during the 30 glorious years of prosperity following World War II, but the whole culture fell ever more strongly under the spell of redistribution and egalitarianism in the decades that followed, as a result of the Charter, and this ideological spell has not disappeared.

This is the only plausible explanation for the willful blindness of Scott Brison (and of the current Trudeau government) in the face of the Canadian federal public service mess. They cannot be ignorant enough not to understand the catastrophic effect of cancelling C-4 – the first significant effort in some 50 years to contain the noxious effects of the Pearson conceit – but they cannot fathom facing the accusation of being 'anti-progressive' – an accusation they spent 10 years levying against the former government, an accusation that went quite a distance in demonizing it – even though it was a baseless accusation.

The progressive virus has been celebrated with sufficient pomp over the last decades that it has become impossible to appear not to support it. So the new government, whatever its unease, will redistribute yet more largesse onto unionized public sector workers in good conscience "because it is 2016"... because they think it is what public opinion supports ... because opposing it would require wisdom and courage and these virtues are in short supply in Ottawa these days.

## The case for more gumption

In the cases sketched above, failures (1) to confront unwarranted assumptions, flawed arguments, and deceitful and disingenuous persons and groups, and (2) to denounce the fairy tales and myths being derived from them are ascribable to the combination of:

1. a growing lack of critical thinking in the population at large,
2. public information media not providing critical, impartial coverage of issues of national concern, and

3. *pouvoir social à la* Tocqueville, triggering unwarranted information cascades.

Let me explain.

In the first case, this is due to the development of a Canadian *esprit* dominated by political correctness, *molle pensée*, and a tolerance of the most outrageous public statements – formally in the name of tact and civility, but *de facto* as a result of a desire to avoid controversy at all costs.

In the second case, this is the result of the media failing to ensure balanced and impartial coverage of issues of national concern, and choosing to deliberately disinform in the name of certain ideological pursuits or political priorities.

In the third case, the toxic complicity of the intelligentsia with the bureaucratic apparatus, the media, and certain interest groups has generated what Tocqueville calls "social power" – embodied in mechanisms and *dispositifs* that tend to impose a dominant opinion on certain subjects. *Le pouvoir social* shapes dominant views that, however ill-founded, become difficult to contradict because of the fabricated public opinion. Even political power comes to be paralyzed and somewhat impotent (Boudon 2005: 168).[7]

## Lack of gumption in the case of our three impostures

In the case of S.O.S. Montfort activism (and its echo effect in the Ottawa region), much has been the result of the fabrication of public opinion by the local gentility and media elite based on systematic disinformation, and the complicity of a segment of the intelligentsia. The fundamentalist discourse of the gentility was accompanied by much intimidation to force

---

[7] An illustration of a notion underpinned by this sort of social power is the notion of the 'corporate welfare bum' that caricatures any measure to stimulate investment by firms and to boost productivity as a gift to enterprises – evoking some complicity between elected officials and the private sector. Since it is assumed that the interests of management and labour are by definition antagonistic, a gift to management can only hurt labour. It is therefore very difficult to defend any form of subsidy to firms (whatever the benefits to labour and the economy in general that may ensue) when it has come to connote the idea of 'corporate welfare bum'.

opinion-molders to join the ranks of the radical group. Even higher officials at the University of Ottawa felt they had to join the mob for fear of being accused of being *collaborateurs* and of being marginalized.[8]

In the case of mass-immigration-cum-multiculturalism, *le pouvoir social* also played a dominant role, but this time the federal state apparatus was profoundly involved in orchestrating and propagandizing the gospel of diversity as a primary good, and the religion of multiculturalism as immunizing Canadian society from any diffractive tension as a result of mass immigration. This propaganda was so overpowering that any person (as I have personally experienced) daring to question the benefits of indiscriminate mass immigration or the sacredness of the doctrine of multiculturalism was routinely accused of bigotry, racism and discrimination from the 1980s on.

In both cases, one may speak of 'systematic disinformation and brainwashing' – by explicit 'intimidation' in the case of S.O.S Montfort, and by 'indoctrination' into soft 'progressive thinking' in the multiculturalism case. The former approach may have important temporary power, but the latter one is immensely more vicious. It has been able to maintain its dominium on the Canadian *ethos* over the last 20 years (Ekos Canada 2015).

In neither case has the voice of the opposition been able to be effectively heard, nor could the critical thinking of the population be counted on to overcome the social power forces imposing a dominant view.

In the case of the Pearson conceit, the elephant in room is *pouvoir social,* and the toxic elevation of redistribution to the status of social virtue. As a consequence, the artificial creation of an aristocracy of labour in the public sector may be episodically denounced as grossly unfair, but is most generally tolerated because of the mythical elevation of work in the

[8] I was fired from the editorial pages of *Le Droit* for parting company with S.O.S Montfort *not* on the objective of affording as much service as possible in French for the Franco-Ontarian community, but on the choice of means most likely to be useful in this pursuit.

public sector to a special status, carefully cultivated by its being unwarrantedly considered as clergy-like, and the result of a process of selection that recognizes the higher quality of the happy few deserving such high status.

The fact that such pretention is hollow, and such status is unwarranted may be quite obvious to anyone who has had occasion to interact with public servants, but is rarely challenged because of the aura provided by the position of power over the citizenry of a large number of them – from the Supreme Court judges to the clerks interacting with the public – through pronouncements manufacturing unfounded collective guilt or whimsical treatment of vulnerable and dependent denizens driving a sense of dependency and servility into their minds.

## Gumption must be regained

One should not presume that intimidation, indoctrination, and social power cannot be overcome. But it cannot be done without the reinforcement of the sense of mindfulness, the acceptance of the duty to take initiative as part of the burden of office of the stakeholders, and the leveraging of the whole power of 'culture governance' in the process of confronting the toxic impact of social power – three steps in the regaining of the full power of gumption.

1. There are psychic costs attached to 'mindfulness' leading to confronting – since it is most unpleasant (except for sadists) to engage in agonistic debates with associates – yet confrontation is likely to produce important benefits, and this is the basic rationale for insisting on confrontation to occur. At the individual level, the benefit from confronting is ensuring better performance or limiting the harms generated by under-performance. Breaking this psychic barrier is the first obstacle to overcome if one is to reap the benefit of confrontation (Weick and Sutcliffe 2007: chapter 7).

    These psychic costs are easier to overcome when, as in personnel evaluations, the benefits are easy to gauge – eliminating the costly bad habit of an employee. Both harms and psychic costs attached to eradicating them are considerably greater when bad habits have become generalized in organizations, and a regime of underperformance has crystallized. The costs of the X-inefficiency *à la* Leibenstein (1976) – when a whole horde of employees partake in a culture of underperformance – are becoming immense.

Confronting such a confederacy of bad habits making up a regime is then also quite daunting even if it may be a matter of survival for organizations that have slumped into a state of learned helplessness. When a regime of bad habits has been in place for a while, it often becomes part of the broader culture of a socio-economy, and part of a self-righteous but delusional discourse defending unacceptable arrangements as if they were legitimate. In such cases, the very *ethos* becomes toxic and the language used to defend non-viable arrangements acquires a surreal quality.

The original psychic blockage to mindfulness depends on the depth of the forces generating failure to confront – on whether it is simply a fear of looking bad and of being exposed to ridicule, or the difficulty of running afoul of a bad habit in good currency or of acting in violation of the whole ruling *ethos*, or trying to overcome a cultural propensity to tolerance. In most cases, it is a mixture of these elements that is at work. And rationalizing inaction or a very meek response is usually based on taking refuge in a celebration of tolerance and civility as fundamental virtues.

Tolerance is too often defined as a panacea leading to peaceful coexistence of groups of people with different histories, cultures and identities (Walzer 1997). This is naïve. In fact, the optimal amount of tolerance is not the maximal amount: some perceptions and some behaviours are intolerable, and not being intolerant about them is being complicit in harmful acts. As for civility, it pertains mostly to form, not substance: one may confront in a most civil manner.

Toleration is a sin of opportunity costs that are most plausibly deniable because one may argue that having done nothing actively, one cannot be culpable for what has ensued. This is a case of sophistry. The limit to toleration is defined by gauging the amount of harm that inaction would generate, by the costs of tolerance and the cost of the lost benefits thereby foregone.

Lack of mindfulness is willful blindness, "unsettling or rash lack of concern" – a definition of criminal negligence in the Criminal Code. When made visible, this cost is likely to make inaction impossible and mindfulness into an obligation.

2. However individual mindfulness cannot suffice – even if it is important in administrative pathology (Paquet 2014d) – but it is inconsequential if taking action, *taking initiative* as a result of mindfulness is no longer part of the burden of office of managers, administrators and governors; if one is not led to explore beyond the present arrangements, and to follow through with adaptations that appear imperative in the light of signs of problematic performance in the internal or external contexts.

The notion of burden of office (Tussman 1989) is an essentially contested concept. It admits considerable modification and interpretation in the light of changing circumstances, and may be gauged differently by different parties. Since the burden of office of an official is multi-dimensional and many of these dimensions are incommensurable, this results in much fuzziness when it comes to defining the burden of office of the different stakeholders. It is also difficult to determine how one develops the necessary connoisseurship to be able to despatch one's burden of office when one becomes mindful of the difficulties (Paquet 1997).

The gap between the notions of burden of office of the employer and the employees in the federal public service can only be described as Kafkaesque. For instance, when the Secretary of Treasury Board suggested in 2014 that four competencies could legitimately be required from federal public servants ("showing integrity and respect; thinking things through; working effectively with others; taking initiative and being action-oriented"), to a great many persons, these seemed to be quite commonsensical requirements. Yet, as was pointed out earlier, overnight 17 federal public service unions decided to go to court to fight what they called "disguised discipline" (May 2014).

The notion of burden of office entails a responsibility to launch an inquiry, to take action, to design arrangements that will resolve the problem, to fill the gap, to establish or re-establish the missing coordination links and the required conditions for collaboration. It connotes what one is 'expected to do' and it triggers necessary organizational repairs. Otherwise, stakeholders appear to be incapable of delivering what they are expected to in order to overcome this deficiency. Inaction prevails because nobody is mindful enough to care, and engaged enough to do anything about it.

3. Mindfulness and the burden of office are the first steps, but they need to be contextualized in order to ensure that confrontation is used wisely, i.e., capable of making the highest and best use of the context in the short run, and of catalyzing changes in the context in the longer run. This entails a duty of 'reverence for the context' in the way the surfer respects the wave and uses it, in the short run. Conversely, it entails a duty of 'irreverence' toward existing arrangements and a commitment to redesign these arrangements in the long run – when circumstances change – to ensure 'a capacity to scheme virtuously by making use of the culture governance', of the whole underground of organizations, institutions, feelings, beliefs and powers.

Culture governance helps steer the system through the use of embedded propensities that have evolved over time, and that comprise socially accepted mechanisms, conventions and arrangements that make the highest and best uses of all the intersubjective, interactive and cooperative capabilities in common currency. To put it in another way, "Community is fundamentally an interdependent human system given form by the conversation it holds with itself. The history, buildings, economy, infrastructure and culture are [artifacts] of the conversations and the social fabric of any community" (Block 1993: 30). Culture governance is a product of those conversations, one that evolves a collective sense of what is possible or not; what is or is not acceptable behaviour: for instance what is an acceptable role, or not, for government.

Culture governance is evolving, but it changes slowly. What can be modified more quickly is the power of gumption through more mindfulness and a strengthening of the burden of office of stakeholders. This should contribute to the evolution of an *ethos* where confrontation will become part of the culture, and failure to confront will be recognized for what it is – a toxic sanitization of social intercourse.

Progressing through these three steps will take time. The present culture governance still considers failure to confront, not as a case of intellectual laziness or cowardice, but as a form of tolerance by those 'living' as it were in a fantasy-world of self-righteousness – the words used by Robert Sibley (2013) to define the plague of pneumopathology. Progressives and other ideologues of the same ilk all suffer from pneumopathology. And their self-righteousness provides a protective belt for their fortress against the usual attacks of reasonableness.

\* \* \*

At the turn of the century, as I mentioned above, I was fired as an editorialist of a French daily newspaper in Ottawa – after a successful five year stint in the job – for being unwilling to bow to the gospel of S.O.S. Montfort. This led to tense discussions with the Editor-in-chief about my sense that S.O.S Montfort was an imposter. In these conversations, much remained unsaid on the part of the management of the newspaper, and most certainly there was no recognition ever that the newspaper had betrayed the trust of its readership by not denouncing that imposture, and by disinforming its readers. The matter remained unsettled. We chose not to talk about these matters in the name of tolerance. Convenience trumped intellectual honesty. This was the *sympathique* way to allow the issue to die unresolved.

Fifteen years later, the Editor-in-Chief of the daily in question, now retired, received the Order of Canada, and the appropriate citation mentioned his *"contribution à l'essor de la francophonie en Ontario."* This was well deserved. However, in an interview reproduced in the media on July 1, 2015, the recipient of the Order of Canada chose to connect explicitly the honour received to the S.O.S. Montfort affair, and to explain his position more clearly than he had done 15 years earlier. What he was standing for at the time, he said, was a matter of deliberate choice: at certain moments, a newspaper cannot simply inform, the Editor-in-Chief has to choose between *"la lutte"* (the struggle) and *"l'impartialité"*... and he proudly concluded that he had chosen *"la lutte."*

I could only read this statement as one explaining that he had chosen between informing and dis-informing, but also as a vehement defense of his having chosen to disinform. That was obviously a betrayal of his burden of office as Editor-in-Chief of a daily newspaper.

Moreover, this choice to disinform was not made, it would seem, under duress as a result of pressures of all sorts from the Franco-Ontarian gentility that held so much power over the survival of the newspaper – an agonistic choice that one might have been tempted to forgive.

It was made on pneumopathological grounds, that the honoree claims now in 2015, with a certain pride, to have been the right one. So in the particular case of the S.O.S. Montfort, the Imposture I dossier is now clearer.

I suppose that one day in the future, with the passage of time, one might finally get the Imposture II dossier also sorted out. It might come from a clear admission by the intellectuals, bureaucrats and politicians involved in that shenanigans that systematic disinformation was committed also, this time in the name of an altogether different ideology, and from a better understanding of the ways in which public opinion is manipulated in our doxacracy ... or might one say in the ineptocracy of our *société du spectacle*.

As for Imposture III, it is the purpose of this small book to expose it to some scrutiny.

# References

Bang, Henrik P. 2003. "A new ruler meeting a new citizen: culture governance and everyday making," in H.P. Bang (ed.). *Governance as social and political communication*. Manchester, UK: Manchester University Press, p. 241-266.

Bernard, Roger. 2000. *A la défence de Montfort*. Gatineau, QC: Le Nordir.

Bissett, James. 2009. "The Current State of Canadian Immigration Policy," in Herbert Grubel (ed.). *The Effects of Mass Immigration on Canadians Living Standards and Society*. Vancouver, BC: The Fraser Institute.

Block, Peter. 1993. *Stewardship: Choosing Service Over Self-Interest*. San Francisco, CA: Berrett-Koehler.

Borjas, George. 1999. *Heaven's Gate – Immigration Policy and the American Economy*. Princeton, NJ: Princeton University Press.

Boudon, Raymond. 2005. *Tocqueville aujourd'hui*. Paris, FR: Odile Jacob.

Cohen, Andrew. 2007. *The Unfinished Canadian*. Toronto, ON: McClelland & Stewart.

Collacott, Martin. 2003. *Canada's Immigration Policy: The Need for Major Reform.* Vancouver, BC: The Fraser Institute.

Collacott, Martin. 2010. "Immigrants want less Immigration," *National Post*, March 10.

Cornellier, Louis. 2014. "Contre les collabos linguistiques," *Le Devoir*, July 12.

Coyne, Andrew. 2015. "Greece considers itself a victim, and it's wrong," *Ottawa Citizen*, July 9, C7.

Eberstadt, Nicholas. 2012. *A Nation of Takers – America's Entitlement Epidemic.* West Conshohocken, PA: Templeton Press.

Economic Council of Canada. 1991. *New Faces in the Crowd.* Ottawa, ON: Supply & Services Canada.

Ekos Canada. 2015. *How Canadians view immigration and multiculturalism today.* Ottawa, ON: Ekos Canada.

Gabennesch, H. 2006. "Critical Thinking. What is it good for? (In fact, what is it?)," *Skeptical Inquirer*, 30(2): 36-41.

Gottfried, Paul Edward. 2002. *Multiculturalism and the Politics of Guilt.* Columbia, MO: University of Missouri Press.

Green, Alan and David Green. 2004. "The Goals of Canada's Immigration Policy: A Historical Perspective," *Canadian Journal of Urban Research*, 13(1): 102-139.

Grubel, Herbert (ed.). 2009. *The Effects of Mass Immigration on Canadian Living Standards and Society.* Vancouver, BC: The Fraser Institute.

Higham, Robin and Gilles Paquet. 2013. "Reflections on the Canadian Malaise," *www.optimumonline.ca*, 43(2): 1-12.

Hirsch, Fred. 1976. *Social Limits to Growth.* Cambridge, MA: Harvard University Press.

Hubbard, Ruth and Gilles Paquet. 2014. *Probing the Bureacratic Mind – About Canadian Federal Executives.* Ottawa, ON: Invenire.

Hubbard, Ruth and Gilles Paquet. 2015. *Irregular Governance – A Plea for Bold Organizational Experimentation.* Ottawa, ON: Invenire.

Leibenstein, Harvey. 1976. *Beyond Economic Man.* Cambridge, MA: Harvard University Press.

May, Kathryn. 2014. "Unions grieve new PS performance rules," *Ottawa Citizen,* April 7, A1-2.

Minogue, Kenneth. 2010. *The Servile Mind.* London, UK: Encounter Books.

O'Neill, Peter. 2010. "Is Canada up to the Immigration Challenge?" *Ottawa Citizen,* September 25, A6.

Paquet, Gilles. 1997. "The Burden of Office, Ethics and Connoisseurship," *Canadian Public Administration,* 40(1): 55-71.

Paquet, Gilles. 1989. "Multiculturalism as national policy," *Journal of Cultural Economics,* 13(1): 48-56.

Paquet, Gilles. 2001. *Si Montfort m'était conté... Essais de pathologie administrative et de rétroprospective.* Ottawa, ON: Centre d'études en gouvernance.

Paquet, Gilles. 2002. "Montfort et les nouveaux Éléates," *Francophonies d'Amérique,* 13, p. 139-155.

Paquet, Gilles. 2008. *Deep Cultural Diversity.* Ottawa, ON: University of Ottawa Press.

Paquet, Gilles. 2012. *Moderato Cantabile – Toward Principled Governance for Canada's Immigration Regime.* Ottawa, ON: Invenire.

Paquet, Gilles. 2013. *Tackling Wicked Policy Problems – Equality, Diversity and Sustainability.* Ottawa, ON: Invenire.

Paquet, Gilles. 2014a. *Unusual Suspects – Essays on Social Learning Disabilities*. Ottawa, ON: Invenire.

Paquet, Gilles. 2014b. "'Bilinguisme officiel' pour Ottawa: Non, et voilà pourquoi," *www.optimumonline.ca*, 44(3): 45-55.

Paquet, Gilles. 2014c. "Radiographie d'une grogne: bilinguisme officiel pour Ottawa redux," *www.optimumonline.ca*, 44(4): 1-20.

Paquet, Gilles. 2014d. *Tableau d'avancement III – Pour une diaspora canadienne-française antifragile*. Ottawa, ON: Invenire.

Picot, Garnett *et al.* 2007. *Chronic Low-Income and Low-Income Dynamics among Recent Immigrants*. Ottawa, ON: Statistics Canada, Catalogue No. 11f0019MIE2007198.

Reitz, Jeffrey G. 2011. *Pro-Immigration Canada – Social and Economic Roots of Popular Views*. Montreal, QC: IRPP.

Schafersman, S.D. 1991. *An Introduction to Critical Thinking*. www.creeinquiry.com/critical-thinking.html.

Sibley, Robert. 2013. "Young men can be turned to good or evil," *Ottawa Citizen*, May 2.

Stoffman, Daniel. 2008. "Truths and Myths about Immigration," in Alexander Moens and Martin Collacott (eds.). *Immigration Policy and Terrorist Threat in Canada and the United States*. Vancouver, BC: The Fraser Institute, p. 3-28.

*The Economist*. 2011. "Immigration: The United States v Canada," May 20.

Tussman, Joseph. 1989. *The Burden of Office*. Vancouver, BC: TalonBooks.

Walzer, Michael. 1997. *On Toleration*. New Haven, CN: Yale University Press.

Weick, Karl E. and Kathleen M. Sutcliffe. 2007. *Managing the Unexpected*. San Francisco, CA: Jossey-Bass.

# PART II
# Modeling

The sad state of affairs of the Canadian federal public service lies behind our efforts to understand human resources (HR) in the federal public sector. The inability of the many parties involved to carry out the necessary repairs, and the demise of critical thinking and failure to confront that would appear to permeate the Canadian *ethos* and to cripple any effort to drive the fake out of public administration and detox the HR regime in the public sector – have created a perfect storm.

The cognitive dissonance that characterizes the principal groups of actors in the face of such a governance failure may have been sufficient to comfort and even comatose the public administration tribe, the intelligentsia and the medias, but any reasonably-informed observer must realize by now that willful blindness of any sort can no longer be tolerated.

Yet any inquiry likely to expose the sources and causes of such an HR fiasco cannot proceed without a minimal frame of reference, providing a basis for a sound problem definition, and a general awareness of the principles, mechanisms and contraptions that might ensure good performance, depending on the various work environments and circumstances that exist within the Canada federal public service.

The aim of the second part of this book is to sketch the contours of the world of possibilities in human resources management (HRM) in our modern complex and uncertain world, and to provide a rough idea of the sort of toolbox available to do the job of detoxing the Canadian federal government's HR systems and of designing more effective HR interventions at two levels – through transforming behaviours and architecture, and modifying the public service culture.

The prototype we have in mind is rough and ready: something that brings forth the essential elements that need to be kept in mind when facing the challenge of designing an HR system for a complex, pluralist, dynamic and highly differentiated socio-economic reality such as this one.

We succinctly overview four facets of this performance challenge:

- reminding the reader of some untoward mis-representations and crazy assumptions that have crippled both the problem definition and the design of initiatives in the past, and that remain in good currency in certain quarters – to a sufficient extent to deserve some preventative work to avoid their toxic impact;
- identifying the main general sources of high performance in organizations and socio-economies, and the different registers that need to be harmonized or kept in tension to ensure value-adding, effectiveness and innovation in the Canadian federal public service;
- probing the cultural underground that shapes the very definition of performance and the acceptable ways of feeding the process of social learning likely to ensure perenniality and resilience;
- suggesting the contours of a loose protocol that might guide the design activity in the general direction sketched above, i.e., a direction meant to transform competencies and social architecture, and modify the public culture.

Part II only sketches the contours of the protocol we suggest. Part III provides more details about the ways in which this sort of inquiry might proceed in the case of a few of the major challenges faced by the Canadian federal public service.

CHAPTER 3

# | An MRI of HRM in the Public Sector:
# A Prototype Intent on Complicating Matters

## Ruth Hubbard and Gilles Paquet

> "The slenderest knowledge that
> may be obtained of the highest things
> is more desirable than the most certain
> knowledge obtained of lesser things."
>
> *Thomas Aquinas*

The world of human resource management (HRM) is usually encumbered by a multitude of considerations inherited from the historical background of the particular arrangements in place, and the culture that has presided over the concoction of these arrangements. As a result, it is often difficult to ascertain whether the core mechanisms are working well, because of the interferences of all sorts of conflicting accounts or distorted representations that are being allowed to obscure the fundamentals of HRM which are all about extracting the most enlightened and creative performance from the existing human resources.

It is amazing how often this pivotal concern for performance gets completely sideswiped by other concerns – like traditions, cultural or human-rights considerations, etc. – to the point that the whole discussion about the optimal HRM apparatus can come to be regarded as entirely appropriate and legitimate without the central concern of performance ever being mentioned.

Our objective in this chapter is to sketch the broad contours of a reasoned approach to the fundamentals of HRM that would maintain its core focus on performance, while addressing subsidiary concerns only in the subsidiary ways that they deserve, and without ever allowing them to divert the discussion away from the core performance issues.

This will be done in three steps: first by ensuring that HRM discussions are carried out on the basis of realistic assumptions; second, by ensuring that the design of appropriate HRM strategies takes into account the full range of considerations and instrumental variables of consequence in constructing such strategies; and third, by articulating a protocol and some modest general propositions, based on some lessons learned, that might serve as a *vademecum* in the design of hybrid HRM regimes, likely to generate the most enlightened and creative performance from the existing human resources, given the variety of circumstances with which one is confronted.

In the first section, some preliminaries attempt to explicitly take into account some of the untoward misrepresentations that have cluttered the problem definition process, and have led to insane assumptions and ineffective initiatives in the design of the HRM regimes over time:

- the distortive view that has come to be in good currency in the public administration literature in Canada that human resources choosing to operate in the public sector are performing a clergy-like function, and thereby deserve separate and more generous rules of engagement;
- the fundamental conceit inflicted in the late 1960s by the Pearson government on the HRM process at the federal

government level for the core public sector when it was decided that the federal government should aim at being a 'model employer';

- the circumstances that led the HRM palaver of the federal public sector to completely lose track of the priority of performance; and
- the warnings issued by behavioural economics about motivation governance that has naïvely betted on the happiness of workers as a prime mover in HRM design: it can only lead to disaster.

In the second section, we probe the general sources of high performance in HRM in order to identify the broad range of dimensions that need to be taken into account in constructing a prototype likely to aptly handle an organization as complex and diverse as the Canadian federal public service:

- an immensely more realistic definition of the pool of human resources from which the Canadian public service is drawn, and of the great challenges in ensuring that there would be appropriate matching between the variety of differentiated cognitive abilities required depending on the nature of their tasks and missions, and the cognitive abilities available in the pool of human resources available;
- an awareness of the vast array of structures and mechanisms (formal and informal) available and capable of generating standards, incentive reward systems, norms, levers, etc. likely to frame the many dimensions of the work conditions that are likely to promote high performance on the part of the employees in all circumstances; and
- a recognition of the different burdens of office of the different groups of public servants depending on their level of responsibilities, sector of operations and circumstances, etc.

In the third section, we ascertain the contours of a loose protocol (based on certain modest general propositions developed in the light of past experiences and speculations about possibilities) that might serve as a guide in the design of HRM regimes with a high degree of goodness of fit with the general *ethos* and the particular environments. We also outline a choice of meaningful experiments that might be conducted in different segments of the Canadian public service to improve its enlightened and creative performance. We call what is needed hybrid forms of governance of HRM.

This chapter does not aim to generate a plan, a rigid blueprint or a recipe that could mechanically and blindly be followed, but only to provide some indications about the most toxic pitfalls that might materialize along the way, about the steps likely to be useful in a process of inquiry seeking to help organizations (in this case the Canadian government) find a way forward (through innovation and value-adding), and a view about the most promising opportunities or initiatives likely to nudge the coordinating inquiries in successful directions.

## Preliminaries

### *Discarding the most unreasonable assumption about HR in the public sector*

One of the most fascinating assumptions that has permeated the public administration literature in Canada under all sorts of thin disguises has been that human resources choosing to operate in the public sector are *generis sui* in a special category of human beings that must be regarded as distinct from and nobler than those in employment in other sectors. Public sector employees have a mission; the rest of Canadians simply have a job.

This sort of credo is widely proclaimed by some leading lights in the Canadian public administration literature, and is argued in more or less guarded ways within the bureaucracy to explain why such persons should be paid more or provided with more generous fringe benefits because of their special status.[1] The assumption that public servants are clergy-like is no more realistic than the assumption that they are delivery-boy-like: both assumptions must be explicitly discarded.[2]

Our joint experience over the last 40 years has revealed that, contrary to this view, in all sectors, there is an array of human resources that range in quality from the highest to the lowest, and that to assume otherwise is not only naïve but disingenuous. Statements made or implied by politicians

[1] This sort of representation would appear to be the absolute obverse of the vision of the world that underpins the deliverology philosophy which presumes that public servants are replaceable and substitutable pieces of a delivery machine, as was postulated by the American system of manufacturing.

[2] It is very interesting to note the surreal nature of the tiptoeing going on in the public dialogue between the Treasury Board Secretariat and the public service unions in the federal government in early 2016. Briefing notes to Scott Brison revealed by the CBC (March 8, 2016) show that he was warned in November 2015 that there were serious problems with the public service that would require a 'cultural change' if its turtle-pace of change was to transform into intelligent risk-taking. Both parties are still refusing to admit that: Brison focuses only on the delivery of services to Canadians, and the unions only to the fact that such delivery cannot be improved unless the cuts imposed by the former government (including those pertaining to the excessively generous sick-leave arrangements – a matter on which Scott Brison has stated that he agrees) are cancelled. So even if the new government is aware of the dysfunctionality and poor performance of the existing public service, it does not appear to be willing to challenge these failures frontally. Indeed, the decision by Brison to rebalance the rules of the game in favour of the unions shows he is disingenuous in claiming to be interested in cleansing the Augean stables of the federal public service. Could this mean that the Trudeau government is unwilling to deal with the public sector unions frontally but only obliquely as some cynics suggest: by downgrading the burden of office of the public service to delivery of services, and allowing its HRM to be downgraded accordingly in due course? A less cute perspective is that the Trudeau government is intent on re-instating the Pearsonian conceit of 'model employer', and give to labour unions the upper hand by annihilating the Harper government's Bill C-4 – an announcement made by Brison in June 2016 – the only serious effort to mitigate the toxic impact of the Pearson conceit since 1967 and to propose necessary management reform.

or grand vizirs of the public sector technocracy about the higher general quality of the public sector workforce should therefore be regarded with great suspicion – as meant only to falsely praise and pacify this segment of the workforce, and to unpersuasively defend the ultra-generous salaries and benefits in good currency in this sector.

Higher quality attributes of the public sector workforce (competencies, etiquette, loyalty, even *affectio societatis* – i.e., extraordinary dedication to the burden of office) cannot be claimed unless such a proposition can be validated by independent and objective appraisal, and, to the best of our knowledge, such vindication does not exist and has never been produced.

Therefore, to pretend that such is the case, and to erect a HRM system on such an assumption is a recipe for disaster. Yet the rampant assumption, in good currency in public administration literature, that public sector employees are different in kind – a sort of clergy displaying higher qualities and more worthy character than the rest of the workforce operating in other sectors – has been a staple assumption for decades in Canadian federal circles, to the point that many public administration gurus have suggested that the technocrats in the public service are more knowledgeable and legitimate than the elected officials (Hubbard and Paquet 2015a).

These arguments may be bogus, but nowhere has this sort of statement been challenged by the new Trudeau government. Indeed, if the rhetoric of the new Prime Minister is to be taken seriously with respect to this file, the 1960s Pearsonian philosophy of the federal government having to be a 'model employer' still seems to be the order of the day … at least frontally. Consequently, it would be surprising if a cultural change were to be engineered in the HRM system as long as the governors remain geared to the happiness of the workforce rather than to the performance of the public sector workforce.

## Why has the HRM lost track of performance?

The erosion of the centrality of performance concerns in the public sector is ascribable to a great extent to the strategic development of job descriptions that have become more and more layered with ornate but vacuous verbiage, pretending to be precise about certain aspects of operations but mainly designed to focus on the trivial, gaugeable dimensions of the tasks while most often taking more and more distance from the true responsibilities of employees. This quantophrenic urge to metre the activities of public servants that are most conveniently metred has created a chasm between what is measured on the one hand, and what the burden of office of the employees really is, on the other.

This transmogrification has been the result of a variety of forces the most important of which is unionization. Unionization has contributed significantly to the transformation of work into so-called activities capable of being metered and gauged. The result has been that the notion of 'burden of office' has been diffracted to the point of disappearing into a multiplicity of tasks descriptions that has enabled the very notion of human labour to disappear into bits and fragments of measurable activities that often have only the most tenuous connection to the burden of office that it is meant to approximate.

This stylization process has dissolved the notion of burden of office into a sequence of more or less meaningless tasks that can be precisely metered and mechanically connected à la Frederick Winslow Taylor. This in turn has led to the concoction of precise quantitative targets in the operations of robot-like creatures to the point of paying scant attention to the gauging of the *travail* that humans perform: i.e., coping, mindfully and intelligently (or not) with their tasks, collibrating or reframing their activities in the face of the more and more wicked problems they are confronted with in our complex and uncertain world (Hubbard and Paquet 2014a). This has pushed out and replaced any meaningful notion of performance.

This has generated a growing gap – between the static stylization of job requirements used to hire, 'evaluate' and promote (or not) personnel, and the necessary dynamic gauges of their real performance that would focus on the effective despatch of their burden of office in ways that would ensure the effectiveness, the resilience, and the antifragility of organizations (Taleb 2012) – contaminating the current supposed evaluation of performance.

Behind the cloak of obligatory questionnaires and rituals, and the agony of pumps and theatrics to go through, the process of hiring, evaluation and promotion in the federal public sector has become more and more whimsical (the more so the higher one looks in the hierarchy): more an echo of personal likes and affinities (that pays attention only to the most ethereal notion of merit) than the result of a serious evaluation of cognitive abilities and creative skills of the employee.

Such a process allows for the most extraordinary amount of fanciful caprice and patronage of the like-minded, and can only randomly hope to generate appointments matching cognitive and creative capabilities to the challenges of the tasks.

Any serious in-depth audit of the appointment process of deputy heads, their associates and assistant deputy ministers (ADMs) – to pick the level where whimsicality and non-verifiability are at their apex – would reveal momentous incongruities: from willful blindness in the face of great talent to flagrant rewarding of failure in the name of sheer patronage of the like-minded.

And yet, as we have shown in a recent paper (Hubbard and Paquet 2014b), much work has been done in Ottawa over the last decades that has led to the development of meaningful gauges for those very critical characteristics of individuals, that capture those very cognitive and creative capabilities, and that should be at the forefront of the evaluation of public servants for purposes of hiring or promotion. But such work has never found ways to reshape the hiring and promotion processes in the federal public service.

The more complex the public sector organizations have become, and the more they have had to operate in a turbulent and uncertain environment, the more the job-descriptions-based caricature of performance has become inadequate as a meaningful gauge of the true burden of office – the more inadequate the higher one proceeds up the ladder of management and governance. This is a difficulty that could have easily been handled through gearing all gauges of performance more closely to the notion of burden of office and its dynamics and imprecisions. But those handling HRM in the federal public service have not been receptive to these sorts of complexifications.[3]

Too often convenience comes to prevail over reasonableness, and surreal trivial metrics that have little to do with true performance are elevated to canonical status. As a result, effective concern for true performance is totally evacuated.

The last stage of this effort to Taylorize that human resources work in the federal public sector has evolved with the recent gospel of deliverology brought forth by the new Trudeau government: a pseudo-science suggesting that one can slice the policy funnel into thin slices to which one might attach some specific metrics. In this Manichean world, political parties are supposed to define broad ideological objectives, and the bureaucracy to deliver what the ideologues have chosen

[3] At the time Hubbard was the head of the Public Service Commission (PSC), and when Paquet was a Fellow at the School of Public Services (SPS), Paquet made representations to Hubbard to obtain aggregate data about the different level of capacities of the EX categories with a view to redefining the mission of the School of Public Services to address gaps that might have been discovered through looking at their Slivinski-generated profiles at the PSC in order for the SPS to fill those gaps. Ironically, Hubbard (then embedded in the federal public service culture) refused Paquet access to these data. Hubbard and Paquet have since jointly worked over the last decade to argue for the development of a more robust strategy that would build a stronger foundation for the HRM in the federal public service. One should not underestimate the extent to which these inadequacies cripple the critical judgment of serious members of the tribe of federal public servants when they are in office.

to do by focusing on some sort of time-and-motion studies that have a whiff of Mussolinian flavour – mainly interested in running trains on time (Paquet 2016). In such cases, the multiplicity of spurious measurements quickly becomes a most effective decoy behind which one may exercise patronage in complete security.

In order to launch a process of social experimentation and learning that might generate better performance sooner than later, the best way is to initiate the inquiry into 'the sort of ecology of HRM regimes' likely to work in the Canadian federal public sector. This would entail ignoring altogether the barrage of trivial measurements put in place for the sole purpose of ensuring a big gap between what would ensue and anything that could reasonably be used to determine performance and remuneration. Those latter dimensions then have to be ascertained in more esoteric ways.

## *Motivation governance*

Public sector employees are neither delivery-boys nor clergy. They are very much like other human resources – neither mindless deliverers nor luminaries strictly motivated by the higher good of the country. Their motivation will therefore determine what value-adding contribution they can make, and motivation governance therefore underpins their performance (Osterloh and Frey 2013).

Osterloh and Frey's work has underlined the multidimensionality and complexity of the motivation of public sector employees: preferences may be more or less plastic, they may be more or less sensitive to the design of institutions, working conditions, and quality of human interactions, but they are not always known and may be wrongly interpreted.

This entails a very careful selection process of employees with the right characteristics to achieve high performance, since it might turn out to be quite difficult to influence behaviour later – especially after the employees have been acculturated to norms in use – for those may come to represent a perverse normalcy that can often only generate negative performance effects.

Osterloh and Frey question, with particular care, the bizarre tendency (endemic in Canada since the 1960s) to try to maximize the happiness of employees as a HRM strategy – they regard it as most likely to produce dysfunctional effects.

Without going very far in exploring behavioural economics, it is important to recognize that our view of the world is influenced by the cosmology of Harvey Leibenstein (1976). In his view, markets are imperfect, and contracts are incomplete. Moreover, rationality is a continuum: individuals are sometimes fully rational, but sometimes less than fully rational. This allows for the existence of inert areas, i.e., a range of effort within which the workers can exercise much discretionary effort depending on his/her preferences. Leibenstein suggests that group norms may prevail that involve issues of the group's history, honesty and trust. One can think of such group norms being echo effects of unionization, for instance.

Quite clearly, such circumstances apply to employment in the public sector. Public sector employees, like other workers, operate in a world of incomplete contracts, and selective and not always full rationality. Consequently, given the prevailing norms, they may exert variable effort in the pursuit of unclear notions like what their burden of office might be.

As a result, if high performance is to become the focal point in HRM, one must focus on the gap between high and low performance – not ascribable to allocative inefficiencies, i.e., ascribable to misallocation of resources – but rather rooted in the inert areas of which workers can make strategic use. Leibenstein's guestimates about the size of the waste generated by employees' under-effort are so large that ignoring it would amount to criminal negligence. Empirical evidence quoted by Leibenstein has shown that overcoming X-inefficiencies has generated increases in productivity by 30 percent to 50 percent and more.

However, dealing with this gap entails operating on a broader canvas than the narrow incentive reward system traditionally in use in animal psychology. Leibenstein brings into play some striking features like the "spirit" of an army, the "tear" in the social fabric, the "split personality" of a workforce – all dimensions that probe much beyond the mechanics of stimuli-responses into the much more profound cultural underground (Frantz 2007: 7-9).

## General sources of high performance

In Hubbard and Paquet (2014a, 2014b, 2015a, 2015b), we have suggested preliminary steps to drive the fake out of public administration, and to improve the performance of the public household.

The explicit intent was to eliminate the fuzz factor in the administration of the public sector to ensure that performance would be its primary focus, and that it would not be trivialized to the point of being reduced to rules of deliverology.

In this work, we underline, often in a very sketchy way, the crucial importance of not presuming that:

- the executive branch in any government really espouses a philosophy of HR that places top priority on performance, understands the central importance of appropriate linkages among the various segments of the policy funnel, and that it does so in full cognizance of the central importance of the engagement of workers, and their commitment to meeting the requirements of their burden of office;
- any one applying for a job in the public sector has the cognitive abilities required to occupy the job, therefore making such an assessment obligatory;
- the organizational structures and mechanisms that are adequate for locus $i$ in the public service may not be necessarily adequate for locus $j$, thus entailing the need to design structures and mechanisms that may be different from place to place to ensure high performance; and,

- any one hired in the public sector recognizes the nature of the 'burden of office' attached to that job (and not only the trivia of the job description); making such an awareness obligatory entails that all would recognize that since the burden of office may differ dramatically from place to place and level to level in the public service, different qualifications should be required.

In our view, most members of the public administration tribe are not at all fully conscious of the centrality of the above gaps, and of the handicaps these gaps create for those trying to implement an efficient, effective and innovative public service; neither are they at all fully conscious that any negligence or insouciance at any of these levels could easily lead to an HR regime that fails miserably:

- in relentlessly pursuing high performance by the best recruitment and management possible of the human resources in the public sector through a healthy philosophy of performance;
- in ensuring a sound appreciation of cognitive abilities and capabilities;
- in effecting a partition of the public sector workforce in segments corresponding to differentiated burdens of office;
- in designing the most effective architecture of organizations and institutions likely to best fit with the idiosyncrasies of the different segments, but also in designing the most effective ensemble of mechanisms to act as technical specifications, incentive reward systems, standards, etc., norms and moral contracts likely to frame the dimensions of the work conditions that can ensure high performance; and,
- in understanding the central importance of anchoring any HR system not only in its socio-technical and organizational contexts but also in its socio-cultural milieu so as to take maximum advantage of the *ethos* and culture in place, while avoiding being swamped

by toxic socio-cultural undercurrents that may also be in place.

In order to make performance the dominant reference point in designing the HR regime, one has to be able to identify the family of factors or dimensions that need to be taken into account, and to identify the various ways in which they might be combined. As a first stab at setting the stage for the design work, we propose factoring in four underpinning dimensions of the HR problem that need to be part of any reasonably integrated approach:

- the four different bundles of public servants,
- the individual competencies and organizational arrangements contributing to performance,
- the psycho-social and cultural factors, and
- the types of instruments of intervention regarded as legitimate.

The design challenge entails taking into consideration the plurality of different situations confronted by public administration, taking action to ensure that competencies and organization arrangements are optimized, factoring in all the psycho-social and cultural constraints regarded as givens in the short run, and making the most inventive and imaginative assemblage of instruments of intervention to ensure that the HR system is catalyzed so as to generate the most effective, efficient, value-adding, innovate arrangement possible.

## Bundling public servants

In some earlier work (Hubbard and Paquet 2014a: 136), we have partitioned the Canadian federal public service into four quadrants of a 2x2 table – identifying certain portions of the workforce according to the greater or lesser degree of uniqueness of their work, and according to the greater or lesser value-adding (value destruction) of their work. These four groups – super-bureaucrats, guardians, professionals, employees – obviously require different performance gauges since their burden of office is qualitatively different.

FIGURE 1.

## Human Capital in the Canadian Public Service

| Higher | 3) Professionals | 1) Super-bureaucrats |
|---|---|---|
| ↑ | Main challenge:<br>  Balance professional & political<br>Main job:<br>  Ideas, innovation & horizontality<br>HR goal:<br>  Learning          (40,000) | Burden of office:<br>  Safeguard fabric of society<br>Main job:<br>  Co-governing & enabling<br>HR goal:<br>  Commitment        (< 500) |
|  | 4) Employees | 2) Guardians |
|  | Main challenge:<br>  Reliability & fairness<br>Main job:<br>Productivity<br>HR goal:<br>  Responsiveness     (185,000) | Burden of office:<br>  Loyalty<br>Main job:<br>Management<br>HR goal:<br>  Productivity        (<10,000) |

Uniqueness

Value ————————————————————————→ Higher

This categorization does not generate a sufficiently granular classification of public servants to fully determine performance measurement. Depending on the particular sector in which the bureaucracy operates (natural resources, manufacturing, finance, culture and heritage, justice, defence and public safety, international, etc.) as well as the status of the organization (central agency, department, agency, crown corporation, policy/operations mix, etc.), there may be specific sensitivies, and responsibilities which can be determinant in defining what performance means. In the same spirit, the nature of the performance may depend on different functions (advisory, enforcement, etc.) depending on the nature of the structures within which the workforce operates, and the competencies that are required for the despatch of this sort of work. Additionally, the ambit of the 'burden of office' may leave a smaller or larger margin of maneuverability where judgment can or should be exercised.

Ideally, the configuration of functions, sectors, status, structures, competencies, burdens of office would shape the sort of mosaic of segments of the workforce calling for somewhat different handling. One might expect to be able to gauge with some reasonableness the burden of office of these groups of employees and design a meaningful appreciation of their performance. However, for purpose of convenience, especially at the experimental stage in the design of HRM regimes, it might be easier to experiment with the basic four groups we identified earlier, while being sensitive to the fact that special considerations may call for particular treatment for some specific sub-groups.

## *Organizational form and competencies*

Organizational form and competencies (and their matching) have come to be regarded as two of the most important sources of high performance. Yet they are probably the most neglected aspects in the HR regimes of the Canadian federal public service.

The choice of organizational form imposes obligations on one or more deputy head (DH) to ensure that there is a strong enough link among the various segments of the policy funnel (i.e., policy formulation, program design and service delivery). Examples are the case where a single DH must be sufficiently aware of policy considerations to ensure that the responsible minister is able to be kept in the 'policy formulation' loop (e.g. CRA). In other cases, a group of DHs must collaborate appropriately. In special cases, like the Public Service Commission, an 'independent agency' may also be an essential part of the HR system.

The notion of competency may be clear in certain professions where accredited bodies exist, but these sorts of tasks constitute only a very small segment of the public service jobs. In most cases (outside the world of regulators and the like), the burden of office of public servants is not always precisely defined, and it is often a mix of abilities, competencies, experience, and *savoir-faire* that is required.

We will return to the question in chapter 4.

## Burden of office is not job description

A centralized standard and homogeneous HRM system may well be able to ensure that each member has a clear job description, but this is unlikely to serve well any large, complex and polyphonic organizations like the federal public service in Canada. What is crucial is that members of an organization need to know what is expected of them, and what is their burden of office.

Over the last while, in the federal public service, the precise specification of the dos and don'ts attached to a job have been rich in detail about all sorts of non-essential aspects of the job, but scant about the crucial aspects of it: what is expected to be delivered by the member to the various persons or groups to which the member is accountable. The effort of job descriptions being cast in general terms means that it does not fit well with the specifics of the job in a particular department, at a particular time. Nor can the generic labels attached to functions by the HRM regime be better suited to the true burden of office existing here and now.

On the first front (dimensions of HR), the following features (functions, sector, status, structure, competencies) need to be brought to bear on the definition of the burden of office. On the second front (dimensions of the HRM apparatus), three general ways would appear to be required to finesse the right steering process: technical specifications pertaining to the specific task, negotiated standards with unions and professional orders, and moral contracts of different sorts to capture the more imprecise and yet quite important aspects of the job having to do with *savoir-faire*. Different mixes of these three instruments are bound to be used depending on the nature of the workforce one is talking about. Yet such fine-tuned appreciation is rarely if ever effected even at the highest level.

The maniacal concern for trivial peripheral aspects of the job description serves mainly to cover the poor quality of the selection process except for entry level routine jobs.

## Fitting the right ensemble of dimensions and levers

Given the contextual mapping of the workforce – a mapping that is obviously evolving all the time – the ways in which performance can be appreciated will obviously differ, and the sort of interventions likely to generate performance improvement will also differ.

At this moment, it is not appropriate to delve into great detail into the toolbox of HRM, but it is crucial to recognize that there are three families of levers available:

- α ascertaining or modifying technical specifications and incentive reward systems;
- β having to do with negotiating with relevant stakeholders the standards and norms defining the work conditions; and
- γ defining, in consultation with the workforce, the sort of moral agreements that might frame many of the dimensions of the work conditions that cannot and should not be frozen, but should remain open to as much freedom as possible on the part of the employees, depending on circumstances, in order for them to be able to adapt and reframe according to circumstances.

The first family of levers (α) flow naturally from basic management rights and technological givens. They pertain to dimensions of performance that are non-negotiable as a matter of law, technology or basic employers' expectations. Even though these dimensions of performance would appear rock-solid, they are not.

There used to be a time when essential services constituted a block of services that the employer could mandate. However, more recently the unwisdom of the courts has led to some of those α levers coming to be regarded as matters that fall into β territory.

The second family of levers (β) are those having to be negotiated with union representatives or professional orders, or other representatives of employees either as part of formal collective agreements or other such sets of rules. They are different for DMs and those doing routine work, but in all categories of employment, there are elements that cannot be modified arbitrarily by the employer without consultations and agreement.

Thirdly, and most importantly even is the matter of moral contracts – i.e., more or less unwritten agreements dealing with matters both non-routine and irregular that cannot be handled by fixed rules but that one might like to ensure will be handled by some more or less precise principle that reassures both parties.

These measures of commitment are crucial in any arrangement (even formal contracts) for they constitute the basis of good faith necessary to interpret the terms of formal contracts. While some parties, like unions, will wish to squeeze out any space for moral contracts, the employer will need some arrangements to ensure that, in the case of crisis, there will be a commitment not to let down the other party unreasonably (Paquet 1991/92 re: moral contracts; Paquet and Ragan 2012 re: their use at Lincoln Electric).

## Juggling with all these dimensions as the main HR challenge

Performance as gauged by the burden of office must be appreciated by taking into account the constraints of the context, and the highest and best use of the levers to deal with them. This is bound to suggest a quite different mix of uses of the different families of levers for the different portions of the mosaic of situations with which one is confronted. So this means that there will be no single way to measure performance: variety is going to be necessary. The different circumstances correspond to a pluralism of situations commanding a true plurality of arrangements.

## In praise of hybrid forms of governance[4]

Designing refurbished and differentiated forms of governance for HRM entails prototyping hybrid forms of governance to correct bad historical mishaps and unenlightened policy moves through a recombination and remodulation of contextual, cognitive, organizational and socio-cultural features into arrangements capable of providing greater effectiveness and innovation.

### Scoping design thinking

In 2004, Karl Weick published a paper in which he rooted his reflections on rethinking organizational design in the examination of the testimonies of two well-known designers: Frank Gehry (the famous architect) and Dee Hock (the ex-CEO who designed VISA) – both blessed with an uncanny ability at such work (Weick 2004; Gehry 1999; Hock 1999). The main lesson Weick drew from these reflections is that even though coordination is a central concern of designers – the job of generating contraptions that not only reconcile the pressures from the geo-technical constraints and from the values and plans of the various stakeholders, through coordinating the activities of all those who have a significant portion of the information, resources, and power that need to be mobilized to ensure resilience and innovation – there is a danger that allowing a fixation on some rigid and impatient coordination imperative might impair the whole process of design.

Weick quotes Dee Hock as observing that management is unduly focused on creating "constants, uniformity and efficiency," when what is required in our turbulent world is to understand and coordinate "variability, complexity, and effectiveness." Weick suggests that these modern requirements identified by Hock "are best achieved if design is recast as designing that uses transient constructs, *bricolage*, and improvisation" (Hock 1999: 47).

---

[4] This section borrows freely from Gilles Paquet, *Tackling Wicked Policy Problems – Equality, Diversity, and Sustainability*, 2013.

This emphasis on ongoing and living processes has a Deweyian flavour: John Dewey always refused to use terms with static connotations, like thing or object, to connote human realities and activities. He preferred using the elusive notion of 'affairs'. In the words of a Dewey scholar, "affairs are never frozen, finished or complete. They form a world characterized by genuine contingency and continual process. A world of affairs is a world of actualities open to a variety of possibilities" (Boisvert 1998: 24).

Therefore, for Weick and others, one must design for transience and incompleteness: being satisfied to define the skeleton or bare-bones framework, and to allow an emergent structure to develop around it as partners interact, argue, come together, and learn along the way. This is exactly what Gehry and Hock would appear to have been doing, and this is the spirit that informs a skeletal roadmap for design in three stages and nine steps.

TABLE 2.

## A Skeletal Roadmap for Design

**Stage 1 – *appreciation and design***
a.  New attitude and vocabulary
b.  Inquiring system: espistemology
c.  Mental mapping: some ethnography

**Stage 2 – *experimentation per se***
d.  Thinking with our hands: a bit of process thinking à la Friedmann & Abonyi
e.  Collaboration
f.  Prototyping and serious play: about reframing, restructuring, and retooling

**Stage 3 – *learning per se***
g.  Social learning: gauging according to various metrics
h.  Engagement and storytelling: moral contracts + feedback loops
i.  Etiquette and ethics of prototyping: corridor phenomena

These stages are not a list of mechanical steps that must be followed *seriatim* in a servile manner. The sequence is rather analogous to sequentially introducing families of concerns that are overlaid one upon the other to represent cumulatively (and through an ever more sophisticated and higher-definition image of complex natural or social systems) a mix of different intermingled sub-systems, making up the whole organization or social system.

Each step in our roadmap connotes configurations of 'affairs', of additional ongoing nexuses of activities of different sorts. The cumulative addition of these nexuses of activities in that particular sequence aims both at enriching the perspective, but also at triggering, with every new step being added, some more and more encompassing questioning of the assumptions made in earlier steps, and some consequential continuous tinkering or *bricolage* with the earlier sets of assumptions and activities presented in earlier transparencies.

The first trio of layers (**a, b, c**) roughly connotes a phase of appreciation and description. The different steps define (a) the prerequisite attitude, discourse, and vocabulary required for a meaningful inquiry to proceed; (b) the basic dynamics of the inquiry process that need to be initiated; and (c) the sort of mental map of the issue domain being explored, so as to anchor firmly the design thinking in the existing material and symbolic world of the issue domain.

The second trio of layers (**d, e, f**) corresponds roughly to experimentation *per se*. They correspond to the different stages of exploration in grappling with the new world to be constructed: (d) defines the forms that are adjusted to the circumstances, and meet some basic conditions of goodness of fit; (e) explores their possibilities and acceptability with crucial partners; and then (f) develops workable prototypes by trial and error, in conversations with the prototypes and the partners, and in experiments.

The third trio of layers (**g, h, i**) focuses more on learning *per se*. This is the moment (g) when the learning loops crystallize and when multiple reference metrics emerge; (h) when the engagement of the different partners evolves, moral contracts among partners take hold, and a new discourse takes form that allows the conversation to establish itself on a new basis; and (i) when a new appreciation of the internal and external constraints (on the conversation being conducted and on the selection of the prototypes likely to be most effective) emerges and gains traction.

This somewhat artificial partitioning and stylization has two main advantages: (a) it underlines clearly that, as one proceeds from stage 1 to stage 2, stage 2 forces considerable recasting of stage 1 assumptions and activities, and as one proceeds to stage 3, some trigger is bound to force some recasting of the two earlier phases; and (b) it provides the basis for a modest checklist that might serve as a useful guidepost in the evolution of the design process.

## Design attitude: why, what and how

The different steps and stages in this design process are anything but linear, since feedback loops are, of course, constantly in action. But the new design attitude permeates all these stages and steps. First we explain why the change in attitude is so important. Then we define exactly what is accomplished in preparing the ground for effective design thinking. Third, we indicate how to proceed to engineer what is expected.

### Why

One is not always as fully aware as one should be of the mental prisons haunting the sort of organizational culture in good currency, nor the conventional wisdom that is crippling the work of all stakeholders as potential organization designers. One of the most important mental prisons is the focus on decision.

The focus on decision, as Boland and Collopy suggest, has led to people being completely mesmerized by a concern about choice among existing alternatives, on the assumption that the problem is already well-defined, and the possible alternatives well-known. This is usually not the case. The design attitude recognizes that the problem definition has to be constructed, and that alternatives have to be created and crafted, and that they cannot be assumed to exist *ab ovo*. A course of action aims at creating better alternatives than what would appear to be originally available (Boland and Collopy 2004; Brown 2009).

In order to deal with an approach based on exploring systems which do not exist, what is required is not only a different attitude that singles out these dimensions for careful attention but also a different vocabulary to tackle them. Boland and Collopy have already tried their hand at a provisional version of the new sort of lexicon (Boland and Collopy 2004: chapter 37): collaboration, dialogue, improvisation, prototype, etc. These notions are essential in the designer's mental toolbox.

In all organizations (private, public, and social), the central basic challenge is problem definition. Each stakeholder has his own partial definition of the problem at hand, based on his partial knowledge and particular interests, but these partial and truncated views hardly suffice to define the problems at hand satisfactorily. This mental prison generates a dangerous blindness that obviously leads to the sorts of action that are likely to be misguided when they are based on these partial, reified, myopic, and uncertainty-denying views. Yet such views often succeed in hijacking the problem definition process, and derailing any meaningful inquiry.

Recognizing the full extent of every stakeholder's ignorance, the limitations it entails for their capacity to define the problem adequately, and the danger of premature reification means that ready-made problem definition needs to be replaced by a process of inquiry into problem definition that recognizes that most of the time the problems are wicked: (1) the goals are not known, or are very ambiguous or not agreed to by the stakeholders, and (2) the means-ends relationships are highly uncertain and poorly understood (Rittel and Webber 1973). The new awareness is a prerequisite for any meaningful inquiry.

## What

The development of such a new attitude would call for something as dramatic for those educating the organizational designers as the reframing of management education in North America triggered by the Ford Foundation and the Carnegie Commission in the middle of the last century. This Ford/ Carnegie reframing considerably strengthened the quantitative and analytic approaches, focusing a great deal on decision making. Serious questioning of the excesses that this Ford/ Carnegie twist has led to, however, has arisen of late, not only in management studies, but in the social sciences in general (Starbuck 2006).

Boland and Collopy have defined the basic elements of the design attitude that would seem to be required in our complex world. For them, "a design attitude views each project as an opportunity for invention that includes a questioning of basic assumptions and a resolve to leave the world a better place than we found it" (Boland and Collopy 2004: 9). Indeed, their 2004 book was planned to encourage just such a shift from a decision attitude to a design attitude.

A design attitude focuses on stewarding the inquiring system toward inventing assemblages of arrangements likely to foster better wayfinding and resilience. To accomplish that feat, it is necessary to focus on the meso-level. Organizations and institutions are meso-phenomena, too often poorly described and apprehended, because observers insist on looking at them through micro-perspectives that focus exclusively on individuals as absolutes, and deny the importance of relationships between entities. They are equally poorly understood by approaches focusing exclusively on macro-systems and totalities as absolutes. Organizational design requires a vocabulary and an approach that focuses at the meso-level.

Some exploratory work has already begun to develop not only some modest general propositions about the nature of the combinations of attributes likely to generate the most value-adding arrangements, given the circumstances, but also about what might be a workable approach to gauging whether these propositions hold under different circumstances: for example, when should the focus be on efficiency or innovation as the prevalent guiding force, as might be the case in the current protocols that would appear to dominate the process of design of organizational forms (Grandori and Furnari 2008).

**How**

As one of us has indicated elsewhere (Paquet 2009: chapter 2), the new competencies and skills that need to be developed to enable a design attitude have much to do with *savoir-faire* and *savoir-être*, and learning by doing. Such competencies, based on practical knowledge, have tended to be greatly underrated in a world where technical rationality has wrongly become hegemonic: presuming that knowledge flows only one way – from underlying disciplines to applied science to actual performance of services to clients and society. Substituting for this one-way street, a two-way approach, emphasizing knowing-in-action, reflection-in action (Michael *et al.*, 1980) (where knowledge emerges equally well from groping with situations and from surprises leading to on-the-spot experiments and knowledge creation) is (at least ideally) the way professionals are educated (Simon 1969/1981: chapter 5).

It emphasizes the development of skills and a capacity for a conversation with the situation through reflective practicum (residency, articling, etc.). It is seen to be the only way to impart practical knowledge in a manner that aims at nothing less than transformation and behaviour modification, for some of those skills are literally embodied: *savoir-faire* in the sense of *tour de main* cannot be learned and developed without a change in *savoir-être*, in identity.

It has proven extremely difficult to ensure the requisite training and coaching in these new competencies, for they require the development of perception skills, diagnostic skills, and the like. This explains the explosion of parallel training ventures dealing with those areas that are largely neglected by the formal education enterprise.

Organizational design uses a variety of mechanisms to help institute a living organization that has the capacity to be reliable but innovative, and to be resilient but to learn. It aims at coherence, but mainly at dynamism. This cannot be accomplished by tinkering only with the hard dimensions of organizations (architecture and routines); it must also modify their behaviour and culture. Moreover, depending on circumstances, this sort of intervention will have to be sequenced carefully if it is to be successful.

This is an especially daunting task in the case of the exploration/exploitation split that often underpins the innovation/reliability challenge (March 1991).

It is impossible to tackle this challenge without explicit efforts to transform the culture of the organization. The simple partitioning of tasks or efforts is unlikely to work.

Some principles and mechanisms have proven useful in this sort of work (Paquet 2005: chapter 8):

- maximum participation to ensure the tapping of all relevant knowledge and more collaboration;
- subsidiarity, or the delegation of decision making to the most local level possible;
- some competition to squeeze out organizational slack and promote innovation; and
- multistability, i.e., the partitioning of the organization into sub-systems, so as to be able to delegate the task of doing so to the one most able to handle a shock or perturbation, without the other sub-systems being forced to transform.

As for the most useful mechanisms, they have been:

- the setting up of ever more inclusive forums for effective multilogue;
- the negotiation of moral contracts defining clearly and well, yet informally, the mutual expectations of the different partners;
- the design of learning loops, enabling the partners to revise their choices of means as the experience unfolds, but also to revise the very ends pursued through reframing the organization when it proves necessary; and,
- the invention of fail-safe mechanisms to ensure that the multilogue does not degenerate into meaningless

consensuses, and to prevent *saboteurs* from derailing the collective effort.

The designer must be ready to prototype and to tinker as the process unfolds, but no organization will permit that unless some action plan is first at least hinted at – providing some sense of the nature of the experiment.[5]

Nadler and Tushman have suggested a blueprint and sequence for design that might serve as such a security blanket (Nadler and Tushman 1997). Their work might be stylized as follows (taking liberties with their own sequencing, and taking into account our earlier analyses):

- organizational assessment: functioning, performance gaps,
- design criteria: what the new design should accomplish,
- groupings: options for general grouping,
- coordination requirements: information-processing needs,
- linking: linking mechanisms (formal and informal),
- properties and capabilities of the ensuing assemblages,
- provisional analysis of impacts,
- simulation of the way in which the design would play out in different circumstances: prototyping and serious play,
- operational design required; detailed planning of implementation: support of key power groups, rewarding desired behaviuor, monitoring transition,
- organizational culture (values, beliefs and norms) as means and ends, and
- social learning loops mechanisms as a way to adapt.

---

[5] One recent example of a public service entity that was pushed to restructure and reframe (to, *de facto*, adopt a design attitude) is the Canadian Forest Service (CFS) (part of Natural Resources Canada). It did this in order to assist the Canadian forest industry to transform in the face of strong worldwide forces (Hubbard and Paquet 2015b: 128-130). One critical factor was permission from its bureaucratic leader (an ADM) to explore and take risks. This book argues for an HRM approach that actually encourages and enables this kind of design thinking and design attitude across the board rather than the current one that hinders rather than helps.

\* \* \*

It is reasonable to ask how one can shift from the attitude underpinning the traditional quest for certainty to an attitude of design for transience and incompleteness.

One interesting way in which the new attitude might be generated has been presented in Weick and Sutcliffe's *Managing the Unexpected* (Weick and Sutcliffe 2007). They have identified principles guiding highly reliable organizations in the face of turbulent environments – three of them helping to improve sensitivity and capacity to react quickly to the unexpected, and two of them having to do with the capacity to contain the toxic impacts of these avalanches:

- preoccupation with failure,
- reluctance to simplify,
- sensitivity to operations,
- commitment to resilience,
- deference to expertise.

These principles are built on 'mindfulness'.

Weick and Sutcliffe suggest that these capabilities may be audited, but they may also be nudged into becoming instituted in the organizational culture, and may be managed through leveraging "small wins" into progress of the organizational culture toward greater mindfulness.

In order for mindfulness to take hold, one must however build on a broad awareness of the range of possibilities open to the designer. One may presume that the state of play will remain the same and that all actors will continue in perpetuity to maintain their present role – in the case of unions, for instance. This would reduce considerably the range of the possible. Alternatively, one may postulate that many of the actors may indeed be reshaped and experience a change in their role. If such possibility is entertained, the whole coordination game in HR may be more fundamentally transformed.

This is not the place to indulge in science fiction when one is aiming at triggering transformation in the HRM world in the short run. However it would be naïve not to consider that, if the HR world is transformed, social learning may well entail that participants in the coordination game on the HR front might very well see their status and role modified. We will return to this range of possibilities in the conclusion.

In the meantime, in part III of this volume, we probe two broad aspects of the HRM challenge a bit further: the world of competencies and organisational forms, and the world of moral contracts. They represent the primary material that is likely to have to be redesigned in the refurbished HRM we envisage.

## References

Boland, Richard J. and Fred Collopy (eds.). 2004. *Managing by Design*. Stanford, CA: Stanford University Press, chapter 1.

Boisvert, Raymond D. 1998. *John Dewey – Rethinking Our Time*. Albany, NY: State University of New York Press, p. 24 (quoted by R. Garud, S. Jain and P. Tuertscher. 2008. "Incomplete Design and Designing Incompleteness," *Organization Studies*, 29, p. 351-371).

Brown, Tim. 2009. *Change by Design*. New York, NY: Harper Business.

Frantz, Roger. 2007. *Renaissance in Behavioral Economics – Essays in honor of Harvey Leibenstein*. London, UK: Routledge.

Gehry, Frank. 1999. "Commentaries," in M. Friedman (ed.). *Architecture + process: Gehry talks*. New York, NY: Rizzoli, p. 43-287.

Grandori, Anna and Santi Furnari. 2008. "A Chemistry of Organization: Combinatory Analysis and Design," *Organization Studies*, 29(3): 459-485.

Hock, Dee. 1999. *Birth of the Chaordic Age*. San Francisco, CA: Berrett-Koehler.

Hubbard, Ruth. 2013. "Performance, not model employer," *www.optimumonline.ca*, 44(2): 41-43.

Hubbard, Ruth and Gilles Paquet. 2014a. *Probing the Bureaucratic Mind – About Canadian Federal Executives*. Ottawa, ON: Invenire.

Hubbard, Ruth and Gilles Paquet. 2014b. "Competencies: Part of the Governance Vacuum," *www.optimumonline.ca*, 44(3): 58-76.

Hubbard, Ruth and Gilles Paquet. 2015a. "The Canadian Federal Public Service: Tinkering Can No Longer Suffice," *www.optimumonline.ca*, 45(3): 3-15.

Hubbard, Ruth and Gilles Paquet. 2015b. *Irregular Governance: A Plea for Bold Organizational Experimentation*. Ottawa, ON: Invenire.

Leibenstein, Harvey. 1976. *Beyond Economic Man*. Cambridge, MA: Harvard University Press.

March, James G. 1991. "Exploration and Exploitation in Organizational Learning," *Organization Science*, 2, p. 71-87.

May, Kathryn. 2014. "Unions grieve new PS performance rules," *Ottawa Citizen*, April 7.

May, Kathryn. 2016. "Public Service News: Liberals to repeal hated Tory legislation on PS bargaining," *Ottawa Citizen*, May 26.

Michael, Donald N. *et al.* 1980. *The New Competence – The Organization as a Learning System*. San Francisco, CA: Values and Lifestyles Program.

Nadler, David A. and Michael L. Tushman. 1997. *Competing by Design – The Power of Organizational Architecture*. New York, NY: Oxford University Press.

Osterloh, Margit and Bruno S. Frey. 2013. "Motivation Governance," in A. Grandori (ed.). *Handbook of Economic Organization: Integrating Economic and Organization Theory*. Cheltyenham, UK: Edward Elgar, p. 26-40.

Paquet, Gilles. 1991/92. "Betting on Moral Contracts," *Optimum*, 22(3): 45-53.

Paquet, Gilles. 2005. *The New Geo-Governance: A Baroque Approach.* Ottawa, ON: University of Ottawa Press.

Paquet, Gilles. 2009. *Crippling Epistemologies and Governance Failures— A Plea for Experimentalism.* Ottawa, ON: University of Ottawa Press.

Paquet, Gilles. 2013. *Tackling Wicked Policy Problems: Equality, Diversity and Sustainability.* Ottawa, ON: Invenire.

Paquet, Gilles. 2016. "Some 120 days later: ever more reasons to be apprehensive," *www.optimumonline.ca,* 46(1): 1-5.

Paquet, Gilles and Tim Ragan. 2012. *Through the Detox Prism – Exploring Organizational Failures and Design Responses.* Ottawa, ON: Invenire.

Rittel, H.W.J. and M.M. Webber. 1973. "Dilemmas in a General Theory of Planning," *Policy Sciences,* 4, p. 155-169.

Simon, Herbert A. 1969/1981. *The Sciences of the Artificial.* Cambridge, MA: The MIT Press.

Starbuck, William H. 2006. *The Production of Knowledge.* Oxford, UK: Oxford University Press.

Taleb, Nassim N. 2012. *Antifragile – Things that gain from disorder.* New York, NY: Random House.

Weick, Karl E. 2004. "Rethinking Organizational Design," in Richard J. Boland and Fred Collopy (eds.). *Managing by Design.* Stanford, CA: Stanford University Press, p. 36-53.

Weick, Karl E. and Kathleen M. Sutcliffe. 2007 (2nd Ed.). *Managing the Unexpected – Resilient Performance in an Age of Uncertainty.* New York, NY: Wiley.

# PART III

# Prototyping

The design of a variety of HRM regimes well adapted to the circumstances of the different bundles of federal public sector workers poses a momentous challenge if the main objective is to ensure effective coordination and best performance, while respecting a number of subsidiary constraints to prevent the labour process from degenerating into dysfunction as a result of allowing gross forms of unfairness.

In this work, the challenge is to create a workable assemblage of four main families of instruments available to the designer to shape the sort of HRM suitable for each of the different groups of public sector workers. We discuss the two hard instrumentations – the organizational structure and the combination of adequate capabilities – in chapter 4, and then we tackle the soft ones in chapter 5 – pertaining to moral contracts and burdens of office.

In neither case, is it our objective to survey the whole range of possible purposive arrangements. We are more interested in illustrating the potentialities of this sort of arsenal to enrich the organizational and social architecture of organizations and capabilities (organizational and human capital) in chapter 4, and those of the relational infrastructure, having to do with moral contracts (Paquet 1991-92) and burdens of office (Tussman 1989; Paquet 1997) – rooted in the sociality and culture of the system – in chapter 5.

The reader may already be familiar with the notion of organizational infrastructure; he/she may be less familiar with the notion of moral contracts and even less with the notion of burden of office, that constitute the complement of softer, but no less important, arrangements that supplement the more formal infrastructure.

## References

Paquet, Gilles. 1991-92. "Betting on Moral Contracts," *Optimum*, 22(3): 45-53.

Paquet, Gilles. 1997. "The Burden of Office, Ethics, and Connoisseurship," *Canadian Public Administration*, 40(1): 55-71.

Tussman, Joseph. 1989. *The Burden of Office – Agamemnon and Other Losers*. Vancouver, BC: Talonbooks.

CHAPTER 4

# | Social Architecture and Competencies
## Ruth Hubbard and Gilles Paquet

"A fundamental mismatch exists between
today's workforce and workplace, and the institutions
and policies that support and govern them"
*Thomas A. Kochan*

There are various ways in which the Canadian federal public household may be said to be less than optimally governed. But two specific interfaces are particularly problematic: first, the interface between the public household and the citizenry it is meant to serve, on the demand side, so to speak; and second, the interface between the public household as a quasi-firm and its workforce, on the supply side.

## *The public household/citizenry interface*

On the first front, all sorts of general forces have dramatically modified the interface between the public household and the citizenry over the last 60 years. One such force is a broad increase in the scope of government services provided to the citizenry with the advent of the welfare state, and, consequently, the significant growth in the size of the public household, and in the complexity of its operations. In a society that has become more variegated and where individuals and groups have become capable of expressing their preferences more and more robustly (and even to refer to them as entitlements), the challenge of meeting these diverse expectations has also become more daunting.

Yet as the public household grew, it also became more and more inward looking and self-centred. The organizational challenge of running such a multi-faceted enterprise absorbed more and more energy, and the temptation to adjust the *modus operandi* to make the task less awkward and less daunting triggered the development of more mechanisms of centralization and homogenization of services, and a certain desensitization *vis-à-vis* the idiosyncrasies of the different segments of the population. Effectiveness in reaching the citizen gave way to standardization and ways that were more convenient for bureaucrats. This created a cleavage between the bureaucracy and the citizenry, and a lesser concern for doing the right thing (effectiveness) as opposed to a greater concern for doing the thing right (efficiency) – i.e., according to rules likely to be audited.

To this broad and sweeping bureaucratization wave, one must add, in Canada, a particular ideological bent that materialized in the post-World War II decades (as a result of the *zeitgeist* of the time), the plague of minority governments especially in the 1960s and 1970s, a growth of activism on the union front, and a particular idealistic/romantic 'progressive' virus that took hold of a significant portion of the elected officials, the media and the intelligentsia.

This maelstrom materialized in the form of a series of determining turns of events: (a) the pursuit of a so-called 'model employer' philosophy by the Canadian federal government (with all sorts of concerns extraneous to performance like diversity, equality, and the like overriding concerns for effectiveness); and (b) a particularly weak reaction by government to illegal strike action by postal workers, by granting the right to unionize and strike to nearly all federal employees. These developments have shifted the focus of the public household away, even more, from concerns about effectiveness, performance and productivity, toward doing the thing right (process, inward concerns about labour peace, and the like).

As these forces created a greater and greater disconnect between the operations of the public household and its performance, this schism was rationalized as responding to the fundamental discontinuity between the sort of 'higher' concerns that the public household has to deal with and the usual concerns of interest in the private sector, and the assertion that those 'higher' concerns called for a totally different way to govern in which performance, effectiveness and the like are only part of a much larger equation.

This allowed the insertion of an immense 'fuzz factor' in the administration of the public household as compared with what was happening elsewhere. All sorts of considerations were brought forth and declared of such import that they could 'justify' a generalized lack of concern with effectiveness and performance in the name of those 'other' considerations. Public administration became absorbed with processes, and more and more immunized from concerns about management and performance.

Bureaucracy-centred imperatives became dominant, and an increase in sophistry helped to rationalize whatever aberration or *bizarrerie* needed to be rationalized. Indeed, among the public household clergy, nothing would appear to be more rational than a rationalization. This was to underpin a philosophy of 'anything goes' in the name of the difference of kind between the public and the private sectors. And to those who might object that this was hardly a way to run any business, the answer was simply that government is not anything like business. What ensued has been a centralized system of control that claims to run the public household top down with formal mechanisms that allow so much whimsicality down the hierarchy that Kafkaesque results ensued (Hubbard and Paquet 2010).

For a while such *obiter dictu* would appear to carry the day. It took disastrous performance of major proportion to open the door to the revolution of public choice, and to the temptation to initiate new public management processes. But by the time these disasters materialized, the public administration ideology had sufficiently crystallized that the public administration tribe (academics and practitioners) could enter the battle with the new barbarians (who claimed that much in the public household could share management tools with the private sector) well-armed.

It became an epic battle of an inspired 'progressive' public administration clergy with a 'common-sense' public management posse. That battle has been fought and won quite differently depending on which battlefield is scrutinized. In the public administration literature, victory has been declared *ab ovo* by a clergy that has been satisfied with denouncing the barbarians who do not understand the quintessence of public administration. Everywhere else, the management vacuum of traditional public administration has been recognized, but corporate interests in the public household – quite comfortable with the prevailing fuzz – have understandably resisted: no one has committed hara-kiri, some superficial management improvements have been clumsily added on, but little has been done to eliminate the penumbra and the 'fake' that it makes possible.

## The public household/ workforce interface

On the second front is the interface between the public household and its workforce. This relationship has been allowed to slump into a state generating great inefficiency not only (a) as a result of the complete disconnect between the organization and performance imperatives, because of the lack of pressure to perform, but also (b) as a result of the disenfranchising of performance (and management) as not being central to the concerns of the public household. The focus on 'model employer' was allowed to run awry, letting the human resource (HR) function become dysfunctional: instead of designing an HR function to achieve performance, the HR function was perverted into focusing on catering to the comfort of the workforce as an objective unto itself.

This has entailed a relaxation of the HR regime to the point of allowing (except in certain areas regulated by external bodies) the real matching of the capacities of the human resources and the complexities of the job to become somewhat subsidiary in the staffing function – and the more so the more one climbs the hierarchical levels, since the job requirements tend to become fuzzier there, leaving much more margin for maneuverability at a whim. The reasons for the 'necessary' looseness of the linkage between the capabilities of the human resources and the complexities of the job (especially at the upper end of the HR scale) – it is argued – are the difficulties of gauging these features. More realistically, it can be said that there has been great care taken in avoiding any effort to develop and finesse in any meaningful way to gauge these features because of the new constraints they would entail for executives in the running of the public household.

No one would deny that these features are difficult to define in useful and reliable ways. But in some agencies, like the Canada Revenue Agency, it has proven both possible and tractable a task. As for the corporatist opposition to such gauging (again outside the realm of externally regulated competencies) in the name of higher-order, ethereal and ineffable qualities being necessary to the despatch of different in-kind tasks in the public household, it may be hogwash but it has become a foundational myth in the public administration tribe. Moreover, this myth has been carefully sustained over time, in academe and elsewhere with sponsored studies feeding on financial support from the federal bureaucracy itself (Kernaghan 2007).

This mental prison has been powerful enough to ensure that concern about the matching of capacities with the complexities of the task has been kept at bay – as not relevant to the sort of public household work, especially at the senior levels. The disinterest in finding ways to improve this matching has resulted in poor matching – a problem exacerbated by the churn of senior executives among departments since Right Honourable Pierre Trudeau's days – and the cost of this mismatch, while it has not been quantified satisfactorily yet, can only be conjectured to be enormous.

## Both flawed interfaces reinforce each other

Both these flawed interfaces in the Canadian federal public household are consequential, and they reinforce each other: less concern about performance breeds laxity in matching capacities and complexities of the tasks, and poor matching can only breed ineffectiveness, poor performance and waste.

It is our view that innovation on both fronts *at the same time* could dramatically transform the effectiveness and performance of the public household. There are obviously many ways in which improvements might be achieved on both fronts. But there is much merit in a zone of waste that for a long time has neglected to deal with precise management discussions about mechanisms to achieve better focus on performance and matching, to proceed not with general wishful statements, but with very precise proposals to explain clearly what might be done and how it would work.

The tool we propose on the first front is the creation of external boards of management for all departments and agencies in the Canadian federal government (unless it can be claimed that it might be totally unsuitable for important reasons) – boards that would focus explicitly on performance – not in complete ignorance of the overall mission of the unit but as a subsidiary board charged with performance within the constraints defined by the policy framework and the senior board, and charged with continuous feedback with the senior board (the whole-of-government board), so as to ensure that there is no disconnect between the policy level and the management level, and that mutual social learning ensues.

The tool we propose on the second front is a competencies approach to the HR regime that would ensure the matching of capacities and the complexities of the tasks. It is not a matter of mechanically imposing a particular scheme, but to use a generic framework and vocabulary to develop a made-in-

Canada framework that would fit our particular circumstances and traditions.

In both cases, there will be opposition to these proposals. Some will claim it impossible to implement; others will argue that it would prevent public sector executives from doing their ineffable jobs. We argue that there is a need to set up an inquiring system not only to find the best fit on both the structural and competencies fronts (given the Canadian circumstances), but also to enable the appropriate social learning and the requisite time to learn and adapt well when changeovers are required.

We suggest that these innovations be developed experimentally in half a dozen departments or agencies at first, and that, once the prototypes have been played with sufficiently to finesse them and have proven resilient, but also capable of making the system *antifragile* (i.e., capable of becoming stronger as the challenges they meet are more robust), they be generalized to all departments and agencies where it is suitable (Taleb 2012). This might be accomplished fully within one decade. The main purpose of this transition period is to have ample time to *drive out the fake* – not only to finesse the right organizational instruments that are needed in particular circumstances, but also to allow mental prisons to be unlocked, and the cosmologies to adapt, so that the mental blockages, that have played such a destructive role in preventing these innovations to take hold up to now, can be neutralized and attenuated if not made to disappear completely.

## Boards of management

Boards of management is not a new idea but one whose time has come, albeit in a form somewhat different from what has been proposed up to now by the likes of Peter Aucoin.

Concern about the underperformance of the traditional departments and agencies of the Canadian federal government (but also elsewhere) began to be felt strongly in the 1970s and 1980s but were systematically underplayed by the choirmasters of the public administration enterprise in Canada. Only the financial crisis of the early 1990s – that forced the program review exercise onto the government's agenda – managed to bring forth real concern about increasing service delivery efficiency. It materialized in the form of the 1995 framework for alternative service delivery (Canada 1995).

The key word was 'efficiency'. This framework was not really directed at making government more effective (i.e., doing the right thing), but at making it more efficient (i.e., doing the thing right). This led to a tendency to tinker with the technology of service delivery segment at the tail end of the policy funnel – going from policy formation, program design, to the mechanisms for service delivery – in quasi-complete isolation of what was happening upstream, and, therefore, without the crucially important feedback loop with the policy end of the policy funnel. This echoed the view of some academics like Aucoin who felt, wrongly, that the policy funnel can be tightly segmented into disconnected pieces without important malefits ensuing (Aucoin 1995, 1996).

This sort of deeply flawed thinking was based on a strong version of three ill-founded assumptions:

(a) the separability of policy formation, program design and delivery mechanisms;

(b) the sacredness of accountability to the minister Westminster-style; and,

(c) the presumption that detailed contracts would suffice to ensure that the policies intended by ministers and senior officials are carried out down the policy funnel most effectively.

Aucoin (first in the 1990s) held these assumptions dear, and he was wrong: separability is toxic because it stunts social learning; and ministerial accountability, conceived for a 'Big G' government world, has become attenuated in a 'small g' governance world (where power, resources and information are widely distributed in many hands). In a 'small g' world, detailed contracts do not suffice to link the various segments of the policy funnel – social learning loops are required. The cartoonesque characterization based on the above assumptions may explain why the alternative service delivery (ASD) initiatives built on it failed: one cannot tinker separately with service delivery without some serious rethinking of all the other segments of the whole policy funnel (Paquet 1997). The magi of deliverology still do not get the point.

To make it more likely for departments/agencies (a) to put more of a focus on management and service to the citizenry in an effectiveness-cum-efficiency mode, as well as (b) to maintain a strong traditionally higher-order 'partnering' with government policy work upstream, effective arrangements need to be found: an appropriate structure providing both freedom and flexibility, while accepting the constraint of effective central oversight and accountability for performance that is mission-driven. An effective external but embedded board of management must remain a subsidiary board, and this can be accomplished if the deputy head is always a member of that board, and ensures continuous liaison between the whole-of-government board and the board of management of the department/agency – a liaison that works both ways by providing and receiving feedback at both ends.

Aucoin (now in the late 2000s) may have appeared to have evolved toward a position calling for continuous necessary feedback loops between segments (Aucoin 2007), and Heintzman and Juillet (2012) may also have appeared to concur and adopt a softer position than Aucoin (first period) if only by not addressing the issue head on. In fact, neither paper is entirely clear about the extent to which the authors adhere strongly or loosely to the basic assumption of absolute separability among the different segments of the policy funnel. However, to the extent that they all seem to embrace separability of an extreme sort 'upstream' – between politicians and senior bureaucrats, for instance – to the point of denouncing a culture of promiscuity wherever less paranoid observers would only see effective collaboration, they must be suspected of still harbouring the same ill-inspired devotion to absolute separability, and to an anti-promiscuity bias, all the way along the downstream segments of the policy funnel.

Most certainly the tone of the last paper by Peter Aucoin, (before he passed away) would still appear to embrace somewhat incoherently:

(a) a tightly segmented view of how the different portions of the policy funnel should interface (and, with it, a phobia of promiscuity);

(b) an ultimate deference to the integrated and hierarchical Westminster system as sacred cow; and,

(c) a presumption that one can define detailed contracts among the segments of the policy funnel to ensure that the policies intended by the senior board and senior officials are carried out down the policy funnel most effectively (Aucoin 2012).[1]

It would suggest that Aucoin would not support our sort of board of management: one that does not presume that such detailed contracts can be drawn, and therefore calls for active collaboration among segments of the policy funnel and some promiscuity in order to ensure synoptic social learning, even though *en dernière* instance, the political authority would prevail.

Our sort of board of management is briefly described below.

## What these boards of management would do

In many countries, the experience with boards of management has been initiated with the creation of agencies as an alternative for the traditional departments to escape many of the constraints inherited from department-centred structures that are hierarchical, centrally-controlled organizations, slow to adapt to changing conditions, and inadequately responsive to the interests they serve (Schick 2002).

---

[1] These speculative reflections about what academic disputations might support are of minimal interest, since, in recent times, Canada has experimented in real time and in real life with an initiative that has already been implemented successfully at the Canada Revenue Agency – one that has met with great success, and has led to CRA initiating also a competencies approach to its HR regime as a fringe benefit (Hubbard and Paquet 2014a).

Unlike Aucoin, Schick would appear to see boards of management as focusing on performance and management, but subject to the broad direction of the whole-of-government board (i.e., Treasury Board) and committed to functional integration by working hard at striking a balance, at the operational level, between coordination and subordination, cooperation and conflict.

In the case of the boards of management that we propose, this would entail that they would take responsibilities for finance, human resources, procurement, asset management and information technology, and the like. The two boards would work in tandem with as much autonomy as possible granted to the subsidiary board, but an explicit recognition that, depending on the nature of the work involved, more or less of the above-mentioned activities might be abandoned – more or less fully – to the subsidiary board.

The Canada Revenue Agency (CRA) provides an example. Its mission is to "… administer tax, benefit, and related programs and to ensure compliance on behalf of governments across Canada …" (Canada Revenue Agency 2011: 3). It assesses, collects, and administers hundreds of billions of dollars in tax revenue every year, including directly delivering billions in benefits and tax credits. To do this, in 2012-13, it had the equivalent of about 40,000 people full time and a budget of over $4.25 billion.

For our purposes, CRA's activities can be thought of as involving three levels of players: 1. the whole of government (the 'big' management board (Treasury Board and its supporting secretariat), the responsible minister (the minister of Revenue), and the Governor-in Council); 2. a subsidiary Board of Management in order to keep a clear focus on performance; and, 3. the Agency itself headed by its commissioner (the uppermost bureaucrat).

A subsidiary Board of Management was established to oversee the CRA's organization and administration. The 15-person majority external (including the chair) Board, sits between the responsible minister and the Agency. The accountability of the most-senior bureaucrat (the commissioner) for day-to-day management rests with the Board and its four committees: audit, governance, human resources, and resources (e.g. financial).

The commissioner is *de facto* a member of the Board, and is responsible for the Agency's management, the supervision of its employees and the implementation of its policies and budgets. The Agency's decision-making body (the Agency Management Committee (AMC) chaired by the commissioner) is supported, in turn, by six sub-committees that deal with: strategic direction, resource and investment management, human resources, strategic operations, and tactical operations, including making recommendations on matters to be decided by AMC. The sixth subcommittee – Management Audit and Evaluation – (responsible for oversight of internal audits and program evaluation) reports to the Board's Audit Committee rather than to AMC.

## How these boards of management would work

As hinted at above, the working arrangements between the two boards might be modulated (with a different division of labour and a greater or lower degree of full autonomy for the junior board) depending on the nature of the mission of the unit. But whatever arrangements might be deemed workable, some crucial imperatives would prevail.

Depending on the relative importance of policy work in the daily activities of the unit, more or less of the operational activities may be ceded to the subsidiary board with more or less important *liens* being imposed as constraints. To fix ideas, one may partition the units into three batches (i: those where all the activities mentioned above are ceded completely to the subsidiary board; ii: those where only some of the activities with diverse *liens* are ceded; iii: those where a minimal set of activities – regarded as the *minimum minimorum* required for the system to function – are ceded) according to circumstances and the relative omnipresence of policy concerns or not in the operations of the unit.

Overriding all these idiosyncrasies, it should be understood that (a) the proposed principles of operations of the board of management for the management of the unit would be scrutinized by the senior board and subject to discussion and negotiations, and ultimately to a directive of the senior board establishing what will need to prevail in the final analysis; and (b) a continuous process of exchange of information between the two boards would ensure effective social learning.

Finally, any such refurbished agency/department may remain somewhat constrained by other authorities within the overall governing apparatus – provincial constraints being respected, wide-ranging authority of commissioners of one sort or another, etc.

Again, the CRA provides a concrete example. The government as a whole uses three main levers to situate and control the CRA. They deal with: (a) management overall; (b) the grey zone between management and policy as well as matters materially affecting public finance; and (c) the appointment of members of the CRA Board of Management. The CRA Board maintains an overall degree of control over CRA management (e.g. approval of its corporate business plan and negotiating mandates with unions), including requiring a degree of consistency in presentation of material with respect to public finances (e.g. approval of annual resource requests, and performance results set out in terms of strategic outcomes). It may (via the responsible minister) issue a written directive to that Board on any matter within the Board's authority that affects public policy or could materially affect public finances. It may also (via the responsible minister) receive advice on management matters from that Board.

The oversight framework enables the CRA Board to assess performance with respect to the five areas of oversight that are required (organization, administration, resources, services, and personnel) (Canada Revenue Agency 2013-14). The framework includes expectations for each area, assessment criteria, information considered in arriving at a rating, and ratings of strong, acceptable opportunity for improvement, or unacceptable (requiring immediate attention).

A list of competencies has been developed for the CRA Board chair (e.g. communications and public relations, corporate governance, strategic outlook and alignment) and individual directors (e.g. collegiality and mature confidence, ethics, integrity and accountability, informed and sound judgment) as well as the overall needs of that Board (e.g. change management, complex multi-dimensional client service, human resources and labour negotiations) (*Ibid.*).

Social learning of all key players is enabled in a number of ways: (a) from the formal reporting that is required by the government along with any written directives to the CRA Board or advice from it; this formal reporting feeds into the senior management board and is necessarily potentially affected by it, including by any written directives from the responsible minister and any advice from the Board to that minister; (b) by the use of the CRA Board's performance assessment that 'informs' the objectives in the Commissioner's Performance Agreement as well as the Board and its committees' work plans (Canada Revenue Agency 2011); (c) by the ongoing activities of internal audit and program evaluation, and via the results of the CRA Board's overview of risk and change management.

### Resistance can be overcome, so an experiment is warranted

Any initiative of such a magnitude at the level of the Canadian public service is bound to run into a number of stumbling blocks – the most important ones being anchored in the structure and culture of the federal public service that has generated bad habits and rigidities of all sorts over time. It is both unlikely and unreasonable to anticipate that this sort of situation will not generate opposition from those whose habits and gratifications are challenged.

We have referred in passing throughout the text to some of these mental prisons and other potential blockages to be overcome. They may be summarized in the form of propensities:

(a) to give dominant priority to the policy formation end of the policy funnel to the detriment of management;

(b) to centralize unduly in order to gain control of the process, and to presume that whatever is ordained at the higher level will be carried out down the chain of command; much of the recent literature has shown how ineffective this 'Big G' form of governance is both because of cognitive limitations at the top and behavioural, organizational and institutional obstacles down the implementation road;

(c) to grant clergy-like status to senior executives in the Canadian public household, and to immunize them from the sort of constraints imposed on mere mortals;

(d) to anthropomorphize much of public administration and thereby to ignore important systemic dimensions that have an impact on the capacity to transform the governance of the public household; such systemic dimensions not only prevent individuals from taking reasonable decisions but also extinguish innovative capabilities altogether;

(e) to allow the public household to fall into pneumopathological states – the state of those who are morally insane, living as it where in a fantasy world of self-righteousness, and in denial *vis-à-vis* the toxicity of the arrangements in place; this leads to indulging systematically in plausible deniability and accepting uncritically surreal schemes;

(f) to restrict debates about reform to general principles instead of recognizing that the devil is in the details, and carrying out precise experiments that can demonstrate whether an initiative is indeed or not a good answer to the present challenges.[2]

---

[2] It is not very useful for navigation to be satisfied with recommendations that the public service should be focusing on the long term, that it should not be fearful of failure, that there should be more "independent, evidence-based decision-making" (whatever this may mean), and that the Canada School of Public Service should transform from an innocuous and not very

We have documented all of these over the last few years (Hubbard and Paquet 2010, 2014a; Paquet 2014a). Not taking these factors into account can only increase the risk that the innovative initiatives will be successfully torpedoed.

While it is natural for the bureaucracy to protect its corporatist interests, it is criminal negligence to allow such pressure to remain unchecked when it threatens to sabotage the effectiveness of the public household. So it is essential that critical thinking kicks in, and that the initiative be accompanied by explicit discussion of these toxic propensities in order to ensure that they are tamed to a sufficient extent that they cannot prevent the implementation of necessary reforms.

The fact that a pre-experiment has been run with great success for some 10 years at the Canada Revenue Agency, and that ways were found there to overcome resistance and blockages, should be grounds enough to argue that the time has come to extend the experiment to a representative group of departments and agencies, so as to be able to determine whether these innovations may be safely generalized to the whole of the Canadian federal public service, and whether there should be exceptions to this regime – where and why.

## Competencies

We have been persuaded by our own ethnographic work that a good many Canadian senior public sector executives underperform, and that they are not well equipped to deal with the full range of problems they are confronted with today and are likely to face in the future. Our way to respond to such concerns has not been to create an ideal-type of the senior-executive as leaders, nor to speculate on what

useful institution to become a more daring and controversial think-tank. Fortunately to this somewhat ethereal wish list, David McLaughlin added one useful suggestions "stop the churn of deputy minister turnover" – a practical suggestion that would help much in ensuring that the capacities of the senior executives would match the complexities of the task (McLaughlin 2014).

tablets might be drafted to specify their relationships with politicians clearly.

We have been satisfied to put forward (Hubbard and Paquet 2014b: 118) a list of the sort of concerns revealed by our ethnographic findings, and to conjecture, on that basis, a tableau of the sort of competencies that would appear to be wanting. The list of the missing competencies is referred to somewhat skimpily at the bottom of this page,[3] and was used to develop a tableau of the capacity refurbishment that might fill the gaps observed (*Ibid.*: 127). These gaps in the knowledge, norms and mechanisms at the cognitive, behavioural, organizational and institutional levels are summarized in Table 3 on the next page.

These are neither the only sources of current concern about the senior federal executives, nor the only competencies that may be lacking. Table 3 should be regarded as nothing but a provisional effort at ascertaining the nature of the knowledge, norms and mechanisms that are missing, and of the traits, attitudes and abilities that the public service executives would appear to need to develop in order for the senior executives to be able to dispatch their responsibilities effectively – in well-defined contexts.

The rest of this section sketches an outline of the competencies *problematique*, explores why and how (even though competencies have been talked about much over the last two decades) *de facto*, the competency *problematique* has been effectively shunned in all but limited segments of the federal public service, and reports on an exception to this trend in the case of the Canada Revenue Agency.

---

[3] Decline in open critical thinking, lack of gumption, willful blindness in the face of mental prisons, failure to take initiative, impatience with contextual issues, cognitive dissonance, latent fear, moral vacancy, crippling epistemologies, risk aversion and fear of experimentation, failure to understand systems, reluctance to admit that experts must learn, and disinterest in the face of new perspectives that are difficult to understand.

TABLE 3.

## Agenda for Capacities Refurbishment to Fill the Gaps

| | GAPS | | |
| | Knowledge | Norms | Mechanisms |
| --- | --- | --- | --- |
| **CAPACITIES** | | | |
| **Cognitive** | systems thinking | thinking critically | question assumptions |
| | exploration | ecological rationality | view from a crane |
| | delta knowledge | post-positivist | rethink education |
| **Behavioural** | effort to understand | learning as main goal | experimentation |
| | lateral thinking | calling a spade a spade | design thinking |
| | exposing deceit | *affectio societatis* | code of honour |
| **Organizational** | identify mental prisons | moral contracts | agoras for dialogue |
| | expose the idol of the tribe | seeking antifragility | forbidding fear |
| **Institutional** | context | performance | fail-safe |
| | | quality control | safe-fail |

Source: Hubbard and Paquet, 2014b, p. 127.

## *The competencies* problematique

The concern with competencies emerges from a central interest in matching the capabilities of officials with the complexity (cognitive and otherwise) of the tasks with which they are likely to be confronted. This requires an accurate appreciation of the complexity of the specific tasks to be handled, and a very effective way to gauge the capabilities of humans supposedly charged with these responsibilities. Why? Because the 'fuzzier' the appreciation of the complexity of the task and of the competencies required, and the 'fudgier' the appreciation of the capabilities of the candidate, the more inadequate the decision about selecting a person for the job is likely to be.

These are rather daunting requirements, and may explain why, even though it would appear to be an obvious way to tackle the selection of fully competent human resources, using a valid and reliable competency-based approach, tailored to union-driven departments and agencies, it has proven rather unpopular in the public sector. The difficulties of the task have been the rationale for not proceeding along this avenue, and the end result, thus, satisfied instead with the quite deficient arsenal of instruments that are currently in use to select public sector personnel (Cooper *et al.* 1998).

There is no denying that the work of gauging the complexity of the task, the capabilities needed, and to ascertain that candidates have such capabilities at a level where mission-driven performance matters, is daunting. However a large number of private and public concerns have found it a tractable task (Vazirani 2010; Bozkurt 2011). Our purpose in this section is not to review the extensive literature on these experiences, but only to provide a broad analytical framework[4] to help the reader gain an appreciation for what is involved.

A simple analytical framework trying to match the cognitive complexity of tasks and human capabilities (while taking into account other relevant dimensions) has been developed by Elliott Jaques and his consorts over the years (Jaques 1989, 2002; Jaques and Cason 1994). Our purpose here is neither to develop a full *exposé* of this particular sort of work, nor to adopt *holus bolus* the clinical apparatus Jaques and his consorts have built upon it. We only wish to make use of Jaques' vocabulary to sketch a broad and loose framework to help the reader sort out the important dimensions of this *problematique,* and gauge the general direction in which the selection process for public sector employees might usefully be re-oriented.

The Jaques-type scheme is based on serious efforts to identify strata of cognitive complexity in the nature of the

---

[4] For a full understanding of the differences between an analytical framework with its looseness, a theory with its generality, and a model with its specificity, see Leibenstein 1976: 17ff.

work, on some appreciation of the time horizon involved for those performing such work, on some way to gauge the sort of information processing capabilities that underpin the different levels of human potential capacity, and the way in which this capacity may mature over time.

If one had such reference points, one might be better equipped to design a human resources regime capable not only of ensuring a better matching of human capabilities and work requirements, but also of having some grip on ways to conjecture the likely future path of individual capabilities (given what one knows about the person now), and consequently to ensure the selection of a cadre of senior executive persons likely to perform better.

To repeat, our intent here is neither to produce an encapsulated operational version of the Jaques approach nor to adopt it as a model, but only to use it to highlight what a competency-centred approach would look like and what it might promise.

## Contours: four components

### 1. Complexity of task

The first component of the competencies *problematique* is the development of some appreciation of the degree of complexity of the task. This appreciation leads to identifying various strata or levels of complexity entailing a shorter or longer time horizon (from hours or days to decades) to dispatch the work well. Six levels are used by Jaques,[5] and are listed for illustration purposes:

---

[5] He also alludes to the existence of a seventh level that would be equivalent to the activities of a four star general or a senior level deputy minister and that would require an ability to handle complex conceptual abstract information in a way that requires thinking about and developing alternative paths. An example would be a senior deputy minister with *de facto* responsibility for advising on broad socio-economic or foreign/ international policy.

### VI Activities requiring complex conceptual abstract information

These fall in the realm of the kind of work that, at its most complex, might face a three star general or a journeyman-level deputy minister (for example, the bureaucratic head of a large operating department that does not involve a lot of high-end policy flexibility).

### V Activities requiring abstract approaches using conceptual-abstract data

These would face a two star general or a senior ADM (for example one involved in providing policy advice in the area of labour markets).

### IV Activities requiring parallel approaches (coordinating a number of serial processes)

These would typically confront a brigadier general, a senior director general in the public service or a general manager in the private sector, using critical path analysis to decide what to do.

### III Activities requiring a serial approach (working out alternative plans and choosing the best one)

These would emerge for the manager of a business unit (a lieutenant colonel or major in the military or a junior executive – senior level, non-executive running a multi-faceted office).

### II Activities requiring a cumulative diagnostic-and-then-corrective approach

These activities would arise in the work of a captain or lieutenant or first-line manager in the public service or a corporation.

### I Activities requiring concretely specified output

These activities would take place in the office or on the (shop) floor. They might, for example, be labelled as a higher clerical officer, a clerical officer or a clerical assistant.

## 2. Mental processing capability

The second component is an appreciation of the information or mental processing capabilities of humans. Jaques provides examples that flow from real live answers to an open-ended question about legalizing drugs.[6] And he suggests that one can readily classify such capabilities in four readily observable categories:[7]

**D   Capacity for parallel processing of information**

In this answer, the person developed one line of argument (i.e., for legalization) and then another (on the other hand the line of argument against) and then juxtaposed them in ways that led to a series of steps that might fix the problem.

**C   Capacity for serial processing**

In this answer, the argument was made by providing several points leading from the first to the next and so forth with unfolding consequences before reaching a conclusion.

**B   Capacity for cumulative diagnostic processing**

In this answer, two or three arguments were made together to lead to the conclusion – "I agree with A who said there would be more addiction … And I think the police would be in more trouble … And, of course, there's all the extra hospital costs …" (*Ibid.*).

**A   Capacity for declarative processing**

In this one, one or two unconnected points were made and the answerer went no further – "Legalization would lead to more addiction … and I am against it …" (*Ibid.*).

**3. Complexity of information**

These information processing capabilities may obviously be applied to problems of growing complexity dealing with:

**α:   General principles**

An example would be one that dealt with improving society in general (e.g. easing political relations between two countries) rather than expressing a concern about how best to position a huge multinational corporation so that it was likely to survive over decades to come.

---

[6] These examples and the ones that follow (i.e., describing the complexity of information) are drawn from Jaques 2002: chapters 3, 6.

[7] Whether or not these capabilities can be readily observable, no one denies that these capabilities can be gauged, and that they make a difference in the performance of differentially complex tasks.

### β: Categories of categories

An example would be talking about publicly funding health care systems by beginning with a category of categories (e.g. 'what societies value') and then elaborating upon it by mentioning a number of values in turn (e.g. 'living beyond societal means'; 'health as opposed to education'; the issue of 'limiting access to service'). In other words, not only mentioning the more general idea, but being able to elaborate to illustrate what they mean in sufficient detail to make their idea understandable.

### γ: Categories of intangible entities

An example would be talking about the categories of (i) investment or (ii) production. For each of these two specific categories, examples are listed that demonstrate what that might mean at levels δ and ε below.

### δ: Intangible entities and collection of tangible entities

i) Money or rent

ii) Tools or drawing instruments

### ε: Here-and-now tangible entities

i) A coin

ii) A hammer or a pencil

The third component is the recognition that the applicable capabilities of humans depend on many things and not only on current potential capabilities as measured by the sophistication of the mental information processing a person uses. In the language of Jaques:

$$AC = f\ CPC \bullet K/S \bullet C \bullet RB$$

where
| | | |
|---|---|---|
| AC | = | applicable capability |
| CPC | = | current potential capability measured by the sophistication of mental processing |
| K/S | = | skilled knowledge for the particular problem |
| C | = | commitment for the particular problem area |
| RB | = | ability or disability to carry out behaviours required by society. |

### 4. Potential capability increases

The fourth component is the maturation process of potential cognitive capability as the individual ages. This is the result of an extrapolation based on extensive observations by Jaques and his consorts, and it has led to the inference that, as an individual grows in age, his/her potential capability increases, and therefore his/her capabilities to tackle more complex issues increase also.

## Promises

This highly-stylized presentation is not meant to capture all aspects of the competencies paradigm, but it indicates that, for many specialists and experts, it is silly to rely exclusively on simplistic information like I.Q. measurements or generic academic degrees or casual impressions at stylized interviews – for those are often quite poor predictors – to determine if an individual is suitable for a complex job of a particular sort. Obviously, much depends on how fine-grained the appreciation of the complexity of the work is, and on how reliable an assessment of the competencies of the candidate is available. While these matters are very much under discussion, nobody has declared that success in gauging these features is impossible to achieve. In any case, it would appear that this sort of framework would provide a more useful approach than the reliance on generic ethereal leadership qualities or the like.

Moreover, the more precise one is able to be about the complexities of the task and the competencies of the candidates, the more likely it is that one can design training programs to help fill any gaps in the competencies of the candidates (if they were to become evident) or to initiate some organizational redesign to alleviate some particularly thorny features of the requirements of the tasks – so as to ensure that the goodness of fit may be improved between the organization and the assortment of people with whom it has to work.[8]

---

[8] It might be worth noting that efforts in this direction were attempted in the mid-1990s. At the time, Paquet was involved with the Canadian Centre on Management Development, and had persuaded the principal, Ole Insgtrup,

Whatever the difficulty in achieving good marksmanship using a valid and reliable competencies approach, it would appear unconscionable not to exert some effort in this direction since the alternatives that would appear to be envisaged by emerging and established leaders or by resident philosophers of public administration would not seem to be very promising.

## Competency as a perplexing label

The notion of competency is undoubtedly very complex. It is based on a mix of qualifications and capabilities for complex work, skills pertaining to specialized areas, commitment, and behavioural requirements to do work of quality in the face of tasks of various complexities – in a world where quality is a somewhat imprecise word connoting a degree of expertise, *savoir-faire*, *savoir-être*, and a professional commitment to meet high standards. In that sense, the notion of competency is quite different from the notions of *savoirs* or knowledge, which are only some of the necessary components of capabilities, but most certainly not sufficient components to ensure competency to deliver the sort of high quality services senior federal executives are meant to provide.

As we have seen earlier, there is a propensity for public administration commentators in their disquisitions about competencies to allow themselves to escape the difficulties in gauging the intricacies of the work and the capabilities of the

that it might be worth exploring what competencies of the federal government executives cadre might be relatively weaker and could be improved by aligning courses offered by CCMD to correct competency deficiencies observed in the group. Len Slivinski of the Public Service Commission (PSC) had the data on the very many competencies measured by the PSC for thousands of executives (EXs) over time. It would have been easy to ascertain in which ones of these competencies (deemed necessary at the time) that cadre of EXS would appear to be relatively less well prepared. The data, in aggregate form, would have preserved the privacy of individuals but would have revealed the relative competency weaknesses of the EXs as a whole, and would have guided CCMD in helping to repair them. Unfortunately, the senior authority at the PSC refused to release this information. This defensiveness prevented an early mobilization of CCMD to provide remedial training.

candidates concretely, by jumping into evasive thinking and loose general correlations between very general characteristics. This is the result of an illusion of totality about the work in the public sector: it is seemingly regarded (quite wrongly) as work of a different sort altogether that cannot be performed by ordinary private sector individuals, but must be reserved for a sort of missionary quality workers. Instead of trying to tackle the difficult task of delineating the precise dimensions of the job, public administration specialists are satisfied to look for across-the-board qualities that are purported to grant true missionary competencies (whatever these may be) for all the work in the whole federal government that is regarded as an homogeneous lump of labour (Kernaghan 2007; Hubbard and Paquet 2010).

In fact, competencies are not that generic. One would not necessarily trust one's dentist to defend one in a court of law. So this pressure to simplify and generalize unduly, simply for convenience purposes, has tended to smother, to a considerable extent, the necessity to be fine-grained in dealing with competencies. The propensity by the bureaucratic tribe to centralize and to promote homogeneity of processes – also vociferously promoted by unions – has run forcefully against the requirements for competencies in terms of detailed, underlying capabilities to deal with various forms of complexities of tasks across the federal public service.

## The peculiar capacity for surrealism of the Canadian federal bureaucracy

Much serious work on competencies has been done at the Public Service Commission of Canada over the years since the 1970s (Slivinski and Miles 1996). In fact, in the early 1990s, every person was subjected to a battery of tests upon being considered for admission into the EX category. Part of that exercise established their score on 14 competencies. These results were obviously used in arriving at decisions about entry into the executive category. But such practices were not uniformly regarded positively. Even from within the PSC, there was caution verging on unease about engaging in such evaluation for purposes of appointments or selection because of the difficulty in generating very reliable gauges for both the complexity of the task and the capabilities of individuals (Cooper *et al.* 1998).

Yet concerns about performance had been omnipresent since the 1980s, and there was a strong appetite for ways to improve the general performance of the public service (e.g. the Public Service 2000 exercise that resulted in a White Paper in 1990 and legislative changes in 1992). Moreover, one might have expected that the financial stringency period of the mid-1990s would provide an added impetus to overhaul the ways in which the senior executives were selected, and to develop the competency approach further as a promising road. Indeed, on the surface, this has happened, but with surprising results in the reality of the trenches.

The modern version of the independent Public Service Commission was established to protect the public service from undue political patronage. By the late 1950s, it had become a full service personnel agency. The Treasury Board Secretariat (as the formal bureaucratic support for the employer) had serious reasons to seek involvement in the file, and has increasingly done so since the 1960s. Decades later the Privy Council Office joined in (the Clerk having been made the titular head of the public service). With all those central agencies having a finger in the pie – often operating with different legitimate perspectives and objectives – the pressure to rationalize led the charge toward the development of some frameworks that would enable the centre to gain a sense of control over a growing and ever more disparate mass of public sector employees over time.

The public household was already quite pluralistic – engaged in quite disparate activities and pursuing more or less complementary goals – and this could only be regarded as a nuisance by those at the centre who were dreaming of unifying this fragmented enterprise, and of re-establishing a sense of control over it to ensure economy, efficiency and effectiveness. This *état d'esprit* might have been quite helpful as long as it remained simply a concern for as much harmonization as possible. But, when it became a utopian drive, generating surreal centralized frameworks, as it has done, the damage is considerable.

The situation was described vividly by Clark and Swain in 2005. They denounced the array of utopian centralized and homogeneity-generating reforms that have come (so they say) to prevent the different departments and agencies from delivering the services they were designed to produce. Over time, there have come to emerge macro-plans for government performance (Management Accountability Framework (MAF)) to not just enable macro-level oversight, but to exercise control. Moreover, there was pressure to hook up all the other systems to it. This impacted on the structure of the human resources scheme (e.g. key leadership competencies) that, in turn, needed to fit. This led to pressure on the different regimes to eliminate idiosyncrasies, and to agree on broad, general categories of macro-competencies that had to be vested with a coefficient of vagueness so as to fit all situations (Clark and Swain 2005).

As a matter of consequence, this very vagueness and malleability made competencies so mushy that one could run a three-ton truck through them, while claiming to be in keeping with the spirit of the broad norms. For instance, as a result of this smothering process, the 14 competencies in use were found to be too complex, and were reduced to 4. This led to more and more talk about competencies but defined in more and more ethereal and vague ways. So, concretely, in daily life, real concern about real competency as a driving force in the selection of personnel has become ever more attenuated.

The result has been a somewhat schizophrenic outflow of statements from the Canadian government about what was going on on the competency front.

On the one hand, much has been written in the form of fable-like and inspirational stories (originating from the central agencies and mainly for international audiences) that has celebrated the great success of these operations, and has argued that MAF has led not only to the elicitation of a list of key leadership competencies that drives directly the choice of executives in the public service, but also to the design of the programs of the Canadian School of Public Service, that is meant to provide continuing education for the Canadian federal public sector executives (Forgues-Savage and Wong 2010).

On the other hand, much serious concern has been expressed within the Canadian federal service, in the world of everyday makers (as Henrik Bang calls them), about the inadequacy of the performance of government units as a result of their not being able to do what they should for the lack of personnel able and allowed to do it (Bang 2003). This is the clear message we have received from the Canadian federal executives we conversed with, and it is echoed in a whole literature on the poor performance of the public service (e.g. poor alignment of HR plans with business plans, ineffective dealing with poor performers, etc.).

Any one even cursorily informed about the Canadian federal public service, and the functioning of MAF, human resource management, and the realities of the Canada School of Public Service would be embarrassed by the fairy tales propounded internationally by official Canadian emissaries to international fora. The reality is much closer to the Clark-Swain scenario than to the idyllic state of affairs evoked by federal officials from central agencies.

Demonstrating it, however, is not so easy because of the fact that the federal tribe of senior executives has no interest in denouncing its own inadequacies openly nor the inadequacies of the process that got them to the positions they are in today. One may, however, gauge that the existing system must be somewhat inadequate since it has been openly rejected by a significant segment of the Canadian public service itself as unsatisfactory, and replaced by an alternative HR regime, deliberately focused on competencies.

## An enlightening way to use a competency approach: the CRA case

The Canada Revenue Agency (CRA) assesses, collects, and administers hundreds of billions of dollars in tax revenue every year, and directly delivers billions in benefits and tax credits. In 2012-13, it had the equivalent of about 40,000 people full time, and a budget of over $4.25 billion – about 70 percent of its operating budget committed to the salaries and benefits of its workforce.

It was given the authority to design and develop its own tailor-made framework and systems to manage human resources. Its direct responsibilities were extended to staffing, classification, compensation, labour relations, collective bargaining, training and human resources policy development, to help make its human resource management regime more efficient, effective, and responsive to its business needs. It chose to build a human resources regime that enables the alignment of HR plans and business plans, and focuses on 'competencies' as the common denominator to enable the building and sustaining of an integrated HR regime that explicitly links workforce needs and business needs (Canada Revenue Agency 2011).

Built on the idea that organizational performance results from having the right people, with the right skills, in the right place, at the right time, competency profiles were prepared for relevant positions and approved by the Board of Management that provides management oversight (Canada Revenue Agency 2012a). These competencies have been used as the foundation for all HR functions: resourcing and recruitment; classification; training and learning; career management; performance management; and HR planning.

The CRA competencies are much more fine-grained than the central four key leadership competency (KLC) profile (value and ethics, strategic thinking, engagement, and management excellence). The competency definitions are focused on business requirements, and they are used to ensure consistency across the agency (Canada Revenue Agency 2012b). Moreover, they are constantly revised as the context changes. The most-recently updated list comprises 17 behavioural competencies and 34 technical competencies. It includes definitions for each one along with the core motivation sought. There is a progression scale (i.e., four levels for behavioural competencies, reactive through to strategic, and five for technical ones, basic knowledge through to expert).

Systematic Agency level feedback is reviewed (related to several categories of expectations about the Agency's overall management capacity), areas requiring further work are identified, and next steps that should be taken are indicated (Canada Revenue Agency 2013-14: 3). Those next steps inform the corporate business plan, the objectives of the performance agreement of CRA's uppermost bureaucrat (the commissioner) as well as other work plans. For each category, expectations for good management, key questions that delineate good management practices are identified and provide the basis for the assessment, and the evidence used to make the assessment is reported.

The success of CRA, both in terms of employee satisfaction and assessed performance – however imperfect those measurements might be – have been noted by the Auditor-General under the new arrangements that have freed CRA to focus on performance (Auditor General of Canada 2008).

## Kick-starting the innovation process

### Three major challenges have to be overcome

First, in order to have a locus where the mission of the organization is taken seriously, and where it is going to be made to fit with the environment it is meant to serve, one must envisage the possibility of generalizing what has worked so well with CRA – an agency confronted with a wide variety of stakeholders – i.e., the setting up of external boards of management for departments and agencies.

Without such a structure at the interface between the broad social context and the whole-of-government conglomerate – the equivalent of a subsidiary board of the whole-of-government management board that would take charge of management and performance in a specific area – there is little chance that performance will ever find any true anchor at all and ever be taken seriously.

The broad objectives of the political conglomerate will never be translated well in operational and managerial terms by bureaucrats, whose sole purpose in life is to serve the broad conglomerate that has much broader considerations in mind.

Peter Aucoin (2007) has argued that the board of management experiment that has been successful with CRA should be extended to other departments and agencies, because there is a "vacuum of governance for the management function in government." The point has been re-iterated forcefully by Heintzman and Juillet (2012) who underline the fact that "if departments and agencies have their own local governance instruments that are able to apply the same standards (e.g. MAF) in more direct ways and on a more regular basis ... boards of management could help to 'drive out the fake' in public management and help make something like MAF a genuine management framework for senior leaders – that is, a framework they actually use in their *own* pursuit of improvement in organizational performance, not just something with which they comply for purposes of reporting to central agencies" (Heintzman and Juillet 2012: 367).

This sort of structure would not in any way weaken the accountability chain since the chair of the board of management could appear in front of parliamentary committees upstream, but such a board would also have (as it has in the case of CRA) sub-committees dealing with key management functions downstream – like the human resources function. This would ensure the possibility of dealing *in situ* with the key competency challenge: connecting the complexity of the tasks directly with the process responsible for staffing the positions of those attending to these tasks.

Second, in order for departments with boards of management to be able to define competencies in terms that fit the complexities of their particular mission, there will have to be arduous negotiations with the unions that have taken hold of job categories, and have little interest in allowing competencies to be established (even though they are essential for the good performance of the organization) if, for example, they, in any way, attenuate the lateral interdepartmental movements of personnel. This will also be opposed at the top by executives hoping to hop their way up the executive echelons by zigzagging their way interdepartmentally, with little interest in departmental or agency performance.

This was accomplished at CRA, and, with time, it has contributed to maintaining the continuity and management focus that have obviously contributed to the CRA's success. This would tend to question the wisdom of the merry-go-round of senior executives among departments and agencies without concern for their specific capacities to deal with the different circumstances they provide equally well – a bad protocol developed in the Pierre Trudeau era. However, it would be naïve to presume that it will be easy. Performance is a most detested word in union circles. And the long tradition of the government of Canada wanting to be a model employer has generated a long list of concessions to the public sector unions over time that have translated into a greater and greater schism between the HR regime and performance concerns. The shift to a competency-approach would entail a focus on performance as a priority that will call for nothing less than a cultural revolution.

One may therefore expect the fight to re-institute performance concerns by taking a competency-approach to generate a substantial rear-guard action, but this should not be an alibi for not trying.

Third, above and beyond the creation of boards of management and negotiating the reshaping of the interface with the unions in departments, there will have to be a reframing of the mindset of senior executives in the federal Canadian public service to make this transformation possible. Indeed, this is probably the major challenge.

The group that benefits most from the present "grey zone" – where anything goes and maladministration thrives – is the group of senior executives and uppermost bureaucrats. While the current confusion may damage good governance and public trust (*Ibid*.: 369), it serves the 'tribe' well, and immunizes it from meaningful performance evaluation and assessment. The idea that senior executives and uppermost bureaucrats as a group would not be able to hide any longer behind fuzz and might be forced to meet competency tests and performance tests can only be arresting.

While we may not have the same faith in clarity as a panacea as Heintzman and Juillet, a case can be made that we have a long distance to go in Canada at the federal level before clarity runs into diminishing returns. In the meantime, the defence of the *status quo* would appear to be obscurantist, and the defence of the current amateurish selection of personnel is nothing less than active support for maladministration and malgovernance of management.

Consequently, it may not be possible to adopt a competency-approach without challenging frontally the non-unionized senior executive class and its current clergy-like frame of mind. This terrain is more of a minefield than the one defended by the unions. The reason is that while the politicians have a strong interest in performance, the tribe does not: it is much more concerned (as the public choice literature has shown) in preserving its privileges and authority than in performance. However, for reasons that are not entirely understandable for many, the senior executives and super-bureaucrats have acquired a credibility and legitimacy with the citizenry (as irony would have it because of their purported expertise and competencies) that too often have made their positions regarded as more defensible than those of elected officials (Paquet 2014b). As a result, it can only be expected that the tribe will see a 'competency and performance' approach as quite threatening, and oppose it in Canada.

## Whether or not these obstacles can be overcome in Canada is an open question

What is clear is that up to now there has been a conspiracy of forces at work preventing the use of the competency approach to penetrate the Canadian federal public service, and that this conspiracy of blockers has succeeded only because they have been able to marginalize concerns about effective performance as a guiding beacon in public administration in Canada. The model employer philosophy of the Canadian federal government has focused much more on catering to the legitimate and illegitimate requests of the employees than on extracting value-added from them. At the lower echelons of the public service, this has translated into higher costs and poor service to the population. At the higher echelons, this has meant malgovernance, poor management, and the evolution toward a situation where a good many of the federal senior executives are not well suited to the full range of activities in their jobs.

There has been much reluctance to fully recognize these realities, because admitting it could only trigger the recognition that the whole human resources regime has to be overhauled, that senior executives cannot remain only a whimsically tested and controlled group any longer, and that a significant portion of that group may have to be re-assigned or replaced. So cognitive dissonance has kicked in ferociously.

A confederacy of academics and public administrators from within the Canadian federal public service have explicitly opposed a competency approach: some on the ground say that it might not generate an accurate or reliable enough appreciation of the complexities of the task and of the capabilities of the bureaucrats; others, like unions, as a matter of principle as they have objected to performance measurements; while for many senior executives and super-bureaucrats, such tests would be regarded as nothing less than a crime of *lèse-majesté*. All have held these views as a strategy to preserve a *status quo* that has served Canadians rather badly.

Every decade or so, over the last 30 years, one Quixote or another has raised the question of the performance of the public service, and the confederacy of *deniers* has succeeded in drowning his/her voice. This counter-attack has been based entirely on the assumptions that work in the public sector was incommensurable with work in other sectors, that it was imbibed by intangible benefits to society that could not be easily gauged, and that such work was more in the nature of a response to a calling than anything one might observe elsewhere. Over the last decades, this ideology has not been challenged, even though we have found no one capable of demonstrating that this is the case. It has become an act of faith in the public sector land.

More recently, however, the cosmology on which such an act of faith is built has begun to crumble. Very few citizens now would subscribe to such a credo. Indeed, the lower echelons of the public service have realized it first, and have shifted their defence from sermons on the particularity of their work deserving special treatment, to tactics that used to be the preserve of longshoremen. The senior executives are also beginning to sense that this line of defence is no longer effective, and they are tempted to use the same methods as their union brethren to preserve the *status quo*. Soon this will only leave the academics to defend the sanctity of the tribe of public sector employees – in the same manner as they keep trying to rationalize their own privileges and the right for their work to remain unscrutinized and their performance not seriously appraised in the academy.

\* \* \*

For those who remain untouched by the force of these pseudo-ecclesiastical arguments, the time has come to propose an alternative to the arrangements that would appear to have served the citizenry so badly – keeping in mind that a certain political courage to tackle these issues would appear to be required. This would entail a variety of changes in federal public sector management:

- the promotion of performance to a prime role in public management;
- the creation of effective external boards of management for departments and agencies;
- the delegation to these boards of strong performance mandates, including the need to match capabilities to the complexities of the tasks, and to vigilantly monitor how this matching needs to change when circumstances change;
- the development of ever more expertise in appraising quantitatively and qualitatively the complexity of tasks and the capabilities of individuals and groups to deal with them;
- the development of direct connections between the boards of management and the whole-of-government board to ensure that their works cohere;
- the development of direct connections between the local boards of management and the Canada School of Public Service so that the school can respond to their needs: otherwise each department or group of cognate departments should be authorized (under the authority of the local board) to develop local arrangements for training;
- the streamlining of the process and focus of the selection process for personnel to be enriched significantly to deal fully and thoroughly with cognitive capabilities, behavioural characteristics, gumption, etc., and to avoid falling prey to 'progressive' techniques like the anonymous CV syndrome – adopted in many European countries (see *CV anonyme* in Wikipedia) – that are bound to defang, neuter and sanitize selection processes at the very time when they are in need of strong re-enforcement.

These are only general indications of the direction in which the new management and HR regimes should evolve. This is not the place to flesh out the full complement of features of the new arrangements. It will have to wait for a new instalment. But it should be clear that these new arrangements would fill the governance vacuum that Peter Aucoin pointed to – a governance vacuum that cannot be filled unless boards of management are created for departments and agencies, and a competency approach is adopted to match the capacities of candidates to the complexities of the tasks. It is that simple!

# References

Aucoin, Peter. 1995. "Canadian Public Management Reform: A Comparative Westminster Perspective," (mimeo).

Aucoin, Peter. 1996. *The New Public Management: Canadian Comparative Perspective*. Montreal, QC: Institute for Research on Public Policy.

Aucoin, Peter. 2007. "Management Boards for Government Departments: Addressing the Governance of Management Vacuum," (unpublished manuscript, July).

Aucoin, Peter. 2012. "New Political Governance in Westminster Systems: Impartial Public Administration and Management Performance at Risk," *Governance: An international journal of policy, administration and institutions,* 25(2): 177-199.

Auditor General of Canada. 2008. "Use of New Human Resources Authorities – Canada Revenue Agency" in *December Report of the Auditor General of Canada,* chapter 6, http://www.oag-bvg.gc.ca/internet/English/parl_oag_200812_06_e_31830.html [Accessed August 24, 2014].

Bang, Henrik P. (ed.). 2003. *Governance as Social and Political Communication*. Manchester, UK: Manchester University Press.

Bozkurt, Tülay. 2011, *Management by Competencies.* Istanbul, TR: Risus International.

Canada. 1995. *Framework for Alternative Program Delivery.* Ottawa, ON: Treasury Board Secretariat.

Canada Revenue Agency. 2011. "Canada Revenue Agency: Creating a Performance-oriented Culture," 41 pp.

Canada Revenue Agency. 2012a. "Compentency profiles for the Canada Revenue Agency (CRA) Board of Management," http://www.cra-arc.gc.ca/gncy/brd/s9-2-eng.html [Accessed August 6, 2014].

Canada Revenue Agency. 2012b. "Competency Catalogue: revised November 2012," http://www.cra-arc.gc.ca/crrs/wrkng/ssssment/cmptncy/menu-eng/html [Accessed August 6, 2014].

Canada Revenue Agency. 2013-14. "Summary of the Board of Management Oversight Framework: Assessment of performance 2013-2014," (http://www.cra-arc.gc.ca/gncy/bomof-cscd/2014-2015/BoMOF-Summary-eng.pdf [Accessed August 7, 2014].

Clark, Ian D. and Harry Swain. 2005. "Distinguishing the real from the surreal in management reform: suggestions for beleaguered administrators in the government of Canada," *Canadian Public Administration*, 48(4): 453-476.

Cooper, S., E. Lawrence, J. Kierstead, B. Lynch and S. Luce. 1998. *Competencies – A Brief Overview of Development and Application to Public and Private Sectors*. Ottawa, ON: Public Service Commission of Canada, April 1, http://www.scribd.com/doc/117751856/71746115-CBHRM [Accessed August 6, 2014].

Forgues-Savage, Louise and Sharon Wong. 2010. *Competency Management in Canada's Core Public Administration*. A paper presented to the K.U. Leuven Public Management Institute.

Heintzman, Ralph and Luc Juillet. 2012. "Searching for New Instruments of Accountability: New Political Governance and the Dialectics of Democratic Acountability" in H. Bakvis and M.D. Jarvis (eds.). *From New Public Management to New Political Governance*. Montreal, QC and Kingston, ON: McGill-Queen's University Press, p. 342-379.

Hubbard, Ruth and Gilles Paquet. 2010. *The Black Hole of Public Administration*. Ottawa, ON: University of Ottawa Press.

Hubbard, Ruth and Paquet, Gilles. 2014a. "Competencies: Part of the Governance Vacuum," *www.optimumonline.ca*, 44(3): 58-73.

Hubbard, Ruth and Paquet, Gilles. 2014b. *Probing the Bureaucratic Mind: About Canadian Federal Executives*. Ottawa, ON: Invenire.

Jaques, Elliott. 1989. *Requisite Organization*. Arlington, VA: Cason Hall.

Jaques, Elliott. 2002. "Complexity and Capability in Living Organisms" in E. Jaques. *The Life and Behavior of Living Organisms*. Westport, CN: Praeger, p. 27-44.

Jaques, Elliott and Kathryn Cason. 1994. *Human Capability – A Study of Individual Potential and its Application*. Falls Church, VA: Cason Hall.

Kernaghan, Kenneth. 2007. *A Special Calling: Values, Ethics, and Professional Public Service*. Ottawa, ON: Canada Public Service Agency.

Leibenstein, Harvey. 1976. *Beyond Economic Man – A New Foundation for Microeconomics*. Cambridge, MA: Harvard University Press.

May, Kathryn. 2014. "Unions grieve new PS performance rules," *Ottawa Citizen*, April 7, A1-2

McLaughlin, David. 2014. "Five ways to renew the public service," *The Globe and Mail*, August 22, A11.

Paquet, Gilles. 1997. "Alternative Program Delivery: Transforming the Practices of Governance" in R. Ford and D. Zussman (eds.). *Alternative Service Delivery: Sharing Governance in Canada*. Toronto, ON: IPAC/KPMG, p. 31-58 (reprinted in R. Hubbard and G. Paquet. 2010. *The Black Hole of Public Administration*. Ottawa, ON: University of Ottawa Press, p. 307-330).

Paquet, Gilles 2014a. "Super-bureaucrats as *enfants du siècle*," *www.optimumonline.ca*, 44(2): 4-14.

Paquet, Gilles. 2014b. *Unusual Suspects – Essays on Social Learning Disabilities*. Ottawa, ON: Invenire.

Schick, Allen. 2002. "Agencies in Search of Principles," *OECD Journal of Budgeting*, 2(1): 7-26.

Slivinski, Len W. and Jennifer Miles. 1996. *The Wholistic Competency Profile: A Model*. Ottawa, ON: Public Service Commission of Canada.

Taleb, Nassim N. 2012. *Antifragile – Things that gain from disorder*. New York, NY: Random House.

Vazirani, Nitin. 2010. "Competencies and Competency Model – A Brief Overview of its Development and Application," *SIES Journal of Management*, 7(1): 121-131.

# CHAPTER 5

# | An Agenda for Cultural Change in the Federal Public Service

## Gilles Paquet

*"It only becomes an issue when you
can do something about it."*
*Saul Alinsky*

Transforming the organizational and institutional architecture is not sufficient. One must also change the organizational *ethos* of the federal public service if the forces of dynamic conservatism are to not prevail. This can be done in two stages: first, by challenging the personnel managers' view of employees as 'inert instruments' or simple programmable *automata* – an idea inherited from the heyday of Taylorist personnel management that has survived in certain segments of the federal public service until the 1980s; and second, by injecting into the organizational culture of the federal public service new values, new motivations, and new sources of vitality.

Nicole Côté has explored these problems within the Quebec public service. According to her analysis, what makes the public service personnel unproductive has to do with a mistaken appreciation of what really motivates public servants. She is very critical of the mechanical devices invented by personnel managers to energize their employees (executive development seminars, conceptual refurbishment seminars, institutionalized mobility, etc.) and she puts the blame for low productivity at the feet of personnel management.

By unloading onto personnel managers the job of maintaining uniform human resources management systems, public bureaucracies have freed agency/departmental line managers from the obligation of taking good care of their employees; this has severed the link between the employee and his/her organization. According to Côté, employees are not managed by their steward, but by collective agreements, directives, rules, and so on. It is not difficult to understand why they have become *"irresponsables, i.e., incapables de répondre, car il n'y a personne à qui répondre"* (Côté 1984-85).

Professionalism, collective pride, and the sense of civic responsibility have disappeared from the public service to a great extent. In its place, one finds anomie and alienation, and little trace of any *"goût du travail bien fait."* Yet experiments have shown that corporate culture can be modified and become an instrument of revitalization of the workplace.[1]

## In search of a new covenant

But such quick fixes are not enough. The very nature and *ethos* of the federal public service must also be transformed if it is to be able to react with speed, flexibility and creativity to a topsy-turvy environment bubbling up with surprises.

Big firms, big government and big social agencies have reacted to this sort of pressure in three ways: (1) they have attempted to become leaner; (2) they have deconstructed themselves into smaller and more non-centralized units (organizationally and locationally) in order to become more

[1] *"La qualité des services ... faut s'en parler,"* Actes d'un colloque tenu à Québec les 2-4 mai 1984, Ministère de la Main d'Oeuvre et de la Sécurité du Revenu, Québec, 1984. See in particular the papers by A. Fournier and by M. Pellerin, p. 113-37. The new name for this condition is stress and mental illness.

flexible, more attentive to citizens and clients, and more creative; and (3) in order to become more agile, they have begun to renegotiate with their partners the nexus of contracts and treaties they had forged with them.

The first two responses (downsizing, delayering and dispersing power) have elicited much discussion in the specialized literature and have been critically appraised. Much less work has been done on the third front, especially as it pertains to the relationships between organizations and their employees.

While much has been written about new rapports with customers and suppliers, about outsourcing and sub-contracting, it has not always been realized that "a quieter revolution has taken place. It has redefined employees' roles, and in doing so, has rewritten the implicit contract they had with employers" (Bartlett and Ghoshal 1995; Waterman *et al.* 1994). Employers require maximum nimbleness to survive in this new turbulent and fast-changing economy, so they cannot use employees effectively as passive instruments of production. They must come to regard their employees *as partners* whose knowledge and initiative they need on the front line. And yet, (this is the core of the paradox) at the very time when downsizing, the requirement to do more or different with less, and the need for maximum flexibility and creativity are leading employers to demand more from these 'employee-partners' (including longer hours, more dedication and loyalty); they have also asked them to forgo much of the security that they used to have.

Employment contracts are never easy to rewrite and the process is even more difficult in the public sector where there is no bottom-line to coax parties into workable solutions. This is especially difficult for the whole Canadian public sector at this time, because this rewriting is undertaken at a time when, throughout the socio-economy, a process of "dejobbing" – the disappearance of the "steady job" – is swamping the private, public and social sectors (Bridges 1994; Rifkin 1995).

In order to be able to design an effective process of transformation for the federal public service, one must first examine the public service culture as it stands, and the recent questioning of its efficiency and effectiveness.

## The public service culture in question

The principles associated with the traditional culture of a career in the public service in Canada are nowhere explicitly stated in a form that would be readily accepted by all stakeholders. They have evolved through time, and are embedded in a number of explicit and implicit, legal and psychological contracts. This evolving nexus of implicit contracts has been loosely recognized as *de facto* conventions by most stakeholders, and its existence has even been acknowledged by the courts.[2]

This culture has been synthesized very well by Kenneth Kernaghan "in a pure and idealized form": public servants as permanent employees appointed on the basis of merit, a job-description, generous fringe benefits, job-security and a career-path, expectations of anonymity, impartiality, and accountability to ministers (Kernaghan 1991). Kernaghan has emphasized that four principles "have been – and continue to be – closely linked with the concept and practice of career public service" (*Ibid.*: 554):

- appointments made with a view to preserving political neutrality;
- appointments based on merit of the best qualified candidate;
- appointments from within the public service as far as possible;
- assistance for public servants in selecting career goals and pursuing them.

While it is readily admitted that (1) there may have been differences of opinion as to the exact content of such a covenant among stakeholders, (2) the daily practice may have been at odds with these principles, and (3) these principles may have been

---

[2] See Fraser *v*. PSSRB [1985] 2 S.C.R. 455 and PSC *v*. Millar et al. [1991] 2 S.C.R. 69.

applied or interpreted quite differently from department to department, there is also a general agreement that this culture corresponded roughly and generally to the existing public service culture, circa the 1980s.

In the 1990s, this traditional culture was challenged in two quite different ways. First, there were questions raised in a modest way by a new vision from within: Public Service 2000 (Mulroney 1990; Tellier 1992). Then the traditional culture was hit by strong pressure from without: the harsh new financial and economic realities that forced the directors of Personnel, Treasury Board and the Public Service Commission to question the existing arrangements.[3]

The first challenge, through PS 2000, recognized the need for public service employees:

1) to attend better to the needs of the citizenry and to provide better services to their clients;
2) to make the highest and best use of their creativity, while taking into account the needs of their employers;
3) to improve training and development of their human resources and to put greater emphasis on career planning; and,
4) to develop a new focus for accountability as responsibilities are devolved to managers so they can manage.

This challenge did not shake the traditional culture. Few if any of the actions initiated in the PS 2000 era really questioned neutrality or merit (with the possible exception of the new concerns for equity and representativeness) and the emphasis on career planning was not really challenged; the merit principle might appear to have been relaxed somewhat through the new arrangement, allowing lateral transfers not to be regarded as appointments under the *Public Service Employment Act*, and therefore being exempted from the merit principle.

---

[3] For a statement of the new vision, see *The Way Ahead for the Public Service* (Discussion Paper for the Directors of Personnel Conference, Cornwall, October 4-6, 1994). There were ongoing reflections on this issue in both Treasury Board and the Public Service Commission, and it was regarded as work of the highest strategic priority at the time.

But this loosening up did not have a profound impact on the public service culture.

The second challenge has been much more significant. It was the result of the state's fiscal crisis. While it is difficult to establish clearly the moment the crisis hit the system – because its seriousness was acknowledged at different moments in Alberta, in New Brunswick and in Ottawa – one can reasonably suggest that it emerged as a result of the realization by the different governments that the conventional rules of the game would not be able to deal effectively with the deficit and debt problems.

While Alberta led the parade of provinces in the attack on deficit and debt in the early 1990s, and Quebec was the last to join the parade in 1996, it could be said that the federal Liberal government bit the bullet in the fall of 1994.

The message was clear in the Purple Book and in the Grey Book tabled by Paul Martin, and the full implications of this message for career public service were first presented in the Directors of Personnel discussion paper, in the fall of 1994. This document puts forward a perspective inspired explicitly by David Noer's *Healing the Wounds* and sets out to "define the steps required to achieve a new public service model for Canada" (Noer 1993: 2).

Noer's message is simple and basically two-fold: first, for organizations to face the new realities and acquire the requisite flexibility and nimbleness, the old employment contract guaranteeing much security to the employee must be abrogated; secondly, the traditional employment terms of reference might not have been very healthy in any case (for both the employees and their organizations) because they fostered an undesirable sort of co-dependency between employees and their organization.

The attack on a career in the public service by the Directors of Personnel is stark: they diagnose it as "unrealistic", "not necessary or affordable" and "an unhealthy expectation" (*Ibid.*: 5). Their document suggests the termination of the current policy of conversion from term to indeterminate employment after five years; it puts forward a framework where "employees, not the employer, are responsible for their own employment options, but the employer would provide support to enable the continued employability of staff" (*Ibid.*: 17). One is clearly faced with a new "moral framework" (*Ibid.*: 9) that would have to be renegotiated, and in which the key parameters would have to be clarified and amended in consultation with labour.

Even though this plea for a 'new Public Service model' does not refer explicitly to the general debate about the future of work ("dejobbing"),[4] and avoids confronting head-on the meaning of the new arrangement for some perennial values (accountability), the inescapable conclusion is that the current questioning of the traditional culture necessarily entails the redefinition of many of the fundamental principles on which the career public service had been built throughout Canada.

Strategically, the Directors of Personnel could not and did not come forward with the details of a new model, since the new framework would have to be negotiated with other stakeholders. Yet the document generated a sense of urgency: parameters would have to be clarified very quickly for events are running ahead of plans at this time, and there was a danger that a *de facto* "new model" would emerge that might leave all parties worse off.

There was no consensus on what the "new model" should be, nor on the manner in which the new model would be implemented. However, there were signs that at least two broad options were considered.

In the first case, the debate had begun on the tentative features of the workable model that may be the outcome of this transformation, and officials have speculated in public about the nature of the new public service. In a May 1995 interview, the President of the Public Service Commission,

---

[4] A sample of the papers raising these issues in the popular press might be R.J. Barnet, "The End of Jobs," *Harper's Magazine*, September, 1993; W. Bridges, "The End of the Job," *Fortune*, September 19, 1994; "Rethinking Work," *Business Week*, October 17, 1994; "Redefining Work," (A Dossier) *Challenges*, fall 1994.

Ruth Hubbard, sketched a three-tiered system with a small "core of permanent and highly skilled knowledge workers, supported by a pool of short-term employees who work in government for stints of several months or years and move on"... (plus) a "para-public service that could emerge as various levels of government cooperate on delivering services and as private-public partnerships take over services that were once provided by government" (*Ottawa Citizen* 1995). While this remains vague on specifics, the strategic direction hinted at is congruent with the ruminations contained in the Directors of Personnel document.

In the second case, the debate focused on the implementation process, the final outcome being allowed to emerge from the process. This model has been favoured in Quebec, where an agreement has been signed between the government and a host of public sector unions that sets up both joint ministerial and joint sectoral committees, charged with the responsibility of rethinking the organization of work to reduce public expenditures, while keeping in mind both the welfare of the citizens and of the public employees. This emphasis on process allows all issues like sub-contracting, the hierarchical structure, job classifications, etc., to be debated by these committees, and the collective agreements to be modified according to the consensus reached at this level.[5] In this case, it is not clear that any one particular pattern will prevail in the new framework, nor which ones are likely to.

## The transformation of the public service culture[6]

The context within which this transformation has occurred was bound to have an impact, not only on the methods used to reach this new covenant, but also on its final contours. In this section, we discuss four clusters of forces that have both constrained and shaped the nature of a new public service

---

[5] *Entente sur l'organisation du travail dans la fonction publique intervenue entre le Gouvernement du Québec et les organisations syndicales signataires*, Québec 15 février 1995.

[6] This section draws freely from Paquet and Pigeon, 1995.

model: the limitations imposed and the opportunities raised (1) by the new governance; (2) by the new sociality necessary for a mobilization of the team players in the new dispersed and distributed governance system; (3) by the likelihood that new basic moral contracts would prove tractable and agreeable to all stakeholders; and (4) by the nature of the socio-economic conjuncture.

## New governance, more implicit contracting

In order to ensure the flexibility and nimbleness required by the turbulent environment of the 21$^{st}$ century, a new distributed governance system is emerging. Participants have "a rough sense as to general principles with which unforeseen contingencies will be met," and "corporate culture plays a role here by establishing general principles that should be applied (in the hope that application of those principles will lead to a relatively high level of coordination)" (Kreps 1990).

In this context, much coordination has to be handled by the unwritten or implicit portion of the employment contract, because rule-writing has become more difficult. Indeed, new principles have begun to surface: everyone's employment is contingent on the results of the organization; there is no clear job description; employees shift from project to project; they must manage their self-development and their own career as if they were in business for themselves; and the only commitment of benefits by the employer is to help the employee maintain his/her employability (Bridges 1994; Barnet 1993).

In such market-type employment contracts, explicit provisions allow the employer to modify duties and responsibilities in a major way. There are also easy provisions for severance. Employees may be allowed to choose among various arrangements for severance: from agreement about notice periods to non-compete covenants or other restrictions linked to longer notice periods and higher severance packages for core personnel.

Some observers, like Murray Axsmith, believe that the new governance system need not entail more in the form of implicit contract. The Axsmith model suggests that, as employees become free agents and entrepreneurial suppliers, more and more elaborate, flexible fixed-term written contracts will emerge; these contracts may typically be for terms of three years for core staff, with possibility of renewal; compensation would be made up of a modest base salary, limited benefits, and substantial incentive rewards tied to performance. For shorter-term staff, ranging from one month to two years, compensation would again be a modest base salary, with substantial bonuses linked to performance. Axsmith suggests that these employment contracts may contain "soft" clauses pertaining to expectations for staff, organizational values and the fiduciary duties and responsibilities of employees, but these clauses would have no legal clout; they might at best serve to clarify expectations, and need not be more important than in the past.[7]

While there is much to be said in favour of this shift from bureaucratic to market principles, market ligatures *stricto sensu*, backed and constrained only by explicit written contracts *à la* Axsmith, are unlikely to ensure the requisite coordination in the public service, any more than they can be expected to be satisfactory in the case of partnerships.[8]

We believe this sort of arrangement is flawed in three fundamental ways:

First, however flexible the contract may be, it remains an employee's contract with all the trappings of top-down supervision. This cannot be adequate in a turbulent environment where the organization needs to secure the engagement of the employee as partner on the front line.

Second, this sort of arrangement leaves too little room for the social cohesion and civic commitment required in the governance system. In the market-type employment

---

[7] Many academics and practitioners have developed similar ideas but few have been as influential as Murray Axsmith on the Ottawa scene. One may refer to Axsmith, 1994 and Axsmith, 1993-94.

[8] Gilles Paquet, 1994a; in the case of partnerships, see S.D. Phillips, 1991; J.L. Armstrong, 1991; Kernaghan, 1993.

scenario, "the commitment is to the quality of the work being done. The employee's reputation and future marketability will depend on this" (Axsmith 1992). Yet one of the major points that is made in Steven Rosell's *Changing Maps* (Rosell 1995), based on the important work of James Coleman (1988) and Robert Putnam (1993), is the primary importance of building *social capital* (embodied horizontal and transversal networks of civic engagement, trust, norms and standards) to enhance the performance of a group.

The main challenge of the information age is to construct such social capital, shared values and perspectives in a world where diversity and pluralism are daunting. Market employment contracts will not foster the requisite accumulation of 'social capital'.

Third, the new market employment contract cannot deal adequately with the problems of accountability and loyalty. In the new governance system, the loyalty of public servants cannot be only to the quality of the work done. It must also take into account and balance many transversal and horizontal loyalties: toward one's own "community of practice" – for it is from this network that the support flows for the sequence of contracts that will keep one employed – and toward the citizen or customer that one is serving (value for money is the basis of performance evaluation). And these more horizontal loyalties may conflict with the fundamental vertical accountability to the Minister as representative of the democratically elected government. Accountability and loyalty must therefore be balanced among the citizen, one's "community of practice" and the Minister. This cannot be resolved by a collection of market-type contracts.

Consequently, one must find ways to enrich the implicit content of the employment contract, in order to ensure that the burden of risk-sharing and the responsibility-sharing is not simply shifted completely from the employer to the employee. This sort of drastic switch from minimal to maximal responsibilities for employees may not ensure that the employee's creativity can be mobilized as fully as it needs to be. A middle-of-the road solution between dependency and market-type employment contract must be found if such a sharing of risk is to be renegotiated.

Such a middle-of-the-road solution is unlikely to be negotiated as part of the explicit employment contract. The employer must face too many varied contingencies, and attend to too many idiosyncratic needs on the part of different employees, to be able to attend to those personal needs formally (i.e., through the explicit portion of the employment contract): employers would be in danger of generating a new minimal right for all employees whenever they attempt to provide tailor-made assistance. Therefore, one may expect the development of the requisite foundations for a middle-of-the-road solution in the implicit portion of the employment contract.

## Multiple loyalties, new sociality

Every partner in the new governance system is partially connected with many others, via all sorts of networks. Coordination requires ways to integrate those overlapping networks transversally, in order to allow the individual to balance adjustments in these different dimensions. These loyalties are not equally meaningful and significant, and there are differences of opinion about their relative importance, according to time and place.

For instance, the different value systems in good currency in different countries generate very different trade-offs among loyalties (Hampden-Turner and Trompenaars 1993). What has to be found in the case of Canada is the particular balancing act (among the loyalties to self, network, community, society, and the accountability to citizen, peers, superior or Minister) that will meet with the entrenched beliefs in our value system and provide the basis for effective performance.

Multiple limited identities in an individualistic society entail weak ties. Such ties cannot recreate the traditional community. The construction of a 'new sociality' is required (Schick 1984).

The belief that weak ties (and therefore limited loyalties) can indeed prove to be a valid foundation for a strong community of the new type is rooted in the observation of Mark Granovetter: that weak ties are often more important than strong ties in understanding certain network-based phenomena. Strong ties tend to bond participants that are similar to each other, and information obtained through such a network is often redundant. A weak tie often represents a "local bridge" between parts of the systems that would otherwise be disconnected, and therefore provides much new information from disparate sections of the system. In Granovetter's world, no tie or extremely weak ties are of little consequence; weak ties have maximum impact, and strong ties have diminished impacts (Granovetter 1973).

In our information age, organization is nothing but "an ensemble of interconnected communities of practice," and "learning is the process of becoming a member of a community of practice" (Peters 1994). The challenge proposed by Steven Rosell's *Changing Maps* is to construct a learning network of communities of practice in the Canadian governance system, while keeping in mind that Canadians are more individualist than communitarian.

This means constructing new forms of social cohesion on the basis of weak ties with others. In this complex and fluid informational environment, effective coordination can occur neither by threat nor coercion *stricto sensu* (i.e., via power systems) nor by the operations of the market exchanges *stricto sensu* (i.e., via transaction systems). One has to count a great deal on consensus, on voluntary adherence to norms, and on inducement-oriented arrangements. These are at the core of membership and of shared leadership (Kumon 1992).

This form of sharing is central in the definition of the implicit content of the new employment contract. While there were costs attached to the old implicit contract generating dependency, it cannot be presumed that the optimal amount of protection for the employee is zero, if one wishes to promote learning and creativity. The new sociality must provide some form of basic 'security zone' that is necessary for the entrepreneurial spirit to thrive. The former implicit contract was hierarchical and paternalistic; the new implicit contract is a jointly negotiated, risk-sharing agreement on the minimal security zone necessary for creativity to flow.[9]

## New moral contracts

A number of years ago, we examined the malaise of Canadian public servants in the late 1980s and their loss of drive and initiative.[10] Invidiously, the employment contract had begun to shift, but the contours of the new work arrangements had not yet crystallized. We suggested, at the time, that a possible way out of this quandary was through the renegotiation of two moral contracts, in addition to whatever changes might be required in the explicit employment contract. These moral contracts were meant (1) to enrich the implicit context of the employment contract; (2) to better embed the explicit employment contract in the corporate culture; and (3) to provide guidance in balancing the two basic ingredients necessary for an intelligent organization (freedom of choice and the responsibilities vis-à-vis different communities or the whole of society) (Pinchot and Pinchot 1993).

[9] W.T. Easterbrook has examined the pre-condition of 'entrepreneurship' in bureaucracies and enterprises. While the enterprise form is characterized with a greater dispersion of power, it requires nonetheless some 'security' to thrive. Easterbrook identifies four types of security necessary for enterprise (economic, social, ethical and political). These are the fundamental components that need to be provided by the negotiated implicit contracts. See "The Climate of Enterprise" American Economic Review 39 (1949), p. 322-335; "Political Economy and Enterprise" Canadian Journal of Economics and Political Science 15 (1949), p. 322-333; "Uncertainty and Economic Change" Journal of Economic History 14 (1954), p. 346-360.

[10] Gilles Paquet, 1991-92. A moral contract is nothing more than a convention or a moral code in the relationship between or among partners. For a detailed examination of the way moral contracts and conventions have been analyzed quite differently in the American and the European literature as mechanisms of coordination, see P.Y. Gomez, 1994.

We argued that the addition of these two moral contracts would generate a proactive, entrepreneurial, and responsible public service capable of balancing loyalties and accountabilities in a creative way.

The two moral contracts were:

*Moral Contract I:* the ethics moral contract, called for a redefinition of mutual responsibilities and obligations between the citizenry and the bureaucracy; and,

*Moral Contract II:* the professionalism moral contract, called for a rethinking of the mutual obligation, trust requirement, and *esprit de corps* between the politicians and very senior bureaucrats on the one hand, and the junior public servants on the other.

The situation has continued to evolve since the early 1990s, and it would now appear that a further enrichment of the implicit employment contract is necessary.

First, some action is needed to minimize the negative impacts of the politicians' centralized mindset, the arrogant logic of internal administration, and the unrealistic expectations of the citizenry. This calls (a) for a re-affirmation of the fundamental responsibilities of individuals for their own affairs; (b) for a reconfirmation that the state is to intervene modestly, as a reserve army, only when its action is necessary to help the citizens take care of their specific needs, and not on the basis of entitlements ordained from above; and (c) for the reminder that if and when the state must intervene, it should always be at a level as close to the citizen as possible, where the help can be provided efficiently. In this context, the task of any higher-order governance unit (i.e., regional, provincial, federal, etc.) is to assist the more localized units in carrying out their tasks, and to manage only those functions that cannot be effectively delivered within these forums (Paquet 1994b).

*Moral Contract III:* from these new circumstances emerges the need for *Moral Contract III* (among the citizens, the bureaucrats at all levels, and the politicians at all levels): – the axiom of individual responsibility and subsidiarity in the governance process, which calls for an explicit re-affirmation of the fundamental responsibility of the citizens for their own affairs, and of the crucial *devoir de prudence et de réserve* of politicians and bureaucrats at the time of intervening in the life of the citizenry, on the basis of needs, and not entitlements.

Second, it has become necessary to re-affirm that the debates leading to the development of a new moral framework demand that dialogue and deliberations be civil, free from coercion or any form of organizational violence. A democratic society is built on dialogue and deliberation. The difficult task of framing a just society, taking into account the growing plurality of interests in Canada, is to ensure that the conversation goes on.

The condition for the dialogue to continue is a *Moral Contract IV* (among the citizens, the bureaucrats at all levels and the politicians at all levels), based on tact and civility, and on trust that there is a capacity to suspend judgment until one's own and the other person's assumptions have been explored.

For Mark Kingwell, "if citizens are to talk to one another, they must refrain from saying all the things they have it in mind to say; they must likewise open themselves up to the possibility that a claim made by someone else has merit" (Kingwell 1993, 1994, 1995).[11] We take this to mean not that people should refrain from expressing their views but that they should do so in a way respectful of other points of view. This is a bare minimum, but only with the assurance of at least that much, can we hope to build an organization where personal meaning and mutually beneficial dreams will serve as an anchor at the time of making these difficult balancing acts (Aubert 1995).

*Moral Contract IV*: dialogue, based on the primacy of tact and civility, reaffirms simply the importance of the moral climate for organizational effectiveness and social learning.

While this last requirement may appear trite, one should not underestimate the difficulty of overcoming the existing degree of cognitive dissonance about the existence of organizational violence in the rapports among and between politicians, bureaucrats and citizens, and the breakdown of trust which

---

[11] For a more elaborate presentation of the argument, see Kingwell, 1995.

obviously ensues. Until this reality is squarely confronted, and individuals accept that they cannot change anything unless they are willing to change themselves, it may be difficult to obtain an agreement on *Moral Contract IV* either because it is wrongly assumed that it is a non-problem, that civility prevails already, that everyone that has anything to say is heard, or because, equally wrongly, it may be presumed that the content of such a norm is trivial and inconsequential.

These four moral contracts constitute the necessary conditions for the creation of a new corporate culture capable of ensuring a deliberative and participative governance. They are required if a new workable implicit employment contract of the new public service is to be negotiated. The central question is: how likely are we to be able to count on such moral contracts emerging as new norms in the near future?

* * *

Summarizing the last section in the reverse order in which the issues were brought up, we can say:

- firstly, that much will depend on the sort of wind that will be blowing over Canada and that a reasonable forecast is that those changes will be carried out in a world of slow economic growth and strong socio-political resistance to change;
- secondly, that while much progress has been made in emphasizing the central importance of the new moral contracts (as new partnerships develop to provide the requisite flexibility and nimbleness) and in allowing them to be discussed openly, the stakeholders are still very far from being persuaded that such conventions and norms are necessary, and they are not very well equipped when it comes to guidelines in the process of arriving at workable conventions;
- thirdly, that the very recognition of the existence of multiple loyalties and of the need for a new sociality is neither recognized nor even acknowledged: the rigid top-down Westminster model of governance is still regarded by a fair majority of the stakeholders as the only

acceptable model. Therefore, it is unlikely that the notions of accountability and loyalty will be redefined completely in the next quinquennium, even though, informally, it is recognized as necessary by a large number of observers;

- finally, and this is an echo effect of our third point, even though market employment mechanisms may appear flawed to most, the view in good currency is that they represent the only workable way. The Axsmith model is therefore proposed as the workable protocol to deal with alternative delivery mechanisms, while the upstream policy development continues to be regarded as a natural preserve of the traditional public service. While models such as those developed in New Zealand would appear to question the existence of any obvious border between the policy development domain and the delivery mechanism domain, and while social learning would appear to require an integration of the two domains for an effective evolutionary policy making, the putative boundaries between the two domains remain in good currency (Aucoin 1995).

## From here to the new covenant in six difficult steps

Strategic action to catalyze the transformation process of the Canadian public service culture can be examined under two general rubrics: (1) there is the action required to develop a new philosophy of governance so as to ensure that the Canadian socio-economy will modify its guidance system to ensure goodness of fit with the new realities; and (2) there is the action required to develop a new philosophy of stewardship so as to ensure that the whole process through which we choose, evaluate, and help executives do their work will be modified to make it congruent with the requirements of the new governance. In the case of each rubric, we proceed in two steps: first, we state for the record what would appear to be the new requirements on the governance and on the stewardship fronts, and then, secondly, we put forward some very precise pre-conditions for a coherent strategy to emerge.

Before we proceed, it may, however, be useful to minimize the possibility of misunderstanding by introducing a number of clarifications.

First, these issues need to be addressed at all levels of the public service, as well as by politicians, unions and other stakeholders, but the requisite dialogue would be only a whimsical fantasy unless debates on these issues are legitimized and built into the daily practice of the federal central agencies. Otherwise, the sort of bottom-up process of social learning that is essential would soon die out.

Secondly, and this danger is the exact obverse of the first, it is essential that all the stakeholders take part in the renegotiation of the new covenant right from the start, and that the central agencies not be allowed to appear to hijack the process. Otherwise, again the bottom-up dynamics would soon die out. Consequently, we suggest that the process be designed in such a way as to allow maximum input from below, right from the beginning.

Thirdly, it should be clear that our modest proposals are only a set of preliminary ideas that might deserve attention at a time when the dialogue is beginning on what a new public service model might look like.

## A new philosophy of governance

### General principles[12]

At first, when organizations were relatively small, governance had a fiefdom-quality. The dialogue was very informal, and strongly focused on the leader. This has often been the governance system of small entrepreneurial firms and of small public sector agencies. But as the size of the socio-economy grew, and the problems it had to face grew more complex, organizations had to develop more elaborate structures and more formal rules to orchestrate collective action; from this emerged more or less standardized bureaucratic forms of

---

[12] This section draws freely from Gilles Paquet, "Paradigms of Governance," 1994a.

organization. Large private and public bureaucracies played an important role between the 1940s and the 1970s.

As long as the environment remained relatively stable, bureaucracies thrived: their rules remained valid and effective. However, as the pace of change accelerated, problems became less structured and ever changing, and the bureaucratic system, with its slow capacity to transform its rules, began to show signs of dysfunction. This led to efforts to partition private and public bureaucracies into smaller, self-contained and more flexible units. In the private sector, large companies created a multiplicity of more or less independent, profit-centred organizations, more attentive to the changing needs of the clients and more adaptable to evolving circumstances. With a lag, public bureaucracies have gone the same route with, for instance, the creation of executive agencies in the United Kingdom, or special operating agencies in Canada. Organizations came to be governed to a much greater extent than before by the invisible hand of the market forces.

But the price-driven steering mechanism often proved less than perfect. For instance, it proved insensitive to third-party effects and external economies, and very poorly equipped to appreciate and foster synergies. As a result, an effort was made to re-introduce the requisite amount of cooperation in the governance of organizations through the development of a variety of informal links – *liens moraux* – based on shared values, i.e., the corporate culture. The private sector developed these new informal clan-type organizations very quickly. Public organizations proceeded at a much slower pace. The Public Service 2000 exercise was one of the first occasions drawing attention to the centrality of organizational culture, but for all sorts of reasons we cannot analyze here, it never succeeded in modifying the traditional culture.

Such a modern, bottom-up, clan-type governance system cannot be engineered top-down by the leader: the organization can only govern itself by becoming capable of learning both its goals, and the means to reach them as it proceeds. This sort of governance system is fundamentally built on intelligence and innovation: a capacity to tap the knowledge and information held by active citizens and by active public servants at all levels, and to get them to invent ways out of the predicaments the organization experiences. This new context must be able to ensure that the institutional setting is capable of promoting and ensuring the highest degree of social/organizational learning. This, in turn, requires that all stakeholders become part of the learning and the change process, and are led to effect and support change without hesitation because the institutional setting ensures fair risk-sharing.

## Modest proposals

Our three modest proposals are in line with this new philosophy of governance. They pertain to three aspects of governance that need to be taken in for repairs.

The first one has to do with efforts to give *a second life to the Program Review exercise*, or to the equivalent or similar exercises that have developed in parallel at the provincial and local levels. We have argued elsewhere that initially a philosophy of subsidiarity was underpinning the Program Review, but that the 1994 Program Review exercise was transformed into a simple, cost-cutting process as a result of the pressures generated by the fiscal imperative. However, there may be a small window of opportunity for a refurbishment of the Program Review process as a result of the panic generated by the October 30, 1995 referendum in Quebec (Paquet and Shepherd 1996).

What is most important in the next round of Program Review, and in the parallel exercises conducted at the provincial and local levels, are:

(1) that it be fully geared to answering the six basic questions raised in round one, but especially the first four; it should generate an important degree of re-responsabilization of the citizen, and a massive devolution of responsibilities to the private and social sectors, and to lower-order governments;

(2) that the required analysis and consultation involve in a meaningful way the citizenry on whom public services are bestowed, but also the private and social sectors, and the lower-order governments.[13]

While this may appear to be very far from concerns related to the renegotiation of the implicit employment contract, it is a pre-requisite to any real rethinking of the way in which the public service will be redesigned. Unless one knows as clearly as possible what the responsibilities devolved to the federal government in the new governance system will be, and also what will fall into the bailiwicks of the provinces, the municipalities, the social sector and the private sector, it is difficult to gauge the nature of the transformation of the public service that is required and, what new public service model is called for.

The second proposal pertains to the adoption of *new principles to reflect the multiple loyalties* required for the success of the new governance system. As it stands now, the principles of the Westminster model are inadequate to meet

---

[13] The Program Review was announced in the February 22, 1994 budget and the basic philosophy and guidelines underpinning this review of government operations were spelled out in the form of six tests that departments were asked to apply in the review and assessment of their activities:

| | |
|---|---|
| Public Interest Test: | Do the program areas or activity continue to serve a public interest? |
| Role of Government Test: | Is there a legitimate and necessary role for government in this program area or activity? |
| Federalism Test: | Is the current role of the federal government appropriate, or is the program a candidate for realignment with the provinces? |
| Partnership Test: | What activities or programs should or could be transferred in whole or in part to the private/social/voluntary sector? |
| Efficiency Test: | If the program or activity continues, how could its efficiency be improved? |
| Affordability Test: | Is the resultant package of programs and activities affordable within the fiscal restraint? If not, what programs or activities would be abandoned? |

the needs of the new governance. New guidelines (inspired by the moral contracts mentioned above, but by others as well perhaps) are required to help select, guide, inspire, develop, evaluate and reward public servants in a manner that would recognize these multiple loyalties. Such principles, however, can be operative only if they are the result of a process of organizational learning involving all levels of the public service and all the stakeholders, with central agencies perhaps acting as facilitators.

At a minimum, the Privy Council Office and the Treasury Board Secretariat must give a clear signal that they are extremely open and presumptively favourable to a process of social learning leading to new principles. These should reflect the emerging multiple loyalties being actively developed to redefine the process of hiring, evaluation, remuneration of public servants but also the workable degree of risk-sharing that can be reasonably demanded from public servants to ensure maximum learning. This, of course, will require a reframing of the outlook of those agencies from that of order-giver and rule-setter to that of facilitator and animateur.[14]

The third proposal deals with the process of social learning which underpins the new governance. It calls for an *explicit recognition that public administration deals with wicked problems* where goals are multiple, ambiguous and uncertain, and means-ends relationships volatile and changing. This, in turn, requires that the governance system abandons its demands for infallible, universal, and mechanical methods of problem solving. Yet public administration has been prone to demand such infallibility in the past (Landau and Stout 1979). Such a view is dangerous, for it instills undue optimism into the practice of public administration and such "optimism restricts

[14] While we do not know exactly the content of the report prepared in the early 1990s by Robert René de Cotret and a blue-ribbon panel of experts to suggest ways of restructuring the federal government apparatus, it has been reported widely that much of their recommendations purported to effect major changes in the role of central agencies, very much in line with what is suggested here.

anticipation of error, minimizes its probability, and leads to the concealment of both its occurrence and the severity of its effects" (Landau and Chisholm 1992: 6)

This state of affairs would appear to fit the Canadian scene very well. In a recent debate, Donald Savoie stated clearly the nature of the malaise, even though he did it without seemingly finding anything wrong with it: "in government, it does not much matter if you get it right 90 percent of the time because the focus will be on the 10 percent of the time you get it wrong" (Savoie 1995). In this context, it is hardly surprising that errors and mistakes are denied with such vehemence, and success-fixation revered in a manner that can only lead to a rejection of managerial techniques built on error-correction.

A more reasonable philosophy of governance would not be built on success-fixation. It would recognize that the greater the nimbleness and agility of an organization, the greater the probability of error. This, in turn, calls for the development of technologies, structures, and incentive reward systems, but also for an overall understanding of what the organization is legitimately about, that would take into account these sorts of constraints in designing the new governance.[15]

[15] For a glaring illustration of the deplorable state of affairs in Canadian public administration, see the exchanges between Donald J. Savoie and Sandford Borins in *Canadian Public Administration,* 1995. The *ethos* of Canadian public administration as described by Donald Savoie is one (by contrast with the private sector) with an extraordinarily low tolerance for mistakes. This fixation on success is attributed to "a political environment that is always on the lookout for 'errors'." Savoie's Manichean view of the world suggests, very much like Jane Jacobs' *Systems of Survival* (1992), that there is such incommensurability between the private and public sector that any attempt to reform the latter by using experiences from the former is bound to fail at best, or at worst to generate "monstrous hybrids." Savoie defends the *status quo* and holds the politicians and the political institutions responsible for what may be imperfect in the present system. Instead of focusing on the failings of bureaucrats and the public service, we should focus on 'fixing' our political institutions and then the laws of Parliament. Borins' belief that "by emphasizing clear objectives and written performance contracts, the new public management should increase rather than diminish the accountability of public servants to ministers and of ministers to Parliament" may be

This requires that the new public sector governance system (1) be designed to incorporate technologies to detect error quickly, for artificial systems like organizations cannot necessarily restore themselves; (2) be structured in such a way that the requisite 'security zones' and 'empowerment levers' are in place so that the learners have both a firm ground on which to stand and the tools necessary to take the sort of action called for as a result of learning; it is our view that this can only happen if some negotiated risk-sharing arrangement among the stakeholders has been arrived at; (3) be designed to ensure that the process of learning from errors and of 'progressive reduction of error' are explicitly legitimized.

The emphasis must be clearly put on the dynamic, cognitive efficiency and effectiveness of organizations: this tends to de-dramatize error and to promote 'reduction of error' as a modest objective worth pursuing in the new modest state. This is what being a learning organization is all about.

Some have argued that the sole pressure of the threat generated by market competition suffices to drive employees to maximum performance. This is based on an unduly restrictive and reductive view of human beings, and one that is mostly wrong. Human beings have a broad range of sensitivities and needs: they demand both support and

---

equally simplistic given the 'wicked' nature of so many problems faced by public servants, and the impossibility of ever writing complete and all-comprehensive contracts in a turbulent world. Consequently, much will depend on 'moral contracts' or implicit arrangements and conventions and these are not always given their due by the new public management literature. For instance – this is a point suggested by Savoie's paper, though not raised explicitly by him – there may be a need for new moral contracts between the government and the opposition, and the government and the media before one can escape the trappings of success-fixation. What would appear to emerge from this debate is that neither the *status quo* nor narrow-minded managerialism will do. The 'wickedness' of management problems (which is not only a feature of public sector issues) demands that a third way be explored between the pure Savoie and the pure Borins' positions. Indeed, this is exactly what we have tried to develop.

stimulation. Ignoring these sensitivities is bound to force the system to operate much below capacity.

The implicit part of the new employment contract must deal with both the support side (the 'security zones' that even entrepreneurs need in order to be creative and the 'risk-sharing' that will provide the maximum incentive to embrace change and to disseminate new knowledge) and the stimulation side, (i.e., the motivation of employees, by recognizing that it is not driven only by coercion and threat, but even more by a commitment to the pursuit of novelty) (Scitovski 1976).

Indeed, the substance of the new covenant has to be very much determined by the negotiation of both the required additional stimulation from below and from above: the nature of the security required for the employee to perform the task creatively, and the nature of the enticement to pursue novelty and to go beyond one's limits that is required for the full creative capacity of the employee to be tapped.

## A new philosophy of stewardship

### General principles

The critical challenge facing the public service is a direct consequence of the complexities and intricacies of the new kind of work required by the new governance. The inter-relationships among all levels of government, departments, stakeholders and citizens, as well as among jobs and functions within the public service, are bound to be more complex and quite unspecified. The job is to ensure that the new governance system works well. Stewardship is about breathing life into structures. But it is crucial to recognize that "it is fruitless to be a leader in an organization that is poorly designed": stewardship entails, therefore, some concern for design and continuous interaction with the construction of the governance system (Senge 1990).

Even though we will refer mostly to persons in positions of authority, it should be clear that stewardship is not the preserve of executives, senior managers and supervisors. Stewardship is a process (neither a task nor a position) in which persons at all levels of the organization must partake. By focusing on those who are expected to effect change, we wish to emphasize two main points: (1) that those in authority may, because of their authority, make or break the new governance; and (2) that those who wish to institute change cannot do it at arms' length and be themselves untouched by the change. Stewardship is not about manipulating an object outside of and independent of the leader: "senior managers who labor under this misconception don't learn to play their complementary part and therefore unconsciously undermine the reorganizations or cultural change they initiate" (Kaplan *et al.* 1991).

For stewardship is about cultural change. And to modify a culture, three main ingredients are necessary: a capability for meaning-making, a capacity for community-building, and much honesty and an ability to inspire trust and confidence.

First, the new governance system requires making sense of people's experience by putting it into a larger context, thereby providing a sense of purpose, a story of why people do what they do; and, a way to shape the organization by building a shared vision with the many stakeholders. Meaning-making is about reflecting meanings that existed in the partners, and connecting them to one another in new ways appropriate to the demands of the new situation (Drath and Palus 1994).

Second, community-building is about establishing, developing, maintaining, sustaining and nourishing relationships within and between organizations. It is all about skillfully working interfaces where dilemmas, inconsistencies, contradictions and paradoxes are omnipresent. This requires the mastery of dialogue, the capacity to suspend judgment, and to question one's assumptions.[16]

---

[16] Hervé Sérieyx describes the leader as community builder very well: "*Le véritable acteur de l'entreprise en réseau est un accoucheur (il sait faire émerger une innovation), un fécondateur (il sait enrichir ses découvertes de celles des autres), un facilitateur (il met l'innovation en oeuvre sans déstabiliser l'organisation quotidienne), un guetteur (il apporte des idées venues d'ailleurs); c'est un peu un concierge le 'doorkeeper' qui fait circuler l'information entre des parties relativement séparées de l'entreprise), un intégrateur (il met en relation des acteurs complémentaires), un connecteur (il branche ensemble réseaux et autres "susciteurs de vie," "entreteneurs d'influx")* (Sérieyx 1993).

Thirdly, stewardship cannot emerge unless one can promote "adaptive capacities rather than inappropriate expectations of authority," for it entails "influencing the community to face its problems." This cannot be accomplished without some sort of 'social contract' between the leader and the community: "leadership as influence promotes influence as an orienting value, perpetuating a confusion between means and ends" (Heifetz 1994; O'Toole 1995).

The heart of the matter is not goal-seeking and control, but intelligence and innovation: the definition of standards and norms, and the negotiation of a moral, intellectual and emotional norm-holding pact, built on a multi-level dialogue. The whole institutional process becomes itself the learning process and the source of the redefinition of norms and standards as a result of experience (Zaleznik 1991).

### Modest proposals

Bringing about the kind of leadership necessary for the new governance system to take hold requires a thorough renewal of our way of selecting, evaluating and coaching leaders.

The first proposal has to do with the *selection, promotion and deployment of executives*. It calls for revisions in the current practices to ensure (1) that the selection be done according to criteria that echo the profile of the new leader; and (2) that the selection is made through a process involving various stakeholders.

While this requires no change in legislation or policy, it would call for a significant modification in practice: the definition of the profile of the executive position and the choice of the incumbent would be made in effect not only by the supervisor and the Public Service Commission, but also by representatives of the different stakeholders (employees, peers, major client groups, etc.) under the guidance of the PSC to ensure due process and impartiality. While current practices already encourage the composition of some of the interview boards comprised of some of the stakeholders, our proposal goes much further: it calls for the stakeholders to be involved in defining the selection profile, in arriving at a short list, checking references, etc. – with employees being present at each step of the process.

The inclusion of the stakeholders would force dialogue among them, which can only help anchor the process of organizational learning. Critics will argue that this would require time and dilute management's authority to deploy personnel as it seems fit. That is precisely the point. Meaning-making, shared vision, community building, and organizational learning cannot occur without dialogue. Dialogue takes time and is costly. But poor selection, based on a very partial identification of needs and leading to demotivated employees, can only translate into organizational sclerosis or in-fighting, reduced productivity, low creativity and innovation, and dissatisfied clients. This is much more costly.

Our second proposal deals with how, *once appointed, managers are supported, coached, mentored and developed.* At the risk of generalizing, the current model is one of 'sink or swim'. Executives are expected to be quick studies, and to possess almost instantly all the knowledge and skills of their new positions. Some managers at all levels are known to boast not only that they expect instant high performance, but expect such performances instantly under the most extreme and demanding conditions. This sort of situation has led to organizational disaster, and would, if anything, be exacerbated by a shift to the market employment model.

This proposal calls for personal development to be regarded as a planned process of learning, through feedback, coaching and mentoring, as well as other self-directed activities. Personal development becomes part of a contract where responsibilities are not shoveled onto the employee entirely, but shared by employer and employee. It would require a paradigm shift: from the boss knows to the steward learns. It would also require that managers develop a new appreciation for all the phases of the learning cycle – questioning, finding possible answers, testing to see if they work, and reflecting on the lessons learned (Handy 1989).

Our third proposal calls for *a new process of evaluation for executives*, and a rethinking of the whole incentive-reward system for this category of personnel. Just as the stakeholders must be involved in selecting executives, so they must also be involved in evaluating them. The 360 degree appraisal must become the norm and, as a result of it, a process of dialogue and values clarification must be instituted (Hoffman 1995).

Deputies and central agencies will be expected to reward both formally and informally those persons who meet all aspects of the new leadership profile and to avoid celebrating those who excel in certain areas only to the detriment of others. If one may use the Jack Welch approach as a template, it would suggest a system where several key leadership dimensions are evaluated, and where even if an executive has had a very positive impact on the bottom-line, he or she will be released if their treatment of employees does not reflect the values espoused by the corporation. This is called 'walking the talk', and our experience with hundreds of executives in the classrooms of the Canadian Centre for Management Development tells us that such an approach would be supported by most executives, who feel that several key leadership factors are ignored when the time comes to reward and promote individuals.

This third proposal is the kingpin of the transformation process. No change will occur if employees continue to perceive that rewards go mostly to those whose policy skills and political savvy are geared entirely to serving mindlessly the whims of their superiors, irrespective of their capability for meaning-making, their capacity for community-building and their ability to inspire trust and confidence, and to deal with people at all levels.[17]

[17] As Hervé Sérieyx would put it: *"demander à des fonctionnaires de travailler autrement sans prévoir de distinguer ceux qui acceptent d'accomplir cette mutation et ceux qui s'y refusent, sans transformer les systèmes de notation, de promotion, de rémunération, d'intéressement, c'est réduire le renouveau du service public à un sympathique encouragement du type 'Allez-y les petits gars.' Cette 'boy-scoutisation' des stratégies de changement est souvent perçue par les acteurs les plus dynamiques du renouveau du service public comme sa pire limite et, à moyen terme, comme son plus sûr germe d'échec"* (Sérieyx 1993).

* * *

One may reasonably ask why we have felt we had to roam over such a vast territory in our reflections on the search for a new covenant for the public service. The main reason is that we believe that the traditional employment framework cannot simply be replaced by a nexus of market employment contracts, and we had to provide some basis for the development of the new 'moral framework' that will be required as an essential complement to the market contracts.

This process depends first on the recognition that a nexus of market employment contracts will not suffice. This is a point we have made forcefully and, we hope, persuasively. As to the content of the required complementary moral framework, we have argued that it would have to provide (1) ways of dealing with multiple loyalties by public servants in the modern age; and (2) ways of affecting the moral contracts for the new moral framework to coalesce. We also emphasized the point that the task would be more difficult than had been anticipated because of the likely period of slow economic growth and the high degree of social rigidity that would appear inevitable in the years ahead.

To forge the new moral framework, we have suggested that one must proceed in six steps. Each of these steps will be very difficult because each calls for a genuine revolution in the mind, a *nouvelle manière de voir*.

On the governance front, we feel that wide-ranging consultations can lead (1) to a reconfiguration of the new federal public service (Program Review Phase II); and (2) to the replacement of the Westminster model by a more modern version, taking fully into account the multiple loyalties of public servants; we also suggested that (3) a major redirection in the guiding principles of public administration toward a social learning process is absolutely necessary.

On the stewardship front, we have sketched the general features of the new stewardship in the new non-centralized, distributed governance system and we have suggested some dramatic modifications in the machineries that govern (1) the entry and promotion of executives in the federal public service; (2) the nature of the support and training they get in the process; and (3) the process of evaluation and the whole incentive-reward system for executives.

These changes point the way to a new moral framework that would appear to fall half-way between the old model and the nexus of market employment relations that has been suggested by some as the only workable alternative. This new moral framework will be based on a looser series of ties among a larger number of stakeholders. It will not easily accommodate dependency, but will emphasize the central importance of the *avventura comune* as the binding factor, or at the very least what Aristotle identifies as *concord* ("a relationship between people who ... are not strangers, between whom goodwill is possible, but not friendship ... a relationship based on respect for ... differences") (Oldfield 1990).

This may provide for the federal public service what has been provided by successful private sector enterprises for their employees: not a naked market-based employment contract, but a two-tier contract, with a tacit unwritten but centrally important component to ensure a reasonable degree of risk-sharing between employer and employee. The full burden of risk will not be shouldered entirely by the employer, as in the old moral contract, nor by the employee, as in the market-type employment contract, but will be shared after extensive negotiations involving not only those two parties, but by many of the stakeholders who have such an interest in these negotiations that they will no longer permit that negotiations be carried on without them.

# References

Armstrong, J.L. 1991. "Innovation in Public Management: Toward Partnerships," *Optimum*, 23(1): 17-26.

Aubert, Nicole. 1995. "Organizations as Existential Creations: Restoring Personal Meaning While Staying Competitive" in Thierry C. Pauchant (ed.). *Search of Meaning: Managing for the Health of our Organizations*. San Francisco, CA: Jossey-Bass, p. 151-172.

Aucoin, Peter. 1995. *The New Public Management: Canada in Comparative Perspective*. Montreal, QC: Institute for Research on Public Policy.

"A Vision of the Future," *Ottawa Citizen*, May 14, 1995, A2.

Axsmith, Murray. 1992. "The Emerging Employment Contract," *Transitions*, 4(3).

Axsmith, Murray. 1993-94. "The Work Force: How It Will Change," *Career Options*, 7, p. 5-7.

Axsmith, Murray. 1994. "Contracts to become flexible," *Canadian H.R. Reporter*, February 14, p. 14-15.

Barnet, Richard J. 1993. "The End of Jobs," *Harper's Magazine*, (September): 47-52.

Bartlett, Christopher A. and Sumantra Ghoshal. 1995. "Changing the Role of Top Management: Beyond Systems and People," *Harvard Business Review*, 73(3):132-142.

Borins, Sandford. 1995. "The New Public Management is Here to Stay," *Canadian Public Administration*, 38(1): 122-132.

Bridges, William. 1994. *JobShift*. Reading, MA: Addison-Wesley.

Bridges, William. 1994. "The End of the Job," *Fortune*, September 19.

Bridges, William. 1994. "Rethinking Work," *Business Week*, October 17

Bridges, William. 1994. "Redefining Work," (A Dossier), *Challenges*, fall.

Coleman, James S. 1988. "Social Capital and the Creation of Human Capital," *American Journal of Sociology*, 94, supplement, p. 95-120.

Côté, N. 1984-85. "Pour revaloriser la fonction publique," *L'Analyste*, 8: 21-24.

Drath, Wilfred H. and Charles J. Palu.s 1994. *Making Common Sense - Leadership as Meaning-Making in a Community of Practice.* Greenboro, NC: Centre for Creative Leadership.

Easterbrook, W.T. 1949. "The Climate of Enterprise," *American Economic Review*, 39, p. 322-335.

Easterbrook, W.T. 1949. "Political Economy and Enterprise," *Canadian Journal of Economics and Political Science*, 15, p. 322-333.

Easterbrook, W.T. 1954. "Uncertainty and Economic Change," *Journal of Economic History*, 14, p. 346-360.

Entente sur l'organisation du travail dans la fonction publique intervenue entre le Gouvernement du Québec et les organisations syndicales signataires, Québec, 15 février 1995.

Fraser *v.* PSSRB [1985] 2 S.C.R. 455.

Gomez, P.Y. 1994. *Qualité et théorie des conventions.* Paris, FR: Economica.

Granovetter, Mark S. 1973. "The Strength of Weak Ties," *American Sociological Review*, 78, p. 1360-1380.

Hampden-Turner, Charles and Alfons Trompenaars. 1993. *The Seven Cultures of Capitalism.* New York, NY: Currency Doubleday.

Handy, Charles. 1989. *The Age of Unreason.* Boston, MA: Harvard Business School.

Heifetz, Ronald A.1994. *Leadership Without Easy Answers.* Cambridge, MA: Harvard University Press.

Hoffman, Robert. 1995. "Ten Reasons You Should be Using 360-Degree Feedback," *HR Magazine*, 40(4): 82-85.

Jacobs, Jane. 1992. *Systems of Survival.* New York, NY: Random House.

Kaplan, Robert E., Wilfred H. Drath and Joan Kofodimos. 1991. *Beyond Ambition: How Driven Managers Can Lead Better and Live Better.* San Francisco, CA: Jossey-Bass Publishers.

Kernaghan, K. 1991. "Career Public Service 2000: Road to Renewal or Impractical Vision?" *Canadian Public Administration,* 34(4): 551-572.

Kernaghan, K. 1993. "Partnership and Public Administration: Conceptual and Practical Considerations," *Canadian Public Administration,* 36(1): 57-76.

Kingwell, Mark. 1993. "Interpretation, Dialogue and the Just Citizen," *Philosophy and Social Criticism,* 19(2): 115-144.

Kingwell, Mark. 1994. "The Polite Citizen; Or, Justice as Civil Discourse," *The Philosophical Forum,* 25(3): 241-266.

Kingwell, Mark. 1995. *A Civil Tongue.* University Park, PA: The Pennsylvania State University Press.

Kreps, David M. 1990. "Corporate Culture and Economic Theory" in James E. Alt and Kenneth A. Shepsle (eds.). *Perspectives on Positive Political Economy.* Cambridge, UK: Cambridge University Press, p. 90-143.

Kumon, Shumpei. 1992. "Japan as a Network Society" in S. Kumon and H. Rosovsky (eds.). *The Political Economy of Japan,* vol. 3. Stanford, CA: Stanford University Press, p. 109-141.

Landau, Martin and Russell Stout. 1979. "To Manage is Not to Control: Or the Folly of Type II Errors," *Public Administration Review,* March-April.

Landau, Martin and Donald Chisholm. 1992. "Success Oriented vs Failure Avoidance Management in Public Administration: A Reconsideration, " Paris, FR: Institut de Management Public, Palais des Congrès, mars.

Mulroney, B. 1990. *Public Service 2000: The Renewal of the Public Service of Canada.* Ottawa, ON: Supply and Services, December.

Noer, D.M. 1993. *Healing the Wounds.* San Francisco, CA: Jossey-Bass Publishers.

Oldfield, Adrian. 1990. *Citizenship and Community*. London, UK: Routledge.

O'Toole, James. 1995. *Leading Change*. San Francisco, CA: Jossey-Bass Publishers.

Paquet, Gilles. 1991-92. "Betting on Moral Contracts," *Optimum*, 22(3): 45-53.

Paquet, Gilles. 1994a. "Paradigms of Governance" in M. Cottrell-Boyd (ed.). *Rethinking Government, The Dewar Series: Perspectives on Public Management – Exploration II*. Ottawa, ON: Canadian Centre for Management Development, p. 29-42.

Paquet, Gilles. 1994b. "Reinventing Governance," *Opinion Canada*, 2(2): 1-5.

Paquet, Gilles and L. Pigeon. 1995. "Toward a Transformation of the Public Service," *Optimum*, 26(1): 47-55.

Paquet, Gilles. 1996. "Le fruit dont l'ignorance est la saveur" in A. Armit et J. Bourgault (eds.). *Hard Choices, No Choices: Assessing Program Review*. Toronto, ON: Institute of Public Administration of Canada/Canadian Plains Research Center, p. 47-58.

Paquet, Gilles and Robert Shepherd. 1996. "The Program Review Process: A Deconstruction" in G. Swimmer (ed.). *How Ottawa Spends 1996-97 – Life After The Cuts: Doing Less with Less*. Ottawa, ON: Carleton University Press, p. 39-72.

Peters, Tom. 1994. *The Tom Peters Seminar: Crazy Times Call for Crazy Organizations*. New York, NY: Vintage Books.

Phillips, S. D. 1991. "How Ottawa Blends: Shifting Government Relationships with Interest Groups" in F. Abele (ed.). *How Ottawa Spends, 1991-92: The Politics of Fragmentation*. Ottawa, ON: Carleton University Press, p. 183-227.

Pinchot, Gifford and Elizabeth Pinchot. 1993. *The End of Bureaucracy and the Rise of the Intelligent Organization*. San Francisco, CA: Berrett-Koeler Publishers.

PSC *v.* Millar et al. [1991] 2 S.C.R. 69.

Putnam, Robert D. 1993. *Making Democracy Work.* Princeton, NJ: Princeton University Press.

Rifkin, Jeremy. 1995. *The End of Work: The Decline of the Global Labor Force and the Dawn of the Post-Market Era.* New York, NY: Putnam.

Rosell, Steven A. *et al.* 1995. *Changing Maps: Governing in A World of Rapid Change.* Ottawa, ON: Carleton University Press

Savoie, Donald J. 1995. "What is wrong with the new public management?" *Canadian Public Administration,* 38(1): 112-21.

Schick, Frederic. 1984. *Having Reasons: An Essay on Rationality and Sociality.* Princeton, NJ: Princeton University Press.

Scitovsky, Tibor. 1976. *The Joyless Economy.* New York, NY: Oxford University Press.

Senge, Peter. 1990. *The Fifth Discipline.* New York, NY: Doubleday.

Sérieyx, Hervé. 1993. *Le big bang des organisations.* Paris, FR: Calmann-Lévy.

Tellier, P.M. 1992. *Public Service 2000: A Report on Progress.* Ottawa, ON: Supply and Services, June.

*The Way Ahead for the Public Service.* Discussion Paper for the Directors of Personnel Conference, Cornwall, ON, October 4-6, 1994.

Waterman, Robert H., Judith A. Waterman and Betsy A. Collard. 1994. "Toward a Career-resilient Workforce," *Harvard Business Review,* 72(4): 87-95.

Zaleznik, Abraham. 1991. "L'absence de leadership et la mystique managériale," *Gestion,* 16 (3): 15-26.

CONCLUSION

# | Killing Two Birds with One Stone: a Mental Prison and a Cosmology

## Gilles Paquet

*"Quousque tandem abutere Catilina patientia nostra?"*
*Cicero*

The basic objective of this book is to launch an initiative to drive the fake out of public administration in Canada. This follows a decade of critical work on different aspects of the federal government administrative machinery (Hubbard and Paquet 2010).

To avoid slipping into hollow denunciations, we have decided to use human resources (HR) and HR management systems as illustrations of a mental prison that plagues Canadian public administration at the federal level (the Pearsonian conceit), and of what could be done about it – issues on which we have done a great deal of field work over the last decade (Hubbard and Paquet 2014, 2015). HR concerns illustrate also the full extent of the damage caused by the 'fake' in public administration in all areas where willful blindness and failure to confront waste have become pathological features of traditional public administration. We argue that most often this 'fake' has been instilled by the so-called 'progressive' cosmology and public philosophy that have come to be in good currency during the post-World War II period.

The merits of such a venture in the large are obvious: eliminating the unwarranted waste in the federal government apparatus, improving the performance of the coordination game so that more value-adding and innovation might ensue, both for the public household and for the socio-economy at large, and exposing the perils of the failure to confront such challenges that has also spread around like the plague.

The danger of attacking such a very major source of governance failure as the 'progressive mindset', and of illustrating its toxicity mainly with reference to the particular deficiencies in HR is also obvious: we may win the HR battle but not be persuasive enough with regard to the overall public sector cosmology that was the main target to begin with.

Why then take that risk?

The 50-year old Pearson conceit (deciding that the main priority of the Canadian government was not to make the highest and best use of its human resources in order to better serve Canadians, but to be a 'model employer') is not just a convenient illustration of the broader 'progressive' perversion that has led Canadian governors to betray the trust of their constituents and abandon efforts to ensure the good coordination of the Canadian public household and of the Canadian socio-economy likely to lead to wealth creation – jobs for which they were elected.

The decision by the Canadian government to define as its burden of office the role of 'grand redistributor' in the labour market for the benefit of the aristocracy of labour in the federal public sector may be regarded as a particularly reprehensible instance of its propensity to accept this sort of role from any interest groups capable of inventing a storytelling to support the thesis that their members are the victims of coordination failures.

This is obviously a thankless Sisyphean task (for as Tocqueville has splendidly shown, the more equality is achieved, the more intolerant the pseudo-deprived groups are about the remaining bit of inequality), but this is a mission that reaps immense electoral benefits for the political party in power, and is bound to deflect its attention from the equally thankless but politically unrewarding task of working hard at upgrading its fundamental coordination job.

Let us be clear.

Our reason for being so insistent on the import of the Pearson conceit of 1967 for the whole HR fiasco of the last half century (and of its impending extension into the future by the Secretary of Treasury Board, Scott Brison's forthcoming repeal in 2016 of Bill C-4 that was intent on bringing the Pearson conceit to an end) is that it was and is a particularly blatant consequence of the progressive *état d'esprit* that has prevailed since the 1960s, and resulted in so many other betrayals of the trust of citizens on many other fronts, with equipollent disastrous consequences for Canadian public administration, and, as a result, for the Canadian socio-economy at large.

Killing two birds with one stone was worth trying, but the broader intent (wounding at least the bigger bird of prey) must obviously not be forgotten.

## Progressivism and the age of unreason

### From liberalism I to liberalism II [1]

The spirit of type-I-liberalism thrived in the 19th century. It emerged as a reaction to various forms of coercion imposed by traditional and autocratic governing structures that constrained the scope of individual freedom in what was slowly becoming a more open society. This philosophy was not arguing for anarchy, but for reducing coercion to a minimum. So type-I-liberalism never entailed (except in its radical fringes) a rejection of state action altogether.

[1] The section borrows freely from G. Paquet, 2013, chapter 1.

The type-I-liberalism cosmology perceives that power, resources and information are broadly distributed among a diversity of actors, that no one (including the state) is fully in charge, and that most institutions and rules are not so much the result of rationally planned human action, but the result of some configuration of various forces generating the emergence of a more or less spontaneous order that often acquires a life of its own. As a result, its crystallized shape may not necessarily resemble at all any of the templates originally envisaged by any one of the actors. So the emergence and evolution of coordinating arrangements need not necessarily require a masterminding architect in charge. However, this does not mean that interested stakeholders cannot try to nudge these processes through *bricolage* of all sorts.

While celebrated for its criticism of dictatorship, arbitrary power, intolerance, repression, etc., type-I-liberalism has been criticized as unduly naïve in not recognizing that the actions of individuals may also be irrational, destructive, stupid, and therefore toxic and capable of inflicting important collective damage.

Indeed, such predatory behaviour (whether deliberate or as a result of unintended consequences) was already observed in the latter part of the 19th century, and led to commissions of inquiry (on child labour, poverty, relations between labour and capital, and the like) that revealed abuse and recommended ways to mitigate the collective harms generated by absolute *laissez-faire*.

The growth of labour unions and state regulations constituted a reaction to coordination failures and collective harms that had resulted from the high-tide of type-I-liberalism. The first victim of these correctives was the word 'liberalism' itself – which, over time, was transmogrified, and took on a meaning that was the very obverse of its original meaning.

What is nowadays called type-II-liberalism or 'statism' connotes the idea that freedom is no longer the central concern. What is central in this new view is egalitarianism, and a new vision of the state as being charged with the new superior burden of office of ensuring the sort of equality of outcomes that has come to be regarded in recent times as necessary for citizens to be able to exercise their autonomy and freedom. The role of the state is no longer to protect freedom from encroachment (negative liberty), but to provide, as a matter of entitlement, all that is purported to be necessary for citizens to be able to fully exercise their rights to personal development (positive liberty).[2]

Even though the spirit of 'statism' (type-II-liberalism) was at first directed to correcting gross market failures and social injustices, over time its ambit has become much more encompassing and intrusive. It has reached the point where type-II-liberalism has become a general indictment of type-I-liberalism for having failed miserably in generating effective coordination, through not recognizing that individuals are myopic and gullible, that competition in the marketplace is very imperfect, that public goods are never being produced in 'sufficient' quantity, that private enterprises are manipulative of the preferences of consumers and of the actions of elected and bureaucratic officials, and that, consequently, the objectives of egalitarianism of outcome (regarded as the basic condition for the exercise of positive freedom) have not been fully realized.

[2] *Stanford Encyclopedia of Philosophy*, 'Liberalism', http://plato.stanford.edu/entities/liberalism/ [Accessed February 10, 2012].

TABLE 4.

## A Quick Sample of the Idiosyncrasies of the Two Ruling Cosmologies

|  | Type-I-liberalism | Type-II-liberalism |
|---|---|---|
| Individual | imperfectly informed | manipulated |
| Values | plural | shared |
| Priority | freedom | egalitarianism |
| Competition | rather perfect flexible prices | quite imperfect sticky prices |
| Interventionism | modest | robust |
| Time horizon | long term | short term |
| Trust | private > public | private < public |
| In charge | nobody | State |
| Information | scattered | in hand |
| G action | inquiring system | goals, control, marksmanship |
| Public service | interest group | new clergy |

As a result, it has been argued that the state has to take charge, for only this supra-individual entity, it was argued, could distil and come to embody the notion of 'public interest', and ensure that the basic conditions for effective positive freedom (equality, rights, egalitarian distributive justice, and the like) can be realized.

This type-II-liberalism cosmology took hold in the 1930s as a basis for countervailing state action to deal with the catastrophic Great Depression, but became a much more aggressive new gospel in post-World War II, when intrusive significant state action became something that most citizens came to be persuaded they were entitled to – in good as well as bad times. The main driver of this movement was the declaration of social rights in the 1940s (Gurvitch 1946).

The drift, in the latter part of the 20$^{th}$ century, from a state contribution to correcting abominable disruptions and unacceptable inequalities in periods of crisis, to the state being required by citizens, as a matter of perceived right, to provide insurance and compensation against all unpredictable duress, was consequential. This was the era when the array of claimed 'market failures' (for which citizens felt entitled to compensation), and the claims for state support supposedly required to ensure positive liberty, expanded exponentially. The welfare state led citizens to believe that their sense of entitlement to be protected from any undesirable future was warranted and legitimate, and that the state was the only actor capable of ensuring that it would be done.

## The big coordination-redistribution switch[3]

In the early phase (1971-1995), as we hinted at earlier, coordination concerns still haunted the public sector psyche (along with the sweeping suggestion that New Public Management might be the required response for public administration *per se*), but there were also a large number of more circumscribed structural reforms of all sorts (federally or provincially) that were put forward (Paquet 1997).

The results generated some modest restructuring of the production and allocation apparatuses, but they were not always very imaginative and forward looking. Most importantly they failed to provide any significant and credible remedy to the stagnation of productivity growth.[4]

---

[3] This section borrows from Gilles Paquet and Christopher Wilson, 2016, p. 190-91.

[4] 1968 was the year Trudeau's Liberals said their aim was to create a 'Just Society'. Already, by 1970, Pierre Trudeau had serious reservations about the Canadians' impossibly high expectations. By 1972, after his near electoral defeat and minority government, Trudeau crassly bowed to the 'progressive agenda', and took the limits off the public spending (Bliss 2004: 256-60). Trudeau *le jeune* fell prey to the same trap in 2015-16.

More recently (1996-2014), the situation began to evolve in a dramatically different direction. Redistribution, which had slowly become more and more important during the post-World War II period, came to be regarded in the 1990s as the solution to three daunting public sector challenges:

- the expanded need for mechanisms for recycling of government surpluses;
- the need to factor in the phenomenal ideological drive toward egalitarianism – evolving from social preference to absolute right and entitlement (Kekes 2003); and
- a generalized state of resignation and pessimism on the part of governments – having realized that they had neither the capacities nor the will to transform the unproductive and outdated apparatus of socio-economic coordination – coupled with an understanding that they could at least retain their legitimacy and electorability by compensating the citizenry for the malefits generated by governance failures on the coordination front.

## *Toward unbounded thaumaturgic redistribution*

The 'progressive' have persuaded themselves (and a plurality of the members of the intelligentsia, of the medias, and of the corpus of elected officials) that the failures of the coordination game could be ignored, and that their redistributive magic would keep the game going if only a surplus could be found (or borrowed) to buy peace from all those claiming to be the victims.

Instead of addressing the source – the problems of inefficiency and ineffectiveness in the production and distribution of goods and services – efficiency became denounced as a cult (Stein 2001), and waste came to be almost sacralised as a 'virtue' in public opinion when it was presented as the price of compassionate comforting for an interest group as long as it was not big business. As a result, claim for protection by all sorts of inefficient and ineffective

Canadian agents against more productive foreigners became a mantra of Canadian policy in many sectors.[5]

Even as the entitlement epidemic reached boundless proportions in Canada and elsewhere (Paquet 2013: chapter 4), and redistribution latched into mindless escalation that has allowed the worst aspects of Olsonian decline of nations to unfold (Olson 1982) – it would appear to sound no alarm.

This sort of redistribution goes on unchallenged because it is somewhat subterranean, i.e., it is effected through sleights of hand by government agencies, announced through press conferences to the winners, while the losers are not even aware that their government has shafted them.[6]

The 'failure to confront' the demons of envy and the demise of critical thinking have increasingly left our socio-economies at the mercy of the irresponsible greed of interest groups. Storytelling reached new heights in recent years, and Occupy,

---

[5] As we go to press in the summer of 2016, the Kafkaesque nature of this sort of federal government intervention in the market for dairy products was observed operating without attracting any headlines or critical comments (except from one sane columnist). At a time when the world is awash in excess milk and dairy products as a result of the end of the European production quotas last year, and a recent report announcing that the Canadian dairy farmers average costs of production declined by 2%, the Canadian Dairy Commission – the federal politburo that determines what consumers pay for their milk, cheese, ice cream and yogurt – increased the price of industrial milk by 2.76% in July 2016 after another increase of 2.2% in February. This is an increase of some 5% at a time when the world price of milk is plummeting. This price increase hurts low income families with children the most, but it also deprives the most efficient farmers of the opportunity to expand production and export. Inefficient farmers are unreasonably rewarded by higher prices, and lower income families with children are gouged by such redistribution gimmicks. Yet the Trudeau government hopes that it might reap the dairy farmer's votes (Yakabuski 2016).

[6] This is the core feature of economic fallacies as explained by Frédéric Bastiat: they are presenting only a portion of reality – what is seen – and forgetting what is not seen, such is the case with all redistributive schemes. While Bastiat wrote about these matters in the first half of the 19th century, it is fascinating that it is in Ottawa that an English translation was produced in the 1930s (Bastiat 1934).

Indignados, the 99 percent against the 1 percent could all voice their dissatisfaction in a self-righteous way, and propose the universal solution to their distress – ever more important silent and subterraneous redistribution of income and wealth in their direction, without ever recognizing the damages such action might generate collectively, nor the fact that the 'us and them' in these new conflicts are persons who would appear to only recognize their entitlements and never any responsibilities. In this shell game, where most groups are kept in the dark, everyone hopes to win but everybody loses.

Intellectuals, media personalities, and university professors have ceased to provide their flows of critical thinking because they are now part of the 'have', and feel gloriously entitled to be there. They only comment in their magical Marxism *linguo* about the legitimacy of all progressive recriminations. The aristocracy of labour has also become part of the upper classes, together with the chattering classes. The entitlements of these diverse groups know no bounds, their willingness to transform is rather low, and their incapacity to accept that it might well be that one cannot agree to all demands from all interest groups without running into financial difficulties would appear to legitimize all claims.

Politicians are on the receiving end of this flow of unreasonable demands from external claimants but also from internal bureaucrats. They know that the redistribution magic is a zero-sum game, and that the make-believe that everybody can win in this sort of game is an imposture. Yet they face a citizenry that has developed impossibly high expectations (as Trudeau *père* had realized in 1970) and, for not bowing to these unreasonable expectations, they almost lost power (Bliss 2004: 256).

The alternative, as Trudeau *père* also recognized in 1972, was coping by *mentir-vrai* – disingenuity, disinformation, outright lies, and supplying symbolic resources, because they are cheap, in lieu of real resources, etc. The populace swallowed a lot of this in the 1970s, and the temporary successes of Trudeau *père* ensued, but the ensuing costs for

Canadians were immense. The same 'pharmakon' would appear to work 40 years later. The parading of *majestés de pacotille* and the promises of boundless gratification for the ill-defined middle class would appear to have been an effective smokescreen during the first year in office of the Trudeau *le jeune* government. Yet there are limits to the *politique du spectacle,* and the *fuite en avant par la redistribution* will eventually hit a brick wall as it did in the 1970s.

So the Pearsonian conceit and the progressive deceit about redistribution magic – our smaller and our bigger birds of prey – will eventually have to be dealt with.

## Containing the Pearsonian conceit

Whatever might be the merit of much of our work in Part III of this volume, it would appear that the Trudeau *le jeune* government is intent on not bringing an end to the awful Pearsonian age of trying to be a 'model employer', i.e., the era of bribing the Canadian public sector by unreasonable gratification to make the personnel happy, instead of trying to make the highest and best use of the human resources available.

Scott Brison has now announced that Bill C-4 will be rescinded. It should make the unions happy but it should also ensure that nothing substantial shall be done to detox the HR systems. It remains to be determined how long it will take for Trudeau *le jeune* to wisen up to the toxic nature of the Pearsonian philosophy, and whether electoral tidings may get him, like his father, to hold his nose and maintain this philosophy in place even in the medium term. The disastrous impact of the Pearsonian philosophy is therefore likely to persist, and the continuous decline in the effectiveness of the state is likely to ensue.

We mentioned earlier the possibility of bringing the whole HR system under the supervision of one minister. While there is merit to this sort of carpentering, it would be naïve to expect an epiphany from such bureaucratic sleight of hand. It might even encourage the maintenance of unwarranted centralization and harmonization of conditions of employment in the federal public service – something that would likely be deleterious.

Nothing can bring back concerns about efficiency, effectiveness, productivity, and innovation in the public household but the vigilance of a permanent Program Review Committee. There is no substitute for the existence of constant questioning of existing programs to ensure that they are still needed, that their delivery is delegated to the most appropriate authorities, and that we can afford them.

The last time such an exercise was conducted was the last chance the Canadian federal government had to regain control of its household, and to refocus on the coordination game. The fact that Program Review was then hijacked by financial authorities, and transmogrified into a simplistic, cost-cutting exercise in the 1990s was deplorable. It neutered most of the positive impacts one might legitimately have expected from the exercise (Paquet 1996; Paquet and Shepherd 1996).

But there is no reason to believe that a permanent office charged with program review at the Privy Council Office could not be protected from the raids originating from the Treasury Board Secretariat or the Department of Finance, if the highest authorities in government were to be committed to protecting this key function from being derailed as it was in the 1990s. This much has been learned from the failures of Program Review in the 1990s.

A new permanent incarnation of this process would have the principal merit of upgrading efficiency, effectiveness, productivity and innovation, and promoting them anew as a primary objective of government. But such a success would not eliminate the basic source of the problems.

## Harnessing the progressive deceit

It will not be as easy to harness the progressive deceit at the source of the displacement of the coordination game by the redistribution game that has been underway for the last 50 years. By now, the progressive gospel is deeply rooted in the socio-cultural underground. Indeed, its roots were made clear in the middle of the 19th century by Tocqueville.

## The Tocqueville mechanism[7]

Alexis de Tocqueville has shown that *"les peuples démocratiques ... ont pour l'égalité une passion ardente, insatiable, éternelle, invincible; ils veulent l'égalité dans la liberté et, s›ils ne peuvent l›obtenir, ils la veulent encore dans l›esclavage"* (Tocqueville 1840: 104). The core of *De la démocratie en Amérique II* (*Ibid.*) is a sort of sociology of equality in democratic societies. It argues that the basis of modernity and democracy is rooted in this sentiment of equality.

'Equality' in the sense of Tocqueville is not an observed fact, but it is fundamentally an ideal, an *"imaginary equality,"* an egalitarianism that drives democracy (*Ibid.*: 189). Tocqueville has shown that equality is not only the dominant value in democracy, but that *"le désir de l'égalité devient toujours plus insatiable à mesure que l'égalité est plus grande"*(*Ibid.*: 114): even when a very egalitarian status has been realized in a society, *"on peut compter que chacun de ses citoyens apercevra toujours près de soi plusieurs points qui le dominent, et l'on peut prévoir qu'il tournera obstinément ses regards de ce seul côté"* (Dumouchel and Dupuy 1979 : 49). So, contrary to what one might have suspected, greater equality does not generate less envy, but more.

This sort of passion for equality applies as well to ethnic and cultural groups. And it works with even more force when there is a coexistence of decreed egalitarian rights with considerable *de facto* differences in power, wealth, etc. among the different groups. Strong resentment ensues. It leads not only to cultural 'jealousies' (an innocuous zeal in the preservation of something possessed), but to 'envy' (defined as displeasure and ill will at the superiority of another person in happiness, success, reputation or the possession of anything desirable).

---

[7] This section draws freely from Paul Laurent and Gilles Paquet, 1991.

The rise of egalitarianism as a modern democratic dogma has been exponential over the last decades, and has consequently produced a heightened degree of tension, frustration and envy at the intercultural interface. It has contributed to the accumulation of culture-specific, social capital, and to the further balkanization of modern societies. Moreover, in countries like Canada, where multiculturalism has become a national policy, and where cultural rights have become entrenched in charters and laws, the process of segmentation has been accentuated, and envy has been further promoted in view of the stark contrast between the equality of ethno-cultural groups decreed as the norm, and the realities of intercultural differences (Paquet 1989).

The process of exponential growth of governmental gratification over the last decades, and their hardening into a cumulative ratcheting of non-negotiable entitlements or *acquis* have had toxic effects on the burden of office of citizens as governors — increasing irresponsibility, disengagement and victimology. Egalitarianism as the philosophical underpinning of the entitlement edifice has fuelled the expansion of redistribution.

## The revolutionary philosophy of equability

Harnessing the illusions and toxicity of egalitarianism will require a revolution in the mind, the replacement of the 'mythology' of egalitarianism by a 'philosophy' of equability as an alternative foundational anchor.

This word 'equability' is a term that Merriam-Webster defines as the "lack of noticeable, unpleasant, or extreme variation or inequality." The term focuses on finding the right balance in the practical search for a balance between equality, efficiency, and fairness. Yet this is a word that is not in good currency in Canada, where terms like "entitlements," and "egalitarianism" — words that are quite legalistic and reek of non-negotiability — are the sort of reference points most often quoted.

A shift from egalitarianism to equability as a reference point would transform the doctrinal position of the progressives from an either-or to a more-or-less framework. Equability would raise the possibility of 'acceptable inequalities'. It may not be possible to proceed much further without some relativization of what the progressives have tended to absolutize.

## The governance of equability

The egalitarian illusions that have inspired, bolstered, and supported the entitlement epidemic have been exposed for quite a long time (Kekes 2003). It has been shown that "a society cannot long endure unless it rewards and protects its productive members, and punishes and curbs depredators, cheaters, and free-riders" (*Ibid.*: 206). But even if compassion is an indefensible basis for morality, it remains most seductive. Both Courchene (1981) and Eberstadt (2012) (among others) have shown that egalitarianism-inspired policies generate distortions in the workings of both invisible hands (market for Courchene and morality for Eberstadt) and have argued for taming the entitlement epidemic based on egalitarianism. But, it is fair to say that their message has not been heard.

The difficulty is that these matters have been debated as a black and white dichotomy that appeared to leave no possibility for a compromise position between zero redistribution, and indiscriminate and imprudently generous egalitarianism-inspired redistribution. What needs to be recognized is that modest and prudent redistribution, based on a philosophy of 'equability' (i.e., a philosophy geared to eliminating unacceptable inequalities), may very well be a middle-of-the-road position that could be defended as underpinning reasonable policy choices.

That would entail incurring efficiency (technical and social) costs, but only to the point where they would generate technical, social, and moral benefits that would make such a choice defensible. This would hardly simplify the task, since there is a great amount of imprecision in the data that might help to ascertain what such a stance might mean in real-life situations. But it might be a sufficient guidepost to rein in the entitlement epidemic, and to help to tame it.

The notion that there might be trade-offs, that might be regarded as acceptable to different parties as second-best compromises, would appear to indicate that conversations that would challenge important mental prisons are becoming thinkable.

This sort of debate is unlikely to be initiated as long as the terrain is quasi-fully occupied by beneficiaries, and unabashedly compassionate journalists and experts. These three groups have little tolerance for ambiguity: they thrive on self-righteousness and black-and-white problem definitions and solutions. They have made public administration an inhabitable terrain because of their doctrinaire positions. Indeed, they would rather not even try to tackle normative questions like the workings of the second invisible hand than allow a compromise response to be entertained as plausible – a solution that would be regarded as a betrayal of their creed, even though such a compromise might be politically desirable.

## Modest general propositions

1) **The governance of equability must start with the demythologization of the notions of equality and egalitarianism.**

This is a travail that has been underway for quite a while in the tradition of the indictment initiated by Tocqueville. It has been done in different ways: first, through frontal attacks by Harry Frankfurt (1987) or John Kekes (2003) among others, on the very meaningfulness of such ideals; second, through a probing of the toxic, deleterious, and violence-generating impact of the pursuit of such ideals (Laurent and Paquet 1998; Lussato 1989); and third, through finessing all sorts of attenuation of the basal notions of equality and egalitarianism via the deconstruction of its polysemic nature, the affirmation of necessary trade-offs with many other valuable purposes, and the denunciation of undue reliance on *ex post* relative incomes and resources, rather than on the more fundamental insufficiencies of basic capabilities, ascertained *ex ante* (Sen 1995).

Consequently, it will be a Herculean job to dislodge this passion for equality from its dominant position in the culture, despite all the costs generated by this stance. An epistemological *coup* based on a crippled epistemology is responsible for this dominance, and nothing less than another such *coup* will succeed in slaughtering this sacred cow.

The governance of equability must be rooted in sufficiency and respect as a way to diffuse envy and contain redistribution.

To topple egalitarianism, it is necessary to make it unpalatable and dishonourable, but this is not sufficient. It is also important to contain redistribution as a futile response to the egalitarian drive.

The containment could come from an alternative to the doctrine of equality – the doctrine of 'sufficiency' – the idea that what is important from a moral point of view is *not* that everyone should have the same, but that each should have enough. Frankfurt has developed this alternative more fully in a 1997 paper (Frankfurt 1997). He argues that there is no necessary connection between having a low social position and having a low quality of life. Treating persons with respect entails dealing with them impartially and without arbitrariness. One should not confuse being treated disrespectfully with being treated unequally. And if greater equality is to be regarded as desirable, it should be only because it facilitates the pursuit of other socially desirable aims, not because one regards envy as warranting it. The governance of equability must not be allowed to fall prey to the infernal logic of position and envy.

**2)** **The governance of equability must establish why equability and equability of what, and allow some inequalities in order to avoid worse ones.**

Equability would therefore focus on sufficiency rather than on equality and egalitarianism. This does not make it easier to determine what is sufficient, and what sort of inequalities might be undesirable for other socially desirable aims, but the focus and intent are different: as Frankfurt would put it, the focus is on respect and sufficiency, not on giving a dominant place to envy and equality of outcomes in whatever form.

This does not deny that a significant degree of inequality may be of relevance in the pursuit of other desirable aims, but that corrections to these situations must depend on circumstances. For instance, if there is an agent responsible for a discrepancy generating inequality of condition because the agent has failed to treat each person with respect, it may be objectionable, but not because of inequality of outcome, because of the lack of respect.

The governance of equability must therefore gauge the desirability of many social aims. The way of defining unacceptable inequalities depends not on the degree of envy that it fuels (which in itself is not a defendable basis for anything),[8] but on the extent or degree to which such a state of affairs may impair the pursuit of other legitimate social aims.

This leads to the conclusion that the denunciation of inequality *per se*, and the elevation of egalitarianism to the role of dominant value *are* illegitimate and unwarranted.

---

[8] It is astounding to hear some egalitarian like Ronald Dworkin indulge in speculations about the "envy test" of the ideal distribution of income – one that would lead to no one being envious of any other person – and that he proposes therefore to elevate the vice of envy to the role of moral standard. See John Kekes critical comments on that position in J. Kekes, 2003, 70ff.

Consequently, redistributive policies aimed at taming the destructiveness of envy may have been used unwisely and imprudently. Such imprudence may be particularly toxic when the dynamics triggered by such devices not only interfere with the effective working of the first invisible hand – that of the market – but also the second one – morality. Often, in this latter case, redistribution generates entitlements and changes in belief systems that are fairly difficult to reverse once the common public culture has been tainted.[9]

* * *

It might have been presumptuous to hint in the title of this chapter that our stone might fatally wound both the Pearsonian conceit and the progressive cosmology. While this was the intent, these are resilient toxicities. There have been electoral reasons for the Pearsonian conceit to survive, and cultural reasons for the progressive cosmology to retain its attraction. This does not mean that either mental prison is reasonable or defendable, but they may nonetheless survive.

On both fronts, the forecast is grim: the recent decision to rescind Bill C-4 by the Trudeau *le jeune* government would appear to indicate that little progress can be expected on the HR front, while the progressive cosmology would also appear to remain unchallenged.

It is not only that those ideological positions would appear unchallenged in the public mind, but they also would appear to be self-righteously defended by political, bureaucratic and judiciary authorities despite their toxicity.

Consequently, a reasoned approach to these issues may not suffice. One may have to recognize that we are confronted with the *pneumopathological* – a word proposed by Eric Voegelin and used by Robert Sibley to describe the state of "those who are morally insane, 'living' as it were, in a fantasy-world of self-righteousness" (Sibley 2013). Such a disordered

---

[9] Can one dare to remind some younger readers that it was not unusual in the 1950s for beneficiaries of relief benefits to be ashamed of being in such a situation.

consciousness is not only ascribable to intellectual laziness, but also to other dysfunctions, of which the excessive politeness, political correctness and unreasonable accommodation are not unimportant ones.

To attack the pneumopathological, a certain degree of methodological cruelty is necessary, in the way one has to deal with viruses. Yet it need not be done unceremoniously or sternly. This is why satire – 'sarcasm, irony or wit used to expose abuses or folly' – has been part of our argumentation, and irreverence part of our dialectical tools.

Will it suffice to wake the citizenry up to provoke a reform movement? Probably not! However it might embarrass officials, and make them feel dishonourable to be involved in such shenanigans. If it works, it would be no small accomplishment. As Anthony Appiah has demonstrated, many social and moral revolutions may be said to have originated in some slippage in the code of honour (Appiah 2010).

# References

Appiah, K. Anthony. 2010. *The Honor Code*. New York, NY: Norton.

Bastiat, Frédéric. 1934. *Economic Fallacies*. Ottawa, ON: The Dadson-Merrill Press.

Bliss, Michael. 2004. *Right Honourable Men – The descent of Canadian Politics from Macdonald to Chrétien*. Toronto, ON: HarperPerennialCanada.

Courchene, Thomas J. 1981. "A Market Perspective on Regional Disparities," *Canadian Public Policy*, VII(4): 506-518.

Dumouchel, Paul and Jean-Pierre Dupuy. 1979. *L'enfer des choses*. Paris, FR: Seuil.

Eberstadt, Nicholas. 2012. *A Nation of Takers – America's Entitlement Epidemic*. West Conshohocken, PA: Templeton Press.

Frankfurt, Harry G. 1987. "Equality as a Moral Ideal," *Ethics,* 98(1): 21-43.

Frankfurt, Harry G. 1997. "Equality and Respect," *Social Research,* 64(1): 3-15.

Gurvitch, Georges. 1946. *The Bill of Social Rights.* New York, NY: International Universities Press.

Hubbard, Ruth and Gilles Paquet. 2010. *The Black Hole of Public Administration.* Ottawa, ON: University of Ottawa Press.

Hubbard, Ruth and Gilles Paquet. 2014. *Probing the Bureaucratic Mind – About Canadian Federal Executives.* Ottawa, ON: Invenire.

Hubbard, Ruth and Gilles Paquet. 2015. *Irregular Governance – A Plea for Bold Organizational Experimentation.* Ottawa, ON: Invenire.

Kekes, John. 2003. *The Illusions of Egalitarianism.* Ithaca, NY: Cornell University Press.

Laurent, Paul and Gilles Paquet. 1991. "Intercultural Relations: A Myrdal-Tocqueville-Girard Interpretative Scheme," *International Political Science Review,* 12(3): 171-183.

Laurent, Paul and Gilles Paquet. 1998. *Epistémologie et économie de la relation – coordination et gouvernance distribuée.* Paris/Lyon, FR: Vrin.

Lussato, Bruno. 1989. *Le défi culturel.* Paris, FR: Nathan.

Olson, Mancur. 1982. *The Rise and Decline of Nations – Economic Growth, Stagflation, and Social Rigidities.* New Haven, CN: Yale University Press.

Paquet, Gilles. 1989. "Multiculturalism as National Policy," *Journal of Cultural Economics,* 13, p. 17-34.

Paquet, Gilles. 1996. "Le fruit dont l'ignorance est la saveur" in A. Armit and J. Bourgault (eds.). *Hard Choices, No Choices: Assessing Program Review.* Toronto, ON: IPAC/Canadian Plains Research Center, p. 47-58.

Paquet, Gilles. 1997. "Alternative Program Delivery: Transforming the Practices of Governance" in R. Ford and D.R. Zussmen (eds.). *Alternative Service Delivery: Sharing Governance in Canada*. Toronto, ON: IPAC/KPMG, p. 31-58.

Paquet, Gilles. 2013. *Tackling Wicked Policy Problems: Equality, Diversity and Sustainability*. Ottawa, ON: Invenire.

Paquet, Gilles and Robert Shepherd. 1996. "The Program Review Process: A Deconstruction" in G. Swimmer (ed.). *How Ottawa Spends 1996-97 - Life Under the Knife*. Ottawa, ON: Carleton University Press, p. 39-72.

Paquet, Gilles and Christopher Wilson. 2016. *Intelligent Governance: A Prototype for Social Coordination*. Ottawa, ON: Invenire.

Sen, Amartya. 1995. *Inequality Reexamined*. Oxford, UK: Oxford University Press.

Sibley, Robert. 2013. "Young men can be turned to good or evil," *Ottawa Citizen*, April 29.

*Stanford Encyclopedia of Philosophy*, 'Liberalism', http://plato.stanford.edu/entities/liberalism/ [Accessed February 10, 2012].

Stein, Janice G. 2001. *The Cult of Efficiency*. Toronto, ON: Anansi.

Tocqueville, Alexis de. 1961 (1840). *De la démocratie en Amérique*. Paris, FR: Gallimard (Editions Mayer), vol. II.

Yakabusky, Conrad. 2016. "Supply-managed Canada cries over spilt milk," *The Globe & Mail*, July 21.

# | Sources

Hubbard, Ruth. 2013. "Performance, not model employer," *www.optimumonline.ca*, 43(2): 41-43.

Hubbard, Ruth and Gilles Paquet. 2015. "The Canadian federal public service: tinkering can no longer suffice," *www.optimumonline.ca*, 45(3): 3-15.

Paquet, Gilles. 2015. "Failure to Confront," *www.optimumonline.ca*, 45(3): 16-32.

Hubbard, Ruth and Gilles Paquet. 2014. "Repairing the management vacuum at the federal level in Canada," *www.optimumonline.ca*, 44(4): 75-86.

Hubbard, Ruth and Gilles Paquet. 2014. "Competencies: part of the governance vacuum," *www.optimumonline.ca*, 44(3): 58-73.

Paquet, Gilles. 2009. *Scheming Virtuously: The Road to Collaborative Governance*. Ottawa, ON: Invenire, chapter 8.

Paquet, Gilles. 2013. *Tackling Wicked Policy Problems: Equality, Diversity and Sustainability*. Ottawa, ON: Invenire, chapter 1.

Paquet, Gilles. 2013. "The Governance of Equability," *www.optimumonline.ca*, 43(2): 13-27.

Paquet, Gilles and Christopher Wilson. 2016. *Intelligent Governance: A Prototype for Social Coordination*. Ottawa, ON: Invenire, chapter 7.

# About the Centre on Governance of the University of Ottawa

The Centre on Governance (COG) was created by Gilles Paquet at the end of 1997 as a joint venture of the Faculty of Administration (now the Telfer School of Management) and the Faculty of Social Sciences at the University of Ottawa. From its inception, it was seen as an umbrella organization – a hub for the work on governance taking place in all the faculties of the University of Ottawa. The main objectives of the Centre were to develop: conceptual frameworks for analyzing coordination problems, tools to better analyze governance issues, and a critical approach for repairing governance failures. It was meant to bring together persons who are committed to seeking better responses to contemporary problems of governance in the private, public and civic sectors both within and outside of the University of Ottawa. It aimed from the beginning to be an observatory of emerging trends and experiments in the world of governance.

From the beginning, the COG has been responsible for the publication of *www.optimumonline.ca* – a refereed quarterly on governance and public management. Fellows of the Centre have produced hundreds of papers over the years and generated large numbers of books published under different banners. What follows is a list of the main books and reports produced by the Centre, under the banner of the University of Ottawa Press, then under the banner of Invenire – The Idea Factory, and also under the banners of other publishers. All these books are available from www.amazon.ca.

## The University of Ottawa Press (1999-2010)

D. McInnes. 1999. *Taking it to the Hill – The Complete Guide to Appearing before Parliamentary Committees*

G. Paquet. 1999. *Governance through Social Learning*

L. Cardinal & C. Andrew (sld). 2001. *La démocratie à l'épreuve de la gouvernance*

L. Cardinal & D. Headon (eds.). 2002. *Shaping Nations – Constitutionalism and Society in Australia and Canada*

P. Boyer *et al.* (eds.). 2004. *From Subjects to Citizens – A hundred years of citizenship in Australia and Canada*

C. Andrew *et al.* (eds.). 2005. *Accounting for Culture – Thinking though Cultural Citizenship*

G. Paquet. 2005. *The New Geo-Governance: A Baroque Approach*

J. Roy. 2005. *E-government in Canada*

C. Rouillard *et al.* 2006. *Re-engineering the State – Toward an Impoverishment of Quebec Governance*

E. Brunet-Jailly (ed.). 2007. *Borderlands – Comparing Border Security in North America and Europe*

R, Hubbard & G. Paquet. 2007. *Gomery's Blinders and Canadian Federalism*

N. Brown & L. Cardinal (eds.). 2007. *Managing Diversity – Practices of Citizenship*

J. Roy. 2007. *Business and Government in Canada*

T. Brzustowski. 2008. *The Way Ahead – Meeting Canada's Productivity Challenge*

G. Paquet. 2008. *Tableau d'avancement – Petite ethnographie interprétative d'un certain Canada français*

P. Schafer. 2008. *Revolution or Renaissance – Making the transition from an economic age to a cultural age*

G. Paquet. 2008. *Deep Cultural Diversity – A Governance Challenge*

L. Juillet & K. Rasmussen. 2008. *A la défense d'un idéal contesté – le principe de mérite et la CFP 1908-2008*

L. Juillet & K. Rasmussen. 2008. *Defending a Contested Ideal – Merit and the Public Service Commission 1908-2008*

C. Andrew *et al.* (eds.). *Gilles Paquet – Homo Hereticus*

O.P. Dvivedi *et al.* (eds.). 2009. *The Evolving Physiology of Government – Canadian Public Administration in Transition*

G. Paquet. 2009. *Crippling Epistemologies and Governance Failures – A Plea for Experimentalism*

M. Small. 2009. *The Forgotten Peace – Mediation at Niagara Falls 1914*

R. Hubbard & G. Paquet. 2010. *The Black Hole of Public Administration*

P. Dutil *et al.* 2010. *The Service State: Rhetoric, Reality, and Promises*

G. DiGiacomo & M. Flumian (eds.). 2010. *The Case for Centralized Federalism*

R. Hubbard & G. Paquet (eds.). 2010. *The Case for Decentralized Federalism*

## Invenire (2009-2016)

R. Higham. 2009. *Who do we think we are: Canada's reasonable (and less reasonable) accommodation debates*

R. Hubbard. 2009. *Profession: Public Servant*

G. Paquet. 2009. *Scheming Virtuously: The Road to Collaborative Governance*

J. Bowen (ed.). 2009. *The Entrepreneurial Effect: Ottawa*

F. Lapointe. 2011. *Cities as Crucibles: Reflections on Canada's Urban Future*

J. Bowen. 2011. *The Entrepreneurial Effect: Waterloo*

G. Paquet. 2011. *Tableau d'avancement II – Essais exploratoires sur la gouvernance d'un certain Canada français*

R. Chattopadhyay & G. Paquet (eds.). 2011. *The Unimagined Canadian Capital – Challenges for the Federal Capital Region*

P. Camu. 2011. *La Flotte Blanche – Histoire de la Compagnie de la navigation du Richelieu et d'Ontario 1845-1913*

M. Behiels & F. Rocher (eds.). 2011. *The State in Transition – Challenges for Canadian Federalism*

R. Clément & C. Andrew (eds.). 2012. *Cities and Languages: Governance and Policy – International Symposium*

R. Clément & C. Andrew (sld). 2012. *Villes et langues : gouvernance et politiques – Symposium international*

C.M. Rocan. 2012. *Challenges in Public Health Governance: The Canadian Experience*

T. Brzustowski. 2012. *Why we need more innovation in Canada and what we must do to get it*

C. Andrew *et al.* 2012. *Gouvernance comunautaire : innovations dans le Canada français hors Québec*

M. Gervais. 2012. *Challenges of Minority Governments in Canada*

R. Hubbard *et al.* (eds.). 2012. *Stewardship: Collaborative decentred metagovernance and inquiring systems*

G. Paquet. 2012. *Moderato cantabile: Toward principled governance for Canada's immigration policy*

G. Paquet & T. Ragan. 2012. *Through the Detox Prism: Exploring organizational failures and design responses*

G. Paquet. 2013. *Tackling Wicked Policy Problems: Equality, Diversity, and Sustainability*

G. Paquet. 2013. *Gouvernance corporative : une entrée en matières*

G. Paquet. 2014. *Tableau d'avancement III – Pour une diaspora canadienne-française antifragile*

R. Clément & P. Foucher. 2014. *50 years of official bilingualism: challenges, analyses and testimonies*

R. Clément & P. Foucher. 2014. *50 ans de bilinguisme official : défis, analyses et témoignages*

R. Hubbard & G. Paquet. 2014. *Probing the Bureaucratic Mind: About Canadian Federal Executives*

G. Paquet. 2014. *Unusual Suspects: Essays on Social Learning Disabilities*

R. Hubbard & G. Paquet. 2015. *Irregular Governance: A Plea for Bold Organizational Experimentation*

L. Cardinal & P. Devette (eds.). 2015. *Autour de Chantal Mouffe – Le politique en conflit*

R. Higham. 2015. *What would you say? … as guest speaker at the next Canadian citizenship ceremony*

D. Gordon. 2015. *Town and Crown – An Illustrated History of Canada's Capital*

G. Paquet & R.A. Perrault. 2016. *The Tainted-Blood Tragedy in Canada: A Cascade of Governance Failures*

G. Paquet & C. Wilson. 2016. *Intelligent Governance: A Prototype for Social Coordination*

R. Hubbard & G. Paquet. 2016. *Driving the Fake Out of Public Administration: Detoxing HR in the Canadian Federal Public Sector*

## Editions Liber

G. Paquet. 1999. *Oublier la Révolution tranquille – Pour une nouvelle socialité*

G. Paquet. 2004. *Pathologies de gouvernance – Essais de technologie sociale*

G. Paquet. 2005. *Gouvernance : une invitation à la subversion*

G. Paquet. 2008. *Gouvernance : mode d'emploi*

G. Paquet. 2011. *Gouvernance collaborative : un anti-manuel*

## Éditions Vrin

P. Laurent & G. Paquet. 1998. *Épistémologie et économie de la relation – coordination et gouvernance distribuée*

## Éditions H.M.H.

G. Paquet & J.P. Wallot. 2007. *Un Québec moderne 1760-1840 : Essai d'histoire économique et sociale*

## Government of Canada

G. Paquet. 2006 (en collaboration). *The National Capital Commission: Charting a New Course*

Report of the NCC Mandate Review Panel

## Special research reports

J. Roy and C. Wilson. 1998. *Strategic Localism and Competitive Advantage*

COG. 1999. *Corporate Governance & Spin-in Ventures*

COG. 1999. *The Borough Model: Municipal Restructuring for Ottawa*

COG. 2000. *The Governance of the Ethical Process for Research – A study for the Tri-council*

COG. 2000. *Governance in the 21ˢᵗ Century*, Lead role in the annual symposium of the RSC

G. Paquet. 2001. *Si Montfort m'était conté ... Essais de pathologie administrative et de rétroprospective*

Talentworks Project (under the supervision of Christopher Wilson)

COG. 2001. *Evaluating TalentWorks: Creating a Foundation for Successful Collaboration*

COG. 2002. *Ottawa's Workforce Environment, Report I of Ottawa Works: A Mosaic of Ottawa's Economic and Workforce Landscape*

COG. 2002. *Profiling Ottawa's Workforce, Report II of Ottawa Works: A Mosaic of Ottawa's Economic and Workforce Landscape*

COG. 2002. *Ottawa's Workforce Development Strategy, Report III of Ottawa Works: A Mosaic of Ottawa's Economic and Workforce Landscape*

A. Chaiton and G. Paquet (eds.). 2002. *Ottawa 2020 – A synthesis of the Smart Growth Summit*

G. Paquet and Kevin Wilkins. 2002. *Ocean governance ... An inquiry into stakeholding*

B. Collins, *et al.* 2003. *Assessment of Public Internet Access in Ottawa: Report of Key Findings*

COG. 2003. *SmartCapital Evaluation Guidelines Report*

COG. 2003. *SmartCapital Baseline Assessment*

R. Hubbard, G. Paquet and C. Wilson. 2004. *CIPO: Reaching the World of SMEs*

COG. 2004. *SmartCapital: A Smart Community Assessment*

G. Paquet and J. Roy. 2005. *CIPO as an Innovation Catalyst*

www.ingramcontent.com/pod-product-compliance
Lightning Source LLC
Chambersburg PA
CBHW062050270326
41931CB00013B/3016

9 780776 638348